Sisters of the Midnight Sun

Sisters of the Midnight Sun

A Murder in Arctic Alaska

Rebecca Wright Stevens

COUNTERPOINT • CALIFORNIA

SISTERS OF THE MIDNIGHT SUN

This is a work of nonfiction. However, some names and identifying details of individuals have been changed to protect their privacy, correspondence has been shortened for clarity, and dialogue has been reconstructed from memory.

First Counterpoint edition: 2026

ISBN: 978-1-64009-771-1

The Library of Congress Cataloging-in-Publication data is available.

Jacket design by Victoria Maxfield
Jacket image © Martina Melzer / Alamy Stock Photo
Book design by Laura Berry

COUNTERPOINT
Los Angeles and San Francisco, CA
www.counterpointpress.com

Printed in the United States of America

1 3 5 7 9 10 8 6 4 2

For Elizabeth Kanayurak Pawluk, 1960–2020

I miss your brave spirit and caring, sharing heart.

Sisters of the Midnight Sun

1

You never know who are really your friends
or enemies until the ice breaks.
ALASKA NATIVE PROVERB*

Arraignment of Amos Lane in District Court
Utqiagvik (formerly Barrow), Alaska
August 6, 1993

WHEN I PUSHED OPEN THE HEAVY GRAY DOORS OF the courtroom, heads turned toward me as though it were a wedding, but nobody smiled. I wished I weren't dragging a suitcase, but I'd come straight from the airport because my office said arraignment had already begun. I stashed the suitcase in a back corner and headed up the aisle.

The courtroom usually sat empty on a Friday morning and usually was as quiet as a church, which it resembled with its pinstriped gray carpeting and blond wood spectator pews. Instead of an altar, we had a judge's bench and jury box. Today the place was standing room only, and it buzzed with the murmurs of impatient spectators.

"Amos Lane is his name," Liz, our office manager, had said when she phoned me in South Carolina in the middle of my first vacation in three years. "They're holding him on misdemeanors now, but they think he killed the Ipalook sisters."

"The Ipalook sisters!"

Fred Ipalook Elementary School in Utqiagvik was named for the family patriarch, the first Inupiaq (formerly called Eskimo) school principal.

"Both of them strangled, one raped," Liz said.

I was standing in my parents' kitchen, looking through the magnolia trees blooming on their lawn, trying to register what Liz was saying.

"Listen . . . I know you haven't been out in a while," she went on. "Do you want me to have Anchorage send somebody up temporary?"

It took me a while to answer.

"No, I'll come. It's my territory."

My parents' friends had asked me why I went so far away to defend people who might be dangerous. I had two explanations. The first involved money, the second was hard to explain, so I usually tried to change the subject.

The first was that my daughter was in law school and my son had just started college. Financial aid departments were generous to a widow like me, with meager resources, but the schools were still expensive. I learned that oil-rich Alaska provided good salaries for public defenders, especially if you were willing to go to a bush office, so I sold the old farmhouse near Olympia, Washington, that had been our family home for eleven years; managed to get through the Alaska bar exam; and moved to Arctic Alaska. The second answer was that the midnight sun and the polar night and the white owls and white bears and white foxes of the Arctic fascinated me. Especially the white owls.

Public Safety officers filled the back pews. Their presence tended to put pressure on the magistrate to set a high bail. I knew it would be part of my job today to remind the court and the prosecutor that we were here only on misdemeanors. My new client might be a suspect in these shocking murders but had not been charged with them. No one had. I spotted Ed Ellingsworth, local lead detective, his cadaverous frame drooping over a corner of a pew. A young female reporter sat beside him, plump and giggly. I rather liked the way she never spelled the district attorney's name right. The name was Slusser, but she always wrote *Slusher.* She also garbled some Inupiat words, and used *k*, *q*, and *g* interchangeably, but so did a lot of people. The language is not yet entirely standardized, but then, neither is English. At least she had learned that *Inupiat* was a noun and *Inupiaq* an adjective, though I didn't have the heart to tell her that even this usage sometimes varied place to place and speaker to speaker.

Words that still confused me were the names of the area. When I first arrived, I was told that historic areas in the middle of town were referred to as *Ukpeagvik*, with a *p*, and that the name meant "place where the snowy owls gather." How lovely, I thought—both the name and the glorious creatures themselves. At the time, the town was called Barrow, a proper British name, but then the townspeople voted to return to the ancient name of Utqiagvik, or "place where roots are dug." No doubt both names are accurate, and the difference between them perhaps neither the reporter nor I will ever fully understand, but I preferred the owls.

Two entire middle pews were occupied by members of the Ipalook family, looking stricken and exhausted. There were also many spectators who came to court out of boredom. Utqiagvik didn't have a movie theater. In the front row, there was a group of young women in summer parkas, some with babies folded inside their front zippers.

A faint, comforting scent of seal cooking oil pervaded the room.

My new client, Amos Lane—it would have to be him—sat alone in handcuffs at the defense table, bearing the angry stares at his back. All I could see was that he was a Native man with long black hair and muscular shoulders wearing an orange jumpsuit, and that he needed some company. I passed through the pony gate in the bar and took my place beside him.

His eyes flicked sideways over me, and I saw in his glance that he lumped public defenders together with bailiffs, clerks, police, DAs, judges, and everyone else who put him and kept him in jail.

"You're Amos Lane? My name's Rebecca Wright. I'm the public defender for the North Slope Borough. Let's see what we've got."

Alaska is divided into boroughs rather than counties. The North Slope Borough, an area the size of Wyoming, occupies the northern tier of the state. The Inupiat control the North Slope Borough financially and politically. While many teachers, doctors, and lawyers are *taniks*, non-Natives, they serve at the pleasure of Native authorities—and may be, and have been, asked to leave if they don't serve well.

Without a word, Amos passed me the mess of papers in front of him. There were two misdemeanor complaints filed yesterday, and a petition for misdemeanor probation revocation filed instanter. Now.

The first complaint declared Lane was the subject of a citizen's arrest by one Harold Killbear, whom he had assaulted.

He whispered, "That's bullshit. The guy was beating up his girlfriend and I stopped him, is all. I got witnesses."

I shrugged.

What struck me about the complaint was the "citizen's arrest" part. It signified that no law enforcement officer had witnessed Lane committing any crime. To arrest on a misdemeanor, according to Alaska law, an officer actually had to see the offense happening. Otherwise, the defendant could only be summoned to come into court at a later time. But Killbear could file his own complaint and ask for assistance in taking anyone into custody right away. I recalled that Killbear himself had appeared in court some weeks previously on a charge of DUI. I wondered, if I ever made it so far as my office this morning, whether I would find that the case against Killbear had been opportunely dismissed.

I felt my hackles rising. It was bad enough for Lane to sit alone in a courtroom of people who wanted somebody, anybody, to be jailed for a serious crime, without Public Safety piling on fake charges. I wished I'd had a chance to read over the file or even just talk to him before the hearing. The initial stages of a case of this magnitude had to be done right. And I would have liked to tell Mr. Lane my initial reaction to the Killbear complaint, but we couldn't afford to appear to furtively conspire in front of the crowd. Utqiagvik was so small that each and every person in the courtroom was a potential juror.

"I've heard of you," Lane muttered.

He didn't say whether what he'd heard was good or bad.

I gave him a polite smile. "I've heard of you, too," I said, "all the way to South Carolina." Lane started to inquire what I had heard, but I held up a hand and focused on the next charge.

In this complaint, Johnny Aveoganna accused Lane of stealing some ivory from his home. Uh-huh. I knew Aveoganna. He was a talented and prolific carver of ivory, a friendly and generous man, and a heavy drinker. He sold a lot of ivory. I had bought from him myself, a classic polar bear carved from part of a walrus tusk, and a smaller gull and a seal of fossilized ivory. He also gave away a lot of his work, especially to friends who dropped by for a drink. If Public Safety had found some ivory signed by Aveoganna in Lane's possession, he could be accused of stealing it. At trial Aveoganna could explain the ivory was a gift. Even if Amos had, in fact, stolen the ivory, the easygoing Johnny might call it a gift, just for old times' sake. On the other hand, Aveoganna's ivory was not the tourist-trinket kind that sold cheaply in Anchorage. Its real value could kick the charge up from misdemeanor into felony if Public Safety decided they really wanted Lane and couldn't find anything else with which to hold him, at least until the grand jury met to indict someone in the murder case. Hopefully, as an ultimate last resort, an Utqiagvik trial jury of people who knew Aveoganna as Lane and I did, and Fairbanks didn't, would make short work of the charge.

"Mr. Lane, are you on any kind of parole or probation status?"

"No. I maxed out."

Only the hardcore went the route of serving every day of their suspended time, the time that would be held over their heads when they were released to parole. That Lane had served every day told me that he didn't want anybody, anywhere, having a leash on him.

I picked up the remaining papers, a misdemeanor probation revocation petition, with two fingers and looked at him inquisitively.

"That was just this stupid fight write-up I caught right before I got out. The guy lied. They were going to charge it as a felony, but then we copped this deal and I pled to it as a misdemeanor. They did it mostly so they could release me into alcohol treatment instead of the street."

My head had begun to ache. What he was saying could be true. A lot of inmate squabbles, or misunderstandings by guards, led to empty charges. On the other hand, his previous record might show that he was a dangerous drunk who tended to get violent, and that whatever parole or probation officer had tried to guide him into treatment was doing the right thing.

Beyond those considerations, I grew puzzled that nowhere in this stack of paper was there any reference to the deaths of the two sisters. I had missed a birthday celebration and flown 3,800 miles to represent Amos Lane. If Liz was right and this guy was a suspect in the case, so far no one had come up with any evidence against him. Liz was Inupiaq herself, and she and her extended family members always knew what had happened, who was accused, and who was probably guilty.

Unlike Public Safety, I might add.

I studied his face. "Mr. Lane, I don't recall seeing you in court before. You're not from Utqiagvik, are you."

It was not a question.

"No way," he said. "I'm from Point Hope."

Utqiagvik was on the northern edge of Alaska and was in fact the northernmost community in the United States. Point Hope was home to a few hundred people on the western rim, so remote it made Utqiagvik seem like a world hub. The people of Point Hope had once successfully resisted the federal government's plan of detonating a thermonuclear device to create a harbor on their coast.

Good for them.

Point Hope is also one of the oldest continually inhabited communities on the North American continent. Inupiat have lived there 2,500 years.

MY GOAL IN the moment was to get Lane out of jail. Since he was suspected, rightly or wrongly, of a crime so serious that it had packed the courtroom, the State was attempting to keep him in jail on nickel-and-dime misdemeanors while they tried to gather evidence against him. For these reasons, the DA would be asking the magistrate to set a high bail. If I could somehow persuade the court that a lower bail was adequate and Lane could be released, the entire murder case would be on a different footing, and I could more easily work with him and prepare for trial, if trial was necessary. For my argument, I needed to learn as much as I could of his background, hopefully without resorting to extended whispers.

"Do you have any sexual assaults on your record?" I asked quietly. For the first time he looked at me full-on, as if trying to gauge my intentions. Or my credibility.

"Yes," he said. "That's what I just got out for."

The conviction must have been a serious one to result in such a long sentence. That was why I hadn't run across his name before. He had been convicted and incarcerated before I ever came to Utqiagvik.

"But you were released to alcohol rehab. Were you not in treatment last weekend?"

"They let me out on a pass for the weekend. I got relatives in town."

The light dawned. Public Safety had glommed on to this guy because he had a rape conviction on his record and happened to be in town. That was the sum total of their "evidence." Outrageous. No wonder Liz had called me. But if the guy jaywalked or littered between now and trial, he could end up convicted.

My public defender adrenaline pumped new energy into me. Here was the problem with this case and, in fact, with due process in the North Slope Borough. The legal system was Anglo, and the location was Native. The two didn't fit. Natives had their own system of justice based on accountability, sanctions, and group knowledge of what had happened. The Anglo system of written law, due process, and witnesses and juries—which I had studied and loved—did not work well in a place where community and family values took precedence over written prohibitions, and where even such seemingly universal qualities as time or factual evidence were blurred in the day-warping constant sunlight and the different cultural frame of reference.

For example, a witness might not be able to tell you whether something happened on a Tuesday or a Wednesday because the twenty-four-hour dividing line between the two didn't seem to matter under the midnight sun. The witness might then tell you what he thought you wanted to hear, in order to be polite. A Native witness might not even care how the case came out. What mattered to him was what his grandmother thought about his actions and their consequences.

To further complicate the situation, the Anglo system was administered by attorneys five hundred miles away in Fairbanks and in Anchorage, two hundred miles beyond that. They rarely came to the Slope and, it could be argued, were not concerned about outcomes here. It would be up to me to keep the case on the right track. I had handled murder cases before, in Washington State, and several here in Utqiagvik, but none like this one that had the whole community outraged. I hoped I was up to the task.

"My counselor said I was doing good in the program. He's here, ask him." Lane's voice had taken on a wheedling tone.

I craned my neck around looking for Pete Petersen, the

director of Utqiagvik's rehab facility, SATS (Substance Abuse Treatment Services), wondering how many minutes remained before the magistrate came in. Stern faces in the crowd glared back at me. I spotted the counselor in a back pew and hurried to him.

"I'm just so upset about this," he began, his lisp more pronounced than usual, when I had barely reached his side. "Amos has worked hard in treatment, on his alcohol dependency and some serious grief issues."

I studied Petersen, trying to determine whether the man showed admirable courage in supporting Lane in the face of community hostility or if he was a foolish do-gooder, as I was sometimes accused of being.

"What kind of grief issues?" I asked him.

Now Petersen turned and studied me for a moment, as if assessing whether or not I could handle what he was about to tell me.

"When Amos was fourteen, his mother was dragged into a house by three men. They raped and tortured her until she died."

A chilling shock fell upon me. I looked around the courtroom at the earnest faces of young mothers and concerned Native elder ladies. We are all prey, I thought. Many things had changed in my lifetime, with the advent of television, jet air travel, and the internet, but this one fact remained the same. Amos's mother, the Ipalook sisters, and all the women here were prey—as were our daughters and our granddaughters. But there was no time in the middle of an arraignment to consider my own reactions. I had to move on. I blinked and shook my head.

"I see. That's quite a traumatic history. Mr. Petersen, can you tell the magistrate today that in your opinion as his counselor, Mr. Lane is still in substantial compliance with your program?"

"Yes, and they have no business poking into treatment. We're protected by federal confidentiality statutes. People won't come for treatment if they're not guaranteed confidentiality. If the confidentiality is broken, we'll lose our federal grant."

Here I tried not to smile or sigh. A lot of federal law didn't reach all the way to the Arctic. The distances between Washington, D.C., and Alaska's North Slope were just too great, the cultural differences too telling, the network of agents too thin. An example of the disconnect occurred with the Distant Early Warning Line, the radar installations that once stretched along Alaska's north coast and into Canada, a 1950s Cold War defense against Russia attacking the United States over the North Pole. The DEW Line was gradually replaced by newer technology, and the government abandoned the installations. Local inhabitants made good use of the furnishings left behind. For a while the government sent up agents from the FBI and the Bureau of Alcohol, Tobacco, and Firearms to prosecute these "thefts" of government property. The agents explained to the court that the specially developed materials in the DEW had cost taxpayers millions of dollars. The judge in Utqiagvik asked them, "You came all the way up here because of some plastic bins that the government abandoned?" The agents quit coming.

I felt uncertain whether to call Petersen, whether what he had to say might do us more harm than good.

"Are you prepared to accept him back into the program?"

He nodded.

"Did the State even talk to you before they filed this petition?"

He shook his head.

"Thanks so much for being here," I told him. He was all we had, and we would have to use him. "We'll call on you."

I returned to Lane. One of the clerks had probably tipped the magistrate that I just got off a plane, and he was giving me a few precious moments to prepare as a nod to fairness, but he wouldn't want to keep this many people waiting much longer.

"Are you willing to go back to the treatment program? I don't think I can get you out any other way."

He didn't answer. Amos didn't resemble a choirboy, but he also didn't have "murderer of two" stamped on his forehead, not that you could have told by looking. His black hair had a slight reddish cast and a bit of wiry crimp on the ends. He reminded me that in the nineteenth century there were other whale hunters here than the Inupiat. The men from Nantucket, the "iron men in wooden boats," cruised these waters. The Yankees left behind some offspring and their New England names: Ashby, Coffin, Bodfish, Tuckfield, and Leavitt. The Portuguese, those famous navigators, came here, too. Descendants of both the Yankees and the Portuguese were present in this courtroom. Amos had a broad face with dark, watchful eyes and winged brows. His narrow nose and archer's bow lips reminded me more of the Mediterranean than the Arctic coasts. I guessed young women in Point Hope had found him handsome.

"I'd rather be with my relatives here in town. They were going to be here today, but they got threats over the phone."

Maybe his relatives had indeed been threatened, or maybe he was just telling me so to cover the fact that they hadn't shown up today because they, too, believed he was a murderer.

"All rise," the trooper-acting-as-bailiff commanded us. The plump and perennially cheerful clerk entered from a door concealed behind the blond wood bench platform. On her heels came my former colleague in the wilderness of Arctic children's neglect-and-dependency cases and part-time dog musher, the magistrate, his brown hair for once neatly combed, his earnest face perplexed. Utqiagvik was not quite large enough to have a real district court judge for the misdemeanor court that we appeared in today, and so we had a magistrate, appointed through the court administrative system.

As we got to our feet, I whispered again to Lane, "Are you willing to go back to treatment or not?"

Unhappily, he nodded.

The magistrate bade us be seated. I felt a pang of sympathy for him. He was the only one looking east in a courtroom of angry eyes staring west.

"Good morning," the magistrate said.

No one in the pews responded.

"Good morning, Your Honor," I said, rising to my feet. "Could my client's cuffs please be removed?"

The DA also rose. "Your Honor . . . ordinarily, we would not object . . ." He was stammering a bit. "But this defendant . . ."

Slusser was probably acting on instructions from Fairbanks and looked uncomfortable about it.

The trooper, a lanky and mustachioed fellow, who served as bailiff and order keeper when there were no Public Safety officers available, approached our table expectantly. His main occupation was to escort prisoners between the small Utqiagvik jail and Fairbanks Correctional Center, known locally as FCC, as needed. The trooper had taught himself Alaska administrative law and regulations, especially those dealing with hiring and pensions. After maneuvering both himself and his wife into the best possible pension program opportunities, he expected before long to retire to the Caribbean or the Gulf of Mexico—and court staff asked him daily whether he had picked Cozumel or Cabo.

"Your Honor, we are only here on misdemeanors," I said.

"You can remove the cuffs," the magistrate directed.

The trooper unlocked the cuffs with a friendly wink at me and went back to his stool near the bench.

"It is Friday, August 6, at 10:20 a.m. and we're here on two misdemeanor and one misdemeanor probation revocation arraignments involving Amos Lane," the magistrate intoned. "First, the matter of representation. Mr. Lane, do you want counsel to represent you?"

"Yes, Your Honor, I do." Lane spoke clearly in the direction of the microphone. He had been in court before.

"Can you afford to hire a private attorney, or are you asking that the Public Defender Agency be appointed?"

"I want a public defender," he said, and here he turned again toward me, this time with an up-and-down glance and an insinuating smile. I would have kicked his ankle under the table for his inappropriate behavior if I could have done so without drawing more attention to it.

"I have to determine if you are indigent. Do you want to fill out a financial affidavit, or do you want me to ask you some questions on the record?"

"The record is fine, Your Honor."

While the magistrate asked my client questions about his financial status, I rummaged in my shoulder bag, which also served as a briefcase, for my copy of the bail statute. In Utqiagvik, almost everybody was released to a relative pending trial for three reasons. First, there weren't sufficient local detention facilities to hold them, and transporting detainees all the way to Fairbanks and back for every hearing got expensive for the State. The second was that most defendants had in their extended family a significant other or cousin or uncle willing to take them, who would nag them into showing up. The third reason was that there wasn't really any place for people to escape to. Public Safety watched the airport, and no roads connected Utqiagvik with any other town. There was only the tundra on one side and the ocean on the other, and both were hard to survive alone.

I found the statute I was looking for. Alaska Statute 12.30.020 stated that "bail is a matter of right unless danger to community or flight risk." But having a right to the setting of bail did not mean that the defendant had a right to be released. The requirement of even a small cash bail posting would keep most Utqiagvik clients in jail, since many local people lived a cashless lifestyle.

"Mr. Lane, I find you are indigent, and I appoint the Public Defender Agency to represent you. Counsel, do you want formal reading of the complaints and the petition and advisement of rights?"

"Your Honor, we waive, and ask the court to enter pleas of not guilty to the complaints and a denial on the petition."

"So entered."

With these few words, the court had now completed the main

purpose of this hearing, the arraignment, which consisted of presenting the defendant with the written charges against him, as required by due process and the Constitution. Counsel almost always skipped formal reading of those documents, preferring to go over them privately with the client.

"We now turn to the issue of bail."

Joe Slusser, the DA, got to his feet. "Your Honor, the State calls Public Safety Officer Marten to the stand."

Behind us the pews buzzed like a jar full of bees.

Marten walked up to the witness box and raised his hand, his blue-black uniform wrinkled and his chubby face tired.

The stalking horse, I thought to myself. Ellingsworth, the lead detective, never appeared and never allowed his name to be used until trial, and then only on those cases he considered sure winners for the State.

The witness was sworn and sat.

"Officer Marten, have you had occasion to run a background check on the defendant, Amos Lane?"

"I have."

"And what did you find?"

"Mr. Lane was convicted by a jury of sexual assault in the first degree in September of 1983 in Kotzebue and has been in almost continuous custody since that time, until he was released to the alcohol treatment program in Utqiagvik three weeks ago."

"Why do you say almost continuous custody?"

"Mr. Lane escaped from Fairbanks Correctional in 1985. He was the subject of an extensive manhunt on the tundra near his home village of Point Hope for several days."

"He was subsequently apprehended?"

"He was found almost dead of exposure, with large portions of his feet frozen. About half of the left foot had to be amputated."

Again, the courtroom buzzed.

I resisted the urge to look down at Lane's feet. I did glance, though, at his face. His expression was as cold as the seawater a hundred yards outside the courtroom and the eternal ice at the Pole. I shivered. What an awful fate, I thought, to be pursued by those mechanized hounds, the snow machines, over the trackless tundra. He would have known he risked losing his life or limbs in making that run. With his ancestor-taught skills and in his desperation, he no doubt lasted longer than anybody else would have, just not long enough to get home.

"Does he have any other charges on his record?" the DA asked the witness.

"Yes, he had a misdemeanor assault on another inmate while in custody." Here Marten took from his uniform pocket two folded sheets of paper, which he began to unfold.

I got to my feet. "Your Honor, defense objects to any reference to in-house administrative proceedings in the Department of Corrections. We object to recitations of any material which we have not had an opportunity to review."

"Are you asking for a continuance of these proceedings, Counsel?" the magistrate asked hopefully.

Continuance only meant delays and more time in jail for my client.

"No, Your Honor, we're asking for due process."

The magistrate frowned. That comment verged on impertinence.

I hastened on with a courteous smile. "We're certainly prepared to file a motion for additional proceedings of whatever nature, should they become necessary."

I could feel Lane's eyes on me, appraising, and hoped he did not ask me what proceedings I might have in mind, because I had no idea at the moment. The magistrate ran his fingers through his hair, making it stick out unbecomingly, while he looked miserably down at the files before him.

"The court will allow the DA to question on the material," he finally declared, "but will not consider that particular information in making the bail decision."

Huh? I thought to myself.

"No further questions," the DA said. He knew the in-house stuff wasn't admissible.

"Ms. Wright?"

"No questions," I said, to avoid emphasis. The potential jurors in the pews behind us already had "prior sexual assault" and "frozen feet" burned into their brains.

"The witness may step down. What is the State asking for bail?"

"The State is asking that bail be set at $10,000 cash only, Your Honor. The defendant is a danger to the community because of his record and also a flight risk, since Utqiagvik is not his home."

Ten thousand cash on misdemeanors?

"Ms. Wright?"

"Your Honor, we call Pete Petersen."

Petersen shambled up to the box, looking like an aging hippie in comparison with the uniformed Marten. While he was being sworn, I scribbled notes to myself, struggling with more than the usual number of two-edged swords. If I attempted to generate sympathy for the defendant by referring to the grief issues Petersen had mentioned, the magistrate might conclude that Lane had been traumatized by tragedy into the capacity for rape and murder. If I tried to explain that Public Safely considered Lane a suspect on the murder cases not because of any evidence, of which I had seen none, but because he had a record and was in town, the magistrate might decide that the prior record looked pretty bad to him, too.

"Mr. Petersen, would you summarize for us your education and experience?" I began.

He had a master's degree from a university in South Dakota and had previously worked as an alcohol counselor in several parts of Alaska before coming to Utqiagvik (where he could earn almost twice as much money).

"Mr. Petersen, Mr. Lane has requested that I ask you some

questions about the alcohol treatment program he has been participating in with you, and he waives his right to confidentiality. Are you in fact his counselor and director of the program?"

He was.

"For what kind of problems were you treating him?"

"Alcohol dependency and grief syndrome."

"Mr. Petersen, did Mr. Lane recently have a relapse of drinking?"

I knew this question was leading, but the DA and I rarely interrupted each other with objections on that basis during bail reviews since there was no jury, and most of the evidentiary rules make sense only when a jury is involved. If then.

"He did. It is typical of recovery that patients return briefly to drinking. They immediately suffer consequences. He went directly into the detox unit and lost all his privileges, like mail, visitors, television, and snacks. Relapse is a part of recovery."

I thought that sometimes the treatment people were fools. One relapse in Utqiagvik could leave bodies all over town. Perhaps this one had. But maybe the potential jurors didn't look at Petersen that way. Maybe they thought he was some kind of expert.

"Mr. Petersen, do you consider Amos Lane to be in substantial compliance with your treatment program?"

"I do."

"If the court releases him to you today, are you prepared to accept him back into the program?"

"I am."

"Thank you, Mr. Petersen. I have no further questions, but the district attorney may have some."

I sat down and Joe got up.

"Mr. Peterson, does your program grant day and weekend passes to patients?"

"We do."

"Is there any supervision of patients while they are out on passes?"

"Not exactly. They don't get passes until they have been in treatment awhile and are ready to demonstrate that they can be responsible."

Well answered, Petersen. But the magistrate would worry about unsupervised weekend passes being available to Lane. I didn't much like them myself.

The magistrate asked, "What is defense proposing in the way of bail conditions?"

"Your Honor, we ask that Mr. Lane be allowed to return to the treatment program he needs so much, which will benefit not only him but, in the long run, the community. We ask that the revocation petition be dismissed since, in the opinion of his counselor, the defendant is in compliance with his program. We also ask that trial dates as early as possible be set for the three misdemeanor cases."

The courtroom fell from quiet to silent.

The magistrate said, "Brief recess," and disappeared behind the bench before his clerk had even a chance to say "All rise."

"Thank you, Counselor," Amos Lane whispered. He had doodled a huge firebird on the edge of one of the complaints and beneath it written, "God is love."

"It's a little early for thanks. I don't think they're going to let you out today, unless you can raise some money."

Slusser passed me a scribbled note. "Sorry about this. E.E. wants this guy."

E.E. Ed Ellingsworth. I smiled ruefully at the DA and handed the note back so it wouldn't fall into the wrong hands. Joe was really a sweet guy, unlike some of the attorneys in Fairbanks who dictated to him.

"What was that about?" Lane demanded.

"The DA said he was sorry about raising that administrative stuff from FCC. Sometimes the Utqiagvik DAs disagree with the Fairbanks DAs, but the Fairbanks office runs the show and calls the shots."

He mumbled, "They shouldn't do it if it's not right," and began drawing a rose on the second complaint. I let his remark pass without asking whether his own life had modeled doing the right thing. He was correct. Fairbanks was in the wrong.

"Are you a good attorney? How come you're just a public defender?" Lane asked me.

I sighed but reminded myself the question was fair. Much of Lane's future now depended on me, and he wanted to know whether I could do a good job for him. Some people think public defenders aren't real attorneys, and most believe they serve only because they can't get any other job. I remembered the old joke: "Please don't tell my mother I'm a public defender. She thinks I play piano in a whorehouse."

I look at things differently. Though classmates had often told me I wasn't tough enough to do criminal law, I found it more interesting than contracts or property, and eventually I learned that hard-shell toughness was not required so much as the kind of sinewy stamina that women have in abundance. Plus compassion. Nobody questions why a person who sees a hungry dog abandoned in the rain can't rest until she rescues it, or why people want to help a crying child. Me, I feel sympathy for any creature at bay, for any defendant at risk of being unfairly oppressed in court.

"Ask around, Amos," I told him. "Ask Frank Peter, or Wesley Ahvakana."

Of course, he might not have a chance to talk to Frank or Wesley. They were not in jail, thanks to me.

The magistrate returned, his hair now neatly combed. We all rose and sat. Without lifting his eyes, he gave his decision.

"The court does not believe that the State has shown that the defendant is necessarily a risk to the community. The sexual assault conviction, while serious, is old, and the defendant has served his time.

"In the opinion of his own counselor, Mr. Lane is in substantial compliance with his treatment program, and the court therefore dismisses the probation revocation petition against him.

"The court also has to state that in its opinion, the present charges could be characterized as thin. The court states in addition"—here the magistrate raised his eyes and looked at me, and I saw in him my old colleague in many battles against the Office of Children's Services for the return of children to their families—"the court knows that all you people are not here out of concern for these misdemeanor charges. You people are here because of that other case, a very serious case. And I will also say, your presence is appreciated. Too many women in our community, and across the state, go missing, and the disappearances are never investigated or resolved. Too many Alaska Native women. Some of our villages have no law enforcement at all, and suspicious deaths aren't even reported. You are here because you care about these women, and your presence and your caring are the only things that will bring about change."

Amen, I wanted to say, on behalf of Amos and his mother, and out of gratitude that this judicial officer cared.

"But Mr. Lane has not been charged in that case. No one has."

Hope rose in my throat. As on many other occasions, I held my breath lest I frighten away that precious concept. Lane ceased his studied indifference and almost vibrated with tension beside me. I thought that he seemed more than misdemeanor-level tense. The present charges posed no long-term threat to him, as he surely knew. He had no felony time hanging over his head. Even if he somehow got convicted of one or more of the new cases, he could do the misdemeanor time at the treatment center and hardly notice it. So why was he so nervous? Guilt? Sheer distrust of the system?

The magistrate looked down at his papers again. "On the other hand, because of the number of charges against Mr. Lane, and because he was apparently out of the treatment facility when the alleged incidents occurred—"

I exhaled.

"—the court is concerned with the fact that this facility lets people out on passes with no supervision. The court is always reluctant to interrupt anyone's treatment, but the court feels that the posting of some bail, though not as much as the $10,000 that the State has requested, is necessary."

For the life of me I've never been able to understand how the posting of any sum of money will magically guarantee that somebody will show up for court. Especially since the defendant is rarely the one coming up with the money. Usually, the posting of the money only showed that somebody still loved him or her, or was at least willing to have them in the house. But in the long run, maybe being loved and having a home were what counted the most, anyway.

Now the magistrate finished in a rush. "The court sets bail at $500 cash, as 10 percent of $5,000, on each of the two remaining cases, concurrently, on the posting of which the defendant may return to the alcohol treatment facility, where he is required to remain in compliance with his treatment program, with no weekend passes, or be subject to immediate arrest without a warrant. Trial dates to be set later."

The magistrate, looking now as weary as Marten, gathered his robes about him and swept out, the clerk trotting after him. Slusser and I smiled at each other. The ruling was fair from both points of view. From the DA's, it kept Lane in jail for the time being. From Lane's, it offered a reasonable chance to return to treatment on a relatively small posting if he did, in fact, have relatives to back him with some money, and one of the cases had been dismissed. I was proud of my old colleague's courage in the face of such great community pressure. Some citizens probably hoped Lane would be charged and convicted this very morning, or that he might be released so that they might seek a rougher justice.

I told my client, "I'll come to see you at the jail. We will keep trying to get you out, and we have to talk about that other case."

"Nothing to talk about. I didn't hurt them girls. I never even knew them."

"Good, but we still need to talk. And don't talk to anyone else."

"You ain't telling me nothing I don't already know." He held up his wrists as the trooper approached.

I hated the part when they led the client away. I studied his retreating form for signs of a limp. Little, if any. I gathered up the papers. This case was going to be a dogfight. Public Safety officers were out in force, and the community would not let them rest until someone, anyone, was charged. The Inupiat knew more about the victims and suspects than Public Safety did, but they didn't like to talk to Public Safety, and Public Safety often didn't listen when they did. I was only one person, and I had 126 other clients besides Amos Lane. Each case was its own universe of legal issues, evidentiary problems, and potential motions. To keep up with the caseload, I'd had to learn to work fast, and then faster—to outline and to skim, to do early triages, and to accept the fact that I could touch only most of the bases, not all.

I would try my best for him, but right now we were facing not one but two adversaries, Public Safety and the community of Utqiagvik.

*AUTHOR'S NOTE: *Many so-called Native proverbs are falsely attributed. Genuine proverbs, either Native or English, arise from an oral tradition, have no one specific author, and are difficult or impossible to research. Rather than leave out this important source of wisdom and voice, after careful checking, I have included eight of these traditional sayings. If a reader has information or suggestions about them, please contact me at rebeccawrightstevens.com and I will try to set the record straight.*

2

Men were the 'keepers of the tradition,' and therefore they were thought to be the most important. The women let them think this, but the women knew that if it weren't for them, doing all the hard work putting up supplies to feed the family and planning for the future, the people wouldn't survive.

EMMA SIKKIKOQ MILLS, AS TOLD BY HER GREAT-GRANDDAUGHTER LORETTA OUTWATER COX IN *THE STORYTELLER'S CLUB* (2005)

THE ALASKA COURT SYSTEM SHARED A BUILDING with the Bank of Alaska, a great square block of pale-blue-and-gray steel and glass, three stories high, with a bite cut out of one corner for a cylindrical entrance. A revolving door within the cylinder with rubber gaskets on the bottom operated as a type of Arctic air lock, a barrier between comfortable room temperatures inside and the wind and cold outside, which sometimes dropped to sixty degrees below zero. It was also one of the few buildings in town that had an elevator. The district court, from which I had just escaped, occupied the lower floor. Above was a mezzanine that held only the superior court. When anyone was charged in the Ipalook case, the suspect would appear in superior court. The public defender's office, my office, was on the third floor, between British Petroleum and Probation. We needed more space than we had in our slender rectangle. Liz's desk and the ranks of file cabinets were in the front half of the office, and my associate, Carol, and I each had an office in the back half. Mine included an indoor window box of morning glories.

Public Safety Officer Marten beat me back to the office. He was slumped in a chair beside the front desk, nearly asleep, when I arrived. He had never before shown up at the public defender's office, but then, two well-known sisters had never been murdered in Utqiagvik before. I was relieved to see Liz at her desk, too, her slender form clad in her perpetual jeans and sweatshirt, her pretty yet tough face perhaps just a little puffy under the eyes with hangover. Elizabeth Kanayurak might not always show up for work, but she was quick and bright and knew everybody in town. As an Inupiaq herself, she could have made a lot more money working for the borough, but she had cast her lot with us downtrodden public defenders. We were the only legal office in town that had a Native person on staff, which was a huge advantage. Clients who called us heard her Native voice rather than a *tanik* bureaucrat, and a little trust was kindled. More than once I had been baffled on a case because I couldn't find a certain witness, but Liz was able to locate them because she knew their mother-in-law's cousin.

I appreciated her sticking with us. Heck, I loved Liz. She possessed many of the qualities listed in the traditional Inupiaq "code of ideals," the Inupiat Ilitqusiat, posted in hallways and framed in offices around town: She was loyal and generous and brave. She shared everything she had, from cigarettes to clothes to groceries. Also, she was funny, and often used her humor to keep things running smoothly in our overworked office. Once I overheard her on the phone with a client who was ranting about how he had to talk to me right away, even though I was getting ready for court on another case. "I can get you an appointment," she said, "but it'll cost you a quarter." The client laughed and agreed to come in after court was adjourned.

"Hey, Rebecca, some vacation." Liz raised an eyebrow, meaning there was something on her mind that she didn't want to say in front of Officer Marten.

I patted her on the shoulder, then turned to our unexpected guest. "What's up? You must be really tired, Officer Marten."

"Can you come over to Public Safety? Couple things I need to ask you about."

"Yeah, sure." I figured it must be something about my new client, Amos Lane. "Give me just a minute to off-load here, and I'll meet you there."

Curious, I watched him shuffle away. Public Safety had never begged for my company before.

"Any news about the Ipalooks?" I asked Liz.

She shook her head. "Maybe he has some."

"Have you seen Randy?"

Randy was a local teen Liz and I had been trying to keep on an informal suicide watch because of the extraordinary pressure within his family. His mother was dying of cancer in the Public Health hospital in Utqiagvik, but his dad remained in the village of Anaktuvuk Pass, leaving teenage Randy to cope alone. As if he needed more stress, Randy was a talented basketball player upon whom the team depended. He was also a skilled mechanic who put in way too many hours at a local shop in order to be able to buy his mom special gifts. He was such a good kid, but he was so at risk of feeling overwhelmed. All Alaska teens, especially Native teens—and especially Native teens in bush communities—seemed to be at risk this year. Anchorage papers were full of "teen suicide epidemic" statistics but few good ideas for solutions.

"Not recently. You're going to be working too hard again, aren't you?" Liz said.

"Huh?"

"Now that you've had your vacation, you're going to go right back to working six days a week and sleeping all day Saturday, aren't you?"

"Why? You're not quitting, are you?"

"You never got to have your birthday at home."

I refrained from asking how she had known it was my birthday.

"We're throwing a party for you," Liz said.

I started to say that given the double homicide, I wasn't in the mood for ice cream and cake, especially since local ice cream was made of lard with dried berries mashed into it, but Liz cut me off.

"I ordered up a bunch of booze from Fairbanks. Saturday night. In my garage. Come to the little side door. You will come, won't you?" She was looking at me with a funny shy look. Shyness was not her ordinary state.

"Liz, I'm honored. But heck, I . . ."

"There's something you don't know," she said.

Oh, no, I thought. Maybe she's been charged with possession. Or she is pregnant and wants to stay home. Or the borough's made her a salary offer she couldn't refuse.

"What?" I asked.

"Eskimo parties are the best parties in the world."

Relieved, I laughed. Once again, she'd used her humor to get her way.

"I didn't know that. I guess I'd better check it out," I said.

"You're coming?"

"I can't have you drinking all that booze by yourself."

"Great," she said. "Now you can have the rest of your phone messages."

She opened a drawer and handed me an inch-thick sheaf of pink message slips with a rubber band around them. I took them into my office and laid them down in front of the azure morning glories I had planted in pots by the window so they could climb some twine in the endless Arctic summer sun. I was pleased to see they were thriving.

As soon as I off-loaded my stuff, I looked in on my associate.

Carol was fresh out of law school and made no secret of the fact that she had come to Utqiagvik because it was the only position she could find since she had no legal experience. Apparently she had no experience of any other kind of job, either. Her first day at work, instead of coming to town the day before and finding room and board so she could report on time, she flew in that morning. Around eleven, she interrupted my meeting with a client to ask whether there was any place where she could get a decent breakfast. I was trying my best to help her learn the ropes, reminding myself that if she quit, it would take a while to find someone else, and in the meantime I would have to handle her caseload as well as my own.

"Carol! How's it going?"

Carol sat cross-legged in her chair, reading a file, trying to look so focused that she had not noticed my return. Now she glanced up at me, round eyed, smoothing limp brown hair back from her pale face. "Oh, hi. How was your trip?"

"Good. Glad to be back. When I catch up a bit, we'll . . . sit down with some of your cases." I was turning away when she called after me.

"Oh, I almost forgot. I have a message for you."

I stuck my head back in her door.

"It was . . . Friday. No, it was Thursday—this kid, a Native kid, he said his name was Ricky—no, he said his name was Randy. He seemed kind of upset. He wanted to see you. I told him you were out of town."

"Randy. Nice-looking kid? Long hair? Basketball jacket?"

"That's him."

"How—how upset did he seem?"

Carol shrugged like her job had ended with the delivery of the message.

"Did he want me to call him?"

"Uh, no. In fact, he said not to call. He said he would come back."

Randy wouldn't have been here unless he had an urgent problem that could truly be a matter of life and death. Carol didn't seem to have learned in law school that all messages in a law office were important, and that people's lives could turn on dates and times. I hoped she hadn't made him feel unwelcome. He might never come back, and then we would have to go out and look for him. I would keep on trying hard not to nag Carol, to give her time to learn the many things she needed to, but she didn't seem to be trying hard to learn them.

"Okay, Carol, we'll talk soon."

I patted the doorframe in what I hoped was a collegial manner and left to meet with Officer Marten.

THE NORTH SLOPE Borough Public Safety building and jail was a blue-tiled cube across a stretch of gravel from the courthouse/bank building. These two structures, along with the Alaska Commercial grocery store, Stuaqpak ("Big Shop"), the venerable Presbyterian church, and two Native corporation headquarters, formed Utqiagvik's downtown. I gulped the clean Arctic air greedily after all those hours in planes, glad to walk on gravel instead of pavement. There was no pavement in Utqiagvik because each winter the cold would destroy it.

The receptionist buzzed me through the security door and upstairs to Officer Marten's small office on the second tier, among walrus and caribou heads, and PR posters telling the public that the pretty girl had quit her guy because he wouldn't quit drugs, that TB was everyone's business, and that shoplifting was theft. The building was oddly designed, almost hollow, with a bank of office doors connected by walkways. Marten's door was shut. I knocked, but there was no answer. He'd asked me to rush over there, and now he wasn't around? Odd. The Ipalook case must have had them disorganized. I sat down on a bench, idly picking up one of the public interest brochures scattered on it.

Subsistence, this one was titled. The cover showed racks of drying fish. "Most *taniks*, non-Natives, when they first come to Alaska, don't understand what the word means," I read inside. True enough.

> Many wrongly believe that it connotes a poverty-level existence. But the word *subsistence* actually stands for a proud Native heritage, one that has now been codified into law in many areas of the Anglolegal system that has been introduced into the Far North.

Who wrote this? I liked it.

> To re-state in words that people in the Lower 48 more readily understand, subsistence means to live off the land, like Daniel Boone and Hawkeye, only in a truer, fuller sense. Inupiat people traditionally do not go to a store for food and other necessities. They harvest food from marine and land mammals, fish, migratory birds, and the tundra. For centuries, they have perfected the necessary hunting skills for survival in a harsh land, and the domestic skills of skin-sewing and ivory carving to turn the hunter's harvest into a comfortable way of life. Many Native leaders and politicians have devoted their lives to protecting and continuing these traditions. Because of this history, only Native peoples are allowed to harvest certain marine mammals and the polar bear.

I was turning the page when footsteps approached. Officer Marten, looking like the living dead, unlocked his door. I followed him inside.

"Thanks for coming." He offered no small talk. No smile. He pointed at a folding chair, and I sat.

"Ms. Wright, we've worked together on a lot of cases," he began. "We've always tried to be fair; you've always been honest. I think you're good people. I hope you think I am."

What I thought was that this was an odd preamble, but I didn't say so.

"We've got a problem on our hands with this Ipalook case. We're getting calls from the mayor, the governor's office, and, of course, the media. And when we've got a problem, you've got a problem, right?"

"I'm not sure I follow you."

"We've interviewed dozens of people. We're trying to piece together a time frame. But it was a weekend in the midnight sun, and lots of people were drinking, and nobody gives the same time for the same thing."

"Witnesses always vary," I said. I wanted to say, Especially when the sun shines continuously for eighty days and you can't tell one day from another, and your boyfriend brought home a jug, but Marten knew those facts as well as I did.

"Yeah, but this isn't just a few minutes or even a few hours. Some witnesses remember details that could be important but can't be real sure whether they're talking about Friday night after bingo, Saturday night after the sober dance, or Sunday morning when they woke up."

"Officer Marten, lay it out for me. What details are we talking about?"

"Like the neighbor. Wiley Ungarook. Bernice Ipalook came over to his place to borrow a cigarette."

"Yes?"

"He vividly remembers her coming over because she ended up taking half a pack and he was pissed."

"So?"

"He says he started drinking Friday afternoon, and he can't be sure when she came over. If she came over late Sunday, then she was still alive after Amos Lane checked back into SATS, and he couldn't have killed the sisters."

"I see."

"So maybe it was the boyfriend who killed them, John Adams,"

Marten went on. "He and Bernice had a big fight that weekend. We know that. She threw her ring in his face. He told the bus driver about the fight on his way back home. Was he jealous because Lane had been to visit?"

"What time was Adams riding the bus?"

"Last bus Saturday night. Around eleven. So there was plenty of time for Lane to show up after Adams left."

I thought a minute. "But if somebody told him Lane was there after he left—even just watching TV or playing cards—he could have walked back to the girls' house later. Mad."

"Now you're getting the picture, Counselor. If we had one good, sober witness who could testify that the girls were alive Sunday night, your client would be in the clear. But Wiley Ungarook just can't quite remember if Bernice borrowed cigarettes Saturday morning, Sunday morning, or Sunday night. I suppose it could even have been Monday morning, when Adams was at work and Lane was back at SATS. Also, you know, there are some hardcore druggies in town. It could have been one of them who killed those poor girls."

"Lane had no motive," I said. "Adams may have had a motive, if they quarreled."

"That's why we need your help," Marten said.

"My help?"

"We know your client, Amos Lane, was out on a weekend pass from treatment last weekend. We need to know who he spent time with while he was out. If you could give those names to us, just between you and me, and they check out, we could quit focusing on him and go on to other suspects. The fiancé, for one."

"He mentioned at arraignment that he had relatives in Utqiagvik who didn't show up because they had received death threats. But he didn't give me any names, and I don't know if I would go so far as to call them alibi witnesses."

"Who are the relatives? I need the names." He took up pad and pencil from his desk.

I couldn't advise my client to give names at this point, since, obviously, if the witnesses' stories didn't check out, he would be in worse shape. With that kind of assistance from counsel, he might well end up indicted for two murders. Why was Marten even asking?

"I don't know any names. I don't even know for sure there are any relatives."

I was trying to think fast but not succeeding because of my own fatigue, plus jet lag. Conventional wisdom said never have your client talk to law enforcement about anything. Period. But in my experience, there sometimes occurs that odd case in which you have a chance, an early window of opportunity, if you judge it right, to help your client and steer a case in a different direction by volunteering information.

"Lane hates Public Safety," Marten said. "We know you know that. You just don't know all the reasons why, like we do."

I could feel my head tilting, spaniel-like, in an effort to understand where he was going with that comment.

"Rumors. Village rumors, is all," he went on. "But some village rumors turn out to be true, and we have to check all of them. There are other women missing on the tundra. And the thing is—"

I tilted back the other way and focused. I knew from the social workers that too many Native women, both Inupiat and Yupik on the tundra and Athabascans in Fairbanks and the interior villages, went missing each year, and too few cases were adequately investigated. In Alaska, victims and perpetrators both often disappeared into the vast expanses. This reality had to change, but resources were inadequate.

"—his name was linked with some of them."

Was Marten trying to tell me that Amos Lane, who had just doodled "God is love" on a misdemeanor complaint, had murdered not only the Ipalook sisters but other women? But Marten had initially said they wanted to clear him of suspicion in the Ipalook case so they could focus on the fiancé of one of the sisters.

I thought back to what Amos's grief and alcohol counselor had told me at the arraignment about the horrific rape and murder of Amos's mother, and once again a chill crept up my spine. I tried to concentrate on what Marten was asking.

"What exactly is it you want me to do?" I asked.

"Give me the witnesses now. Your client will never know. Nobody else is going to know, I promise you. But this grieving family and the community might be closer to having some answers."

We stared at each other in silence a moment. Then I repeated, "I don't know any names, and if I did, I wouldn't tell you. You know as well as I do that's protected client information."

I heard a noise behind me and twisted in my chair. Detective Ed Ellingsworth had joined us.

"Come on in, Ed," I said. "I guess I should have been expecting you."

Ellingsworth took two folded metal chairs from the wall and, in elaborate slow motion, opened them and sat on one, draping his long legs on the other.

"Now, Miss Becky, don't get in a spin," he said, drawling more heavily than usual. I disliked him calling me Miss Becky, and he knew it. To tell the truth, I could hardly stand to be in the same room with this man. I hadn't cared for his oily imitation cuteness when I first met him, and began to actively dislike him when I learned about the Russian girls he invited to visit him to try out as possible brides, even though he had a wife somewhere in the Lower 48.

"If you have a bona fide offer, make it, and I'll take it to my client, but don't expect anything on the side. If it turns out Amos had mud on his boots or a wart in the wrong place, you know the grand jury will indict him."

Ellingsworth reached over and opened a top drawer in Marten's desk, and I saw the glowing red eye of a running tape recorder. With a hidden device, in violation of Alaska law, they had tried to record me giving them confidential client information.

If I'd given them anything, they could blackmail me with it into other kinds of cooperation. If it became known that I'd given them confidential information, the Alaska Bar Association would sanction me severely.

Ellingsworth shut off the machine with a bony forefinger. "Sorry, little lady. This case is driving us nuts. If you can help us here, we'll dismiss all them cases and he'll walk today. I promise."

"You don't have the power to promise anything. Only the DA can promise. And you're offering to dismiss two misdemeanors so you can indict him on a double homicide?"

"If he's innocent, he's got nothing to worry about."

"You mean like Theo Johnson had nothing to worry about?" I said, and wished I hadn't.

Theo Johnson was the reason my dislike of Ellingsworth had escalated into hostility. Theo was a young kid who got drunk one night and barricaded himself and his girlfriend into their cabin. Instead of letting him sleep it off, as was usually done in such situations, Ellingsworth brought in a SWAT team and set up a siege. When officers fired on the shack, Theo fired back, and in the melee an officer got hit. For Theo's sentencing, Ellingsworth brought in officers and their families from all over the Slope to put pressure on the court. Perhaps I should have faked a heart attack just to get a reschedule. Poor Theo received twenty years to serve and was shipped off to a for-profit prison in Arizona, far from his Native home.

"Theo Johnson was a cop-shooting son of a bitch who got what he deserved," Ellingsworth said, straightening up. The footrest chair clattered to the floor.

"Ed," Marten said.

"Tell you what," I said. "Get your Fairbanks DA to offer Lane immunity, and we'll see how much information he has. Maybe he saw the fiancé kill the sisters. Who knows? Then you can get some sleep."

The room fell silent. Come to think of it, the entire building seemed to have gone on hold, listening to the loud voices on the second tier. Ellingsworth sat bolt upright on his remaining chair. Marten looked ready to crawl into a corner. I got to my feet.

"If you ever try this stunt again, we're all going straight to Judge Jeffery, to see what he has to say about it," I said.

"Can't blame us for trying to do our jobs," Ellingsworth said, sounding a bit sheepish.

"Breaking the law is your job?"

"Sorry, Miss Rebecca. I really am," Marten said. "It's a hard case."

For a brief moment, I pitied them. Marten, anyway. It's a public defender job hazard that you learn compassion for almost everybody. The pressure on Public Safety was enormous. Probably neither one of them had slept more than a few hours since the murders.

"See y'all later," I said, heavy on my own drawl, and left them staring wearily at each other.

I trudged back to the office, upset about Public Safety's illegal maneuver. My threat of contacting Judge Jeffery, however, was an empty one. Judge Michael I. Jeffery had no supervisory authority over Public Safety. He could rule only on cases and motions brought before the court, and nothing had been filed yet about the murders of Bernice and Wanda Ipalook. The DA's office didn't directly supervise Public Safety officers, either, though it often advised them on procedure. To call Ellingsworth on the carpet, I would need to contact the director of Public Safety for the North Slope Borough, or the mayor who appointed the director, both of whom would probably encourage the lead detective to continue doing whatever he thought he needed to do to find the perpetrator of the awful crime.

But I was more than upset; I was concerned. I had never known Public Safety to push this hard for evidence. If they couldn't find any evidence, might they make some? Sometimes hair was found where it had been "overlooked" before. Often jailhouse snitches coincidentally overheard just what Public Safety needed them to overhear.

Bernice and Wanda had been murdered in daylight in a small, isolated village where everyone knew everyone. Even Natives didn't attempt the five-hundred-mile trip to Fairbanks over the roadless tundra. I didn't know whether it was possible to get to Deadhorse or Nome—the nearest towns—by small boat, because no one except local whaling crews ever went out in small boats in the Arctic, which meant that in all likelihood, the killer was somewhere among us.

3

The Yupiaq would agree with Chief Seattle (1790–1866), who stated that "This we know: the earth does not belong to man, man belongs to earth. All things are connected like the blood that unites us all. Man did not weave the web of life, he is merely a strand in it. Whatever he does to the web, he does to himself."

ANGAYUQAQ OSCAR KAWAGLEY IN
A YUPIAQ WORLDVIEW (2006)

I awoke glad to be back in my Little House on the Tundra. I had been lucky to find the place. Available housing in Utqiagvik was not so much in short supply as nonexistent. Utqiagvik elders limited new construction in order to avoid the "boom-and-bust oil-pipeline syndrome" that afflicted real estate in Anchorage. More than one newcomer—eager to earn what used to be called, before the village reverted to its original name, "Barrow bucks," for the oil-inflated salaries—had in desperation rented walk-in closets for living space until a room could be found. Some tried living in their offices after hours and nearly went mad in the effort. Living without a home was difficult enough, but for those unaccustomed to the geography of the North Slope, there was the added challenge of living in a place without woods or a park to relax in—or a bar in which to forget it all.

Sight unseen, by telephone, I had initially rented half a duplex, the only housing I could find. The owners evicted me on the spot when I arrived with my Labrador retriever, mixed terrier, and Siamese and tortoiseshell cats. Luckily, just that day the Ukpeagvik Inupiat Corporation, one of the Native corporations that controlled the village, had listed a small, flat-roofed, box-shaped bungalow, maroon with white trim, on the edge of town. Because of permafrost, the ice that underlies all soil in the Arctic, the house was built on stilts and had a plank walk connecting it with the road. If you allowed a building to rest on the ground, eventually its unnatural warmth would thaw part of the permafrost and disastrously tilt the construction, as had happened on many old government buildings. I gratefully paid the exorbitant first month's rent.

There was one neighbor between me and the Arctic Ocean. The family on the corner was well known in town because the patriarch, Clair Okpeaha, had witnessed the plane crash that killed Will Rogers and Wiley Post at Walakpa Bay in 1935. He ran about thirteen miles to bring the news to Utqiagvik. The son, Clair Jr., sometimes shared a duck or hare with me from his hunt. I was ashamed to tell him that I didn't know how to fix game and usually gave them to Liz.

I had a natural gas heater sitting on a raised tiled dais in one corner of the living room. I set its thermostat to sixty-eight degrees, and it guttered away peacefully year-round and never needed adjusting again. Natural gas was cheap because we were so close to the oil fields. Sometimes in a winter storm, snow blew through crevices in the walls and collected in the corners, but the heat never failed. There was, though, an odor, a mild, overripe garlicky smell, that accumulated in clothes, but I got used to it.

The house had a water reservoir in one corner, which a truck filled each week. Since the water was not drinkable, I kept a Sears countertop distiller running in the kitchen to provide drinking water. The curtained bathroom alcove held a honey bucket toilet fitted with disposable plastic bags that were picked up by city employees every three days. This job was called "working the buckets," and I had several clients who earned money this way. The shower stall had an open hole in the floor through which water drained out into the tundra. When I first looked down while showering and saw the ice and snow beneath the house, I expected to feel a draft. But cold settles downward, so the freezing air never reached my warm, wet legs.

The living room held a hide-a-bed couch covered in a flowery print, a large bookcase, and an old TV on a stand. Upstairs, in addition to my futon mattress on the floor, equipped with an electric blanket, I also had a chest of drawers and an Exercycle.

I had everything I needed, plus an incredible, magnificent perk. Above the tundra in front of my house, especially on sunny days, snowy owls glided and soared in their endless search for lemmings. The first time I saw one, I thought I was hallucinating. They couldn't possibly be that beautiful. Wings of snow against the Arctic blue heavens, grace and beauty overhead whenever I had a minute to stand in the doorway and watch. No wonder the ancients had called the area "place where the snowy owls gather." I always think of it that way.

Ordinarily, I slept most of Saturday and worked Sunday. This Saturday I figured I should try to catch up with the backlog, and went in, but hadn't been there long when the DA called.

"I'm going to have to look at the Ipalook crime scene," Joe said. "You wanna come?"

"Sure," I said. "Thanks for including me." Attorneys representing defendants were entitled to information about their cases, according to the rules of discovery, but no one had yet been charged in the Ipalook case. Joe was assuming Amos Lane would be charged and I would be appointed to represent him, so he was cutting a corner and saving time by giving me information as it developed.

"It's over there on the bluffs, behind Arctic Pizza. You'll see the yellow tape. Meet you there."

The office was only a few blocks from the crime scene, so I chose to walk there in the breezes off the Arctic Ocean, which always cleared my head. I needed to be alert. I disliked going to crime scenes, but it was necessary because cases rested on facts, and facts rested on crime scenes. At the scene you might find that a witness could not possibly have seen what they'd told police they'd seen, because of angles of buildings or lack of lighting, but there was no way to know unless you visited the crime scene in person. Only by being in the actual place could you understand how many seconds it would take the perpetrator to reach the front door from the bedroom, how far the sound of voices carried from room to room, or how much the weather could have modified any outside evidence. It was also important to look at the proximity of neighbors, to find out what kind of neighbors they were and what nearby pedestrian and vehicle traffic was like. If there were usually a lot of people in an area and nobody saw what the police were saying happened, then maybe it hadn't.

But I dreaded entering the house where these two beloved sisters had been murdered.

"Over here." Joe waved to me from his faded blue International Harvester Travelall. Public Safety had a fleet of Travelalls—half truck, half station wagon—because they were so tough they seemed immortal, even in the Arctic.

"See," he said, "I've got the notebook the Anchorage forensic team made up."

"Thank you, Joe," I said.

Joe politely lifted the yellow crime scene tape for me, and we crossed the dried mud of the yard, stepping over a pile of rotting canvas squares and skirting an abandoned sink. The house was a large weathered shipping container with plywood add-ons, whose laminations were beginning to buckle. Joe fiddled with a key and Public Safety's padlock until the door yawned inward.

Homes of affluent Inupiat, of whom there are many, were similar to affluent *tanik* homes, but poor Native homes were different from poor white homes. White homes smelled mostly like kids and dogs, maybe potato chips and Campbell's soup, and cleaning products. Inupiat homes smelled like the seal oil used for cooking; gun oil, because they have hunting weapons; and parka fur, which, as it ages, gives off a dusty odor when damp. Local Natives did not usually let dogs into their homes, except for a few pedigreed types. In the very poor homes, where everyone was living in one room and there were no closets, most possessions hung on the walls—pots, clothes, guns, graduation pictures, and bags of food. The honey bucket was partitioned in a corner with only a curtain, but it never gave off an odor because the air was so cold. People went to the rec center for showers.

Joe paused inside the kunnychuck, the protective Arctic entryway, and I almost ran into him. It was little more than a lean-to, and at first, in the dimness, I could see only some jackets and dog harnesses dangling on pegs.

"This is where the first body was found," he said. He moved farther inside, where a crack in the seaming gave light, and opened his notebook to read from it.

> In the Arctic entry Victim A was lying on her left side, head turned south and feet north, with her back propping open the living room door. She was lying on top of her parka and one arm was still inside it. There was a bottle of Crown Russe vodka in the sleeve. She was not wearing any pants. There was a white panty around one ankle. Her t-shirt had been pushed up and the left breast was exposed. A white substance was on her lips that could be dried semen and a sample was submitted for testing. A woman's shoe, black, lay by her right foot, a Reebok high-top tennis shoe. A matching shoe was in the living room. Behind the kunnychuck door was a pile of human feces.

The forensic team had removed everything from the floor and swept it bare. I strained my eyes for any bloodstains or marks. If it developed that the case involved forensic evidence such as blood spatter patterns, and defense could show they had been deprived of the opportunity to test with their own experts, sometimes an entire case could be dismissed.

Joe moved farther into the house, but I remained, wondering about the woman whose final resting place this had been. I knew many members of the family but couldn't recall meeting Wanda or Bernice. Any woman could end up a victim like this. I said a prayer for the peace of her soul and for her sister's, and I added one for Amos's mother, who had died as they had, as though she also were a sister. I thought that all of us who are prey are sisters. Then I tried hard to retreat back into the emotional compartment that made my job possible. There didn't seem to be any bloodstains. Perhaps no blood had been spilled, since she died from strangulation.

In the main room, a contractor's droplight dangled from an extension cord on a hook in the middle of the ceiling, and Joe switched it on. The small living area held a mattress in front of a television set, and I saw beer cans and overflowing ashtrays everywhere. Joe took down the light and moved it around. As it highlighted different areas, I felt as if I were seeing underwater camera shots from the *Titanic*. The light revealed elaborate hand-carved details on the wooden cabinets around the dry sink. Someone had once tried to make this place a pleasant home.

Joe put the light back on its hook, took up the notebook from the counter, and began to read again.

> Victim B was lying flat on her back on a mattress in the living room, head toward the north. She was wearing a yellow t-shirt and no pants. A pink hair dryer was lying under her shoulder and the cord of it was wrapped around her neck. A pair of blue jeans was lying on top of her lower torso. There was a small amount of blood by her head on the west side.

Listening, I tiptoed around with no idea of what I was looking for, trying not to trip on anything fragile. I noticed a patch of mattress had been removed. I peered through the curtains in the honey bucket corner, but apparently it had been taken away. I looked at a picture on the wall that showed a stern-faced man in a white anorak holding a harpoon and standing astride the tail of a beached whale. I stepped into the kitchen area and stared at a plate of congealed spaghetti on the counter. A rumpled empty bag of cookies lay nearby, crumbs scattered around it. A heavy white coffee mug lay on its side near a spreading brown stain. On the stovetop, a skillet looked like it hadn't been washed since last year but reheated and reused.

Something beside the skillet caught my eye.

There was an odd shape I couldn't immediately recognize sticking out between the skillet and the burner. I figured it was probably nothing important but wanted to look at it more closely. At the same time, on instinct, I didn't want to draw Joe's attention to it. He might be a nice guy and a respected colleague, but he was, after all, a prosecutor.

I don't claim to be a trained observer, but one skill I do have is sensitivity to what is out of place. Years earlier, I accompanied my sister, a biologist, on a saltwater-creature census she was tabulating in an estuary in Florida. In spite of her training and greater experience, I was usually first to spot where the sea bottom had been disturbed and a specimen might lurk.

But the real reason this unknown object under the skillet caught my attention was that I had spent nine years as a homemaker and knew that nobody, not even drunks, either Native or Anglo, would cook with something sticking out of a burner. They might cook with old grease or dirty pots, but not with something flammable right in the area of the fire ring.

The boys from Anchorage in their lintless white jumpsuits, the professionals, had processed this whole place. They would have picked up hairs with tweezers, vacuumed for fibers, and photographed every stain and all the cracks. Surely they wouldn't miss anything of significance, would they?

Sure they would. They missed stuff all the time.

The police radio crackled in Joe's vehicle out in the yard.

"Right back," he said, and went out to check on it.

I took down the droplight and held it over the stove. The object was a ripped and frayed piece of plaid cloth. A button was sewn onto it, an unusual button made of sliced horn or antler.

My brain flashed on the black-and-white canons of legal ethics. I had no duty to point the button out to Joe, but at the same time, I had a duty not to secretly confiscate it, though my fingers itched to grab it and carry it off to submit to our own forensic experts before the State saw it. I could only study the odd item and memorize it. I could tell that the center holes of the button were hand drilled because of their irregularity. The cloth had bluish threads sticking out. When I talked to Amos, I would have to ask him whether he had any blue shirts with missing buttons.

"Nothing serious, I hope?" I asked, putting the light back on the hook when Joe returned.

"Nah. Somebody lost a puppy named Furball. It's a quiet Saturday."

"I hope they find Furball."

"There isn't much in here. Let's look at the bedroom."

We stepped inside the only other doorway. This room was barely large enough for a second mattress. A tangle of faded blue-striped and multicolored sheets had been dumped in the middle of the mattress. A gooseneck lamp sat on the floor in one corner, and a pink plastic milk crate holding socks and panties in the other. Along the near edge of the mattress was a scattering of broken toys. One was a small purple plastic pony with a front right leg missing and three inches of platinum-colored fiber mane and tail.

Joe opened the notebook again and bent his strawberry blond head over it. "I hate to show you these, but I guess you'd better look," he said.

He held the light for me while I took the forensic ledger and viewed photographs of the bodies. I couldn't help wincing. The faces were swollen out of proportion by the gases of decomposition, produced during what was Utqiagvik's warmest season, the early weeks of August. They looked not only dead but as though they had never been alive and human. They looked like balloons with lips and eyes smeared on in paint.

"Pretty hard on the family," Joe said, "and it's a special family, the grandfather being so important, and all. You can see why the Fairbanks office is interested in this case."

I nodded miserably.

"Anything else you want to see?"

I shook my head. "Thanks again for letting me tag along."

"Yeah. Anytime. Hell, I didn't want to come here alone," he said.

"I'd sure rather see it with you than with Ellingsworth."

Outside, Joe snapped the padlock shut on the death house and drove me back to the courthouse in the Travelall. I kept thinking about the button in the stove grease. Maybe I had learned more than I wanted to know.

4

Yesterday is ashes, tomorrow is green wood.
Only today burns bright.
INUIT PROVERB

THAT NIGHT I WAS IN NO MOOD FOR A PARTY, BUT I could not disappoint Liz, who rarely disappointed me. The midnight sun beating on my head did not help my mood.

Relatives in the Lower 48 sometimes asked me whether the months of darkness during the polar night were depressing. No, I'd tell them, and try to explain how people put out Christmas lights early to make the houses look cozy. The village was so small that each person was doubly precious, and in the darkness all went out of their way to help whoever needed it. When the buses weren't running and I had to walk to work, I never made it on foot all the way to the courthouse. Someone always stopped to give me a ride, and I was never afraid to get in the car.

But the damned endless summer sunlight got on my nerves. There were no peaceful twilights, no star-dazzled midnights, just sun so bright it made your eyes wince until you could get behind blackout curtains and hide.

I put on my best jeans and the somewhat low-cut scarlet sweater

I wore for going out when I was in Anchorage, and called a Tuttu Taxi. Utqiagvik had two highly lucrative cab franchises, ArctiCab and Tuttu Taxi (*tuttu* means "caribou"). As a state employee, I tried to divide my business between them to avoid showing favoritism.

"They're having a party over there," the Korean driver said when I gave him the house number of my destination. "Lots of trucks already there. Music too loud. Cops gonna come." Just as in big cities, cab drivers knew what was going on. Also, just as in big cities, the cab drivers of Utqiagvik were a cosmopolitan bunch, representing all corners of the earth. I didn't fully understand how or why so many found their way to this place, which was literally the end of the earth. Some were fugitives. Others just needed a place where it was easy to get a job that paid well, at least well enough to bring up the rest of the family. The drivers could have formed a roll call for the United Nations, and riding in a Utqiagvik cab was never dull.

I arrived at Liz's place around ten; paid the driver, who smirked at me; and crunched off in the gravel looking for the door to the garage. I heard Bob Seger's "Night Moves" reverberating from inside. At least there might be some good music. I found the door, took a deep breath, and opened it.

The garage was dark as a bar. Good. There were more people than I had expected, and they were dancing. Balloons and streamers hung from the low ceiling like an upside-down fantasy forest. I shut the door, and "Night Moves" surrounded me.

"Hey, she's here," Liz yelled. Now I had to show my surprise and delight.

Laughing faces appeared out of the dark, some of them blowing bubbles with kids' bubble-mix bottles. I couldn't see very well, but there seemed to be only one or two *taniks* among them. I wished I could skip the greetings and blow some bubbles myself. I got hugged. The Inupiat hug a lot. Somebody thrust something heavy and smooth and damp and cold into my hand. I peered down and realized it was a bottle of champagne.

"Happy birthday, Counselor!" somebody hollered, but Liz called out, "None of that. She's off duty."

She grabbed my free hand. "Come see the spread." She led me over to a table where I could barely make out salads and casseroles, cold meat and deviled eggs, and bottles of wine, whiskey, vodka, and rum. A washtub filled with beer and ice sat on the floor beside it.

"Wow!" I said. "Who brought the champagne?"

"Lucy Renfro. She appreciated you getting her little brother off on that assault case."

"Who's her little brother?"

"Jimbo Matumeak."

"That was years ago."

"So? She didn't forget."

Liz took the bottle of champagne from me, shook it up and down, and handed it to a bystander to be opened.

"Liz, you must have spent hundreds of dollars on the—"

"Hey, just because I don't show up all the time doesn't mean I don't like my job." She laughed at me. "Look, Seismic brought his best equipment."

I stared into the far corner and could just make out the waving arm of local celebrity KBRW radio disc jockey Seismic Isaac Tuckfield, named for his trademark rumbly voice, sitting beside a huge bank of black boxes. Seismic had a second or third cousin in prison. The family's phone was shut off because his long-distance collect calls from Fairbank Correctional had run up a big bill. The man was just a lonely inmate who wanted to talk to his family, so I let Seismic's family receive the calls at the office. Anchorage never questioned the phone bill, and family members got in the habit of showing up in the office on birthdays and holidays to wait for a call from Fairbanks.

"He came for free," Liz whispered. "Usually he gets $500 a gig. He turned down another party to come here."

Uh-oh, I thought. I'm going to cry and embarrass everybody.

But I was distracted by someone shoving something else into my hand, something that felt like paper wound around a bunch of sticks. I smelled spice. I looked down and saw white carnations glowing in the dark. Flowers in Utqiagvik. They had to have been flown in specially from Anchorage.

What the hell. I could no longer hold back the tears.

A glass of newly opened champagne was thrust at me, and I drank it all.

"Hey, who told them that I loved . . ." I started to say to Liz, but Liz had disappeared into the dark.

"No crying on your birthday. It's time to dance," a male voice said.

Former client Eluktoona Brower led me through a dramatic interpretation of "When a Man Loves a Woman," including twirls and dips, with the carnations and an empty champagne glass dangling from my hand. Eluktoona—who was known as Tuna, I dizzily recalled—had been convicted at trial of a far lesser offense than charged.

"Everybody wants you to have a good time tonight and quit working so damn hard," Tuna whispered as the lovely music drew to a close.

"Okay. I'm ready."

He led me to a table on which lay a mound of presents. People gathered around in the comfortable darkness to watch me open my gifts amid showers of soap bubbles and sprays of champagne, and sips from my own glass, which somehow was bottomless. At the third exquisite ivory carving, I cried again.

"That's enough! The rest later," Liz declared. "More dancing."

Liz placed a chair for me near Seismic, and I drank champagne and danced, drank champagne and opened presents, danced some more, and drank some more. It was the first time I had lost track of time in a long time.

I noticed a Native man leaning with one foot up against the wall, watching the dancers. He was tall and lean, had long black hair, and wore a twisted bandanna tied around his forehead. He looked to be thirtysomething. I was fortysomething. Was that too old for him?

"Liz?" I said. "Who is that?"

Liz stood nearby, picking out some of Seismic's music. She looked in the direction I gestured.

"That's Michael Nusunginya."

"Who?"

"Noo-soon-GEEN-ya."

"I want him for my birthday."

"Rebecca, you're drunk. Time to go to the ladies' room."

I stood up, wobbled a moment, and set out at Liz's side, lurching only slightly, obedient as a spaniel.

"How are you doing?" Liz asked as we crossed her cluttered living room.

"You were right about Eskimo parties! Best birthday party I have ever had. Thank you. I love you. You shouldn't have spent all the money, but I'm glad you did. He's nice looking, isn't he?"

We reached the bathroom door and found it locked. Liz knocked until we were admitted into a great cloud of marijuana smoke. As I entered, the several occupants fled past me.

"I wish they wouldn't do that," I whined. "I would never narc on anybody."

"It's just that you work at the courthouse," Liz said, shutting the door behind us. "Most of them don't know the difference between a DA and a public defender."

The far side of the little room was curtained off, and Liz disappeared behind it to use the honey bucket.

"You should be more careful," she said from inside the curtain.

"What?" I was peering into the bathroom mirror at my champagne-flushed face. I looked ten years younger than usual. Maybe fifteen. I would have to include champagne in my self-care ritual. Maybe I was too young for Michael Noo-soon-GEEN-ya.

"Some of those girls might have been using hard stuff. No

kidding, Rebecca—I try to watch out for you, and I gave everybody a lecture before you got here, but you need to learn to watch out for yourself."

A warning bell went off in my head. I tried to deflect it into the champagne fumes, but then remembered what the cab driver had said about police coming if the music was too loud. Liz was right. I didn't want to lose my law license, though I was too drunk to really worry about it right then. I dug in my shoulder bag for a lipstick. Liz came out from behind the curtain, adjusting her sweatshirt.

"So tell me about Michael," I asked.

"Well, he's . . ." she began, and hesitated.

"He's what?"

"Too young for you."

"Is not! When it's this dark, I can look as young as anybody. How old is he, anyway?"

"I guess he's around thirty-five or so. I was just kidding. Nobody cares about age up here. Why? How old are you?"

"You know how old I am. You knew it was my birthday."

"You don't look that old. He's not too young for you. He's too . . . experienced."

"What does that mean? I have experience, too, you know. I haven't spent my whole life being a *tanik* do-gooder."

"Okay. I give up. You're too young and experienced for him."

"So tell me about him," I persisted. "Is he married?"

"Not that I know of, but he might have a kid around town."

I was not getting the answers I wanted.

"Who is his family?"

"One of his sisters is on the city council. A brother works for Bowhead Transport Corporation. The barges."

"So . . . why shouldn't I get to know him?"

"I didn't say that. He's okay. I like him. He's always helping people out—fixing cars, building houses. But you have no idea how you're going to get teased if you go with him."

"Why teased?"

Now I felt Liz was enjoying my ignorance. Well, let her.

"You white eyes come up here with all your degrees and think you're going to fix everything, and then it takes the whole village to get you trained to the job."

"What on earth are you talking about?"

"There are just so many things you don't know."

"Give you a quarter to tell me."

"Well, like . . . parties aren't the only thing Eskimos are best at."

I blinked at my enhanced, if slightly fuzzy, image in the mirror.

"Think about it," she said. "No Victorian bullshit. No candy-is-dandy or wining and dining. No puritanical shaming, no Freudian creep-outs up here. Just hey, it's a long night and let's you and me try to make each other—"

Somebody banged on the door. Liz admitted a beautiful young Native girl with waist-length jet-black hair, wearing a black T-shirt over black leggings. The two of them launched into a rapid-fire conversation in Inupiaq. I brushed my hair while the girl went behind the curtain and then reemerged.

When the girl had closed the door behind her I said, "You were saying?"

But Liz seemed to have lost her train of thought. She sat down on the polka-dot-upholstered makeup stool, folded her hands on the little counter, and gazed into the mirror. She looked way more serious than she ever looked in the office.

"Sometimes I worry about you," she said.

"Why? Because I think he's good looking?"

"It's not him. It's . . . Utqiagvik. It's not really Utqiagvik, it's . . . you're too drunk right now to listen. Probably not a good time to try to explain."

The champagne buzz in my head surged impatiently while she continued. I wondered which good songs I was missing.

"You work hard, and you . . . meet a few people, and you think you know the place. At least you're friendly. Unlike some of the others. But there's so much you've never really been a part of or understood . . . like Amos Lane, for example."

Now I tried as best I could to pay attention. Liz might tell me something about the case that she had learned from her contacts, something that Public Safety didn't know.

"You shouldn't be representing him."

"But I—"

"Oh, I know you think it's your duty, and so on, with your *tanik* law. But Inupiaq law has been around for thousands of years before you guys came. Some people shouldn't be represented. They should be cast out."

Cast out? I knew that casting out used to be a sanction for people the community judged guilty of an offense. But was it ever still done? Were people cast out onto the tundra? Onto the ice? I thought of the killing-cold ice water a few hundred yards away, glittering in the midnight sun—an ocean as beautiful in the summer as the Mediterranean or the Caribbean, yet capable of chilling the life from you in minutes.

Liz hushed.

Alaska Natives had been here long before anyone else, I knew. The grafted-on Anglo system was far from perfect, as were many of its players. But it seemed to me that, worldwide, due process was the best way to go. Even guilty people were entitled to be heard, not to be overcharged, and not to be oversentenced like poor Theo Johnson, whom Ellingsworth had persecuted because the kid had defended himself from the detective's SWAT team. But perhaps Theo Johnson would have been better off with Native law. Maybe a group of elders would have lectured him and put him on an island with no booze for a while. I'd had a couple of teenage clients placed in rehab programs with a similar format, almost a modern version of "casting out."

"But Amos Lane might be innocent," I blurted out.

Her eyes met mine in the mirror, and she said something in Inupiaq.

"What was that?" I asked.

She didn't answer but walked to the door and opened it, waiting for me.

"Wait . . . wait . . . I never went."

Liz waited silently for me while I took my turn behind the curtain and washed up. We returned to the musical garage. So long as I kept one hand on the wall, I could walk just fine.

This time I didn't sit in my chair. I stood in the shadows near Seismic's blinking black boxes, wondering hazily what I was going to do and glancing at Mr. Nusunginya. Leaning against the wall, he looked to be only momentarily at rest, like a hunter ready to step out of cover and fire. His face was shadowed by the wings of his long black hair, but I had the impression his gaze was watchful, knowing. Somehow he reminded me of the men in the historic photos hanging in the hallway at the Naval Arctic Research Laboratory, the men who went out on the Arctic Ocean in fragile-looking skin boats with a fierce joy in their eyes.

With champagne courage, I walked over to where he stood silently watching the dancers.

"Hello. My name is Rebecca. I don't think I know you."

He startled slightly, like an animal in a cage might do, then said courteously, "Happy birthday. I'm Michael."

"Thank you. I know. Michael Noo-soon-GEEN-ya."

He laughed. "My cousin Liz," he said.

"She's your cousin?"

"Almost everybody in this room is my cousin, one way or another."

"She warned me about you."

"Maybe I should warn you about her."

I decided that I might as well take the whole plunge, forgetting that women from South Carolina never ask men to dance.

"Would you dance with me? It is my birthday."

He took my hand, and we danced to "Wonderful Tonight." He didn't say a word. His arms felt hard. I liked his long black hair.

After that we put two chairs near the black boxes and shared the next bottle of champagne that somebody brought over and dropped in my lap. Eventually he talked a little. He said he was a heavy equipment operator for the city. He lived with his sister and nieces and nephews. He was born in Utqiagvik and had lived for several years in Fairbanks and Anchorage.

"But you came back to Utqiagvik?"

"Everybody that's born here comes back eventually. You've been here four years, right?"

I nodded, surprised that he knew.

"You divorced?"

"Widowed."

"What happened?"

I hadn't expected him to ask. Most people didn't. I drew a breath and thought how to answer and, to my dismay, felt moisture welling in my eyes again. Oh, no, I thought, I don't want to be a crying drunk and spoil my own birthday party. For so long I had tried not to think about Kent's death. The heavy caseload helped keep those thoughts away. In the dark of Liz's garage, the memories flooded back through champagne gates.

"Car wreck," I said, remembering the sound of the police radio in the driveway. Everyone instantly recognizes that sound. It never means good news. The trooper used that odd word. "On the freeway . . . He expired."

There were two things I hadn't been able to do. I couldn't bring myself to take his dinner from the warming tray where it had waited for him, the breast and thigh of fried chicken, plus two biscuits, green beans, and a little pot of gravy. I couldn't look in the closet and bring out clothes for him to be buried in. Friends who came to the house had taken care of the warming tray, and my mother picked out a blazer and slacks, the only dress-up clothes he owned, for him to wear in the coffin.

Eventually, I was able to sort and distribute his books. He was a teacher, and other teachers could use them.

My six-year-old son, whose only frame of reference for death was the TV show *Bonanza*, had asked me whether I was now the "Widder Wright." Yes, I was the Widder Wright, and had been for several years, but with two small children, there hadn't been much time to grieve.

Michael was getting up. He didn't want to sit by some weeping *tanik*.

I understood.

I watched as he walked over to Seismic and whispered in his ear. Seismic flipped through a rank of CDs and selected one. Creedence Clearwater Revival's "Bad Moon Rising" finished, and the chords of Willie Nelson playing "Blue Eyes Crying in the Rain" enveloped us.

Michael came back and took my hand. It wasn't dance music, but he held me in his strong arms, and we moved around the floor while I got the shoulder of his shirt wet. Nobody stared at me; nobody pointed. I got the impression people in Utqiagvik were not surprised by grief and that tears were okay, even at a party.

When the song was over, we sampled Liz's bountiful buffet, filling our plates with deviled eggs and scoops of cheese ball, piling on top cashews and olives and homemade chocolate chip cookies. We sat quietly and munched on the goodies and watched the dancers.

Michael asked me to dance again to "Save the Last Dance for Me," but I wasn't able to move with the music as well as I had earlier in the evening.

Liz interrupted. "You have another gift," she said.

Liz and Michael were both smiling at me like I was a little kid.

"A secret friend is giving you a limo ride home. You and Michael."

I had encountered Utqiagvik's limo service during my initial arrival at the airport. Only the limo could carry my suitcase plus crates holding two dogs and two cats. Debra, the owner/driver, told me that night she was saving her "Barrow bucks" until she had enough to buy a ranch in New Mexico. I found out only later that she was rumored to do more for Utqiagvik customers—at least for the men, according to their wives—than drive them around.

Debra kept herself blond and slender. She lived in a tiny white house near the airport that had window boxes on all sides filled with plastic tulips. One night someone tried to burn it down. Firemen turned out to douse the fire with water drawn from the high school swimming pool. They said that footprints in the snow might match the boots of the wife of one of Debra's frequent fares. Debra kept right on working and saving her money and living in a house with a big smoke stain on one side and singed tulips in the window boxes.

You could argue that Debra made a significant contribution to the community. Residents who got cabin fever during long winters but couldn't afford to pay thousands of dollars to fly out for a vacation in Hawaii, or even for a few days in Fairbanks, could scrape up enough money to ride around in Debra's limo, with a bottle. And Debra.

"Special condition—Michael gets dropped off first," Liz said.

Michael laughed. "That sounds like Tuna," he said.

Liz loaded the carnations and one more champagne bottle into my arms, and the presents onto Michael. Everybody cheered and leered while we made our way out to where the limo waited in the gravel, dazzling white in the evening sunlight.

Nothing like making a spectacle of yourself in front of half the jury pool, I thought, wishing fervently for darkness.

"Congratulations," Debra said as she drove us away. Whether to Michael, to me, or to both, I wasn't sure.

"To the freshwater lake," Michael said. "Nobody said we had to go straight home." Michael opened the bottle and held it for me while I sucked a couple of sips, hoping not to lose consciousness, or chip a tooth when we bumped over a pothole. The edge of consciousness where I lingered was pleasant.

Our blond pilot flew our shining machine out upon the tundra, beneath gilt-edged clouds and incandescent rays streaming over us like an illustration in the Old Testament. I now fully understood why so many spent so much to ride around with Debra, with or without extra services. In the upholstered back seat, I couldn't feel the gravel beneath the wheels, and from behind the tinted windows, the tundra looked like Eden.

"Have you almost got enough for your ranch?" I called out to Debra.

"Bless your heart, honey, for remembering," she said. "Almost! About five-eighths enough."

"Good for you!"

We drove in silence through sudden fog and emerged beside the freshwater lake that lay south of town. Michael helped me out and held my elbow like I was teenager wobbling to prom in her first heels. Good thing, too, or I probably would have fallen face down. I tried not to grin too hard.

The tundra is not flat, not in the way that salt marshes are flat, nor even as flat as the rolling prairies of Kansas. The tundra is small depressions and frost heaves in endlessly interlocking whorls. There is some grass, but the vegetation is mostly miniaturized shrubs, a bonsai garden that is the devil to walk in. The plants don't wave in the wind like grass. They wiggle.

But there was something else. Holding Michael's hand, I knelt and reached out to touch a stalk of hairy gray fuzz holding up purple flowers, and bent close to inhale their sugary scent. How could such a delicate flower emerge from all this gravel and ice? I had seen a picture of it in a guidebook and read that it was called a woolly lousewort. Surely beauty's brave standard-bearer in the Arctic slush should have a more elegant name. Perhaps there was a better word for it in Inupiaq.

I stood up, shaking my head in wonder, and gazed around the horizon. Toward the south there was not a single road between us and Fairbanks, five hundred miles away. I shivered, strangely thrilled.

"Look," Michael said. "*Nigliq.*"

I turned in the direction that he pointed and saw geese settling on the far side of the lake.

"Geese," I said. "They're beautiful."

"They're delicious," Michael said.

"How do they keep from getting eaten by wolves on the ground?" I asked.

"They fly."

"I mean, the babies in the nests on the ground. There's no shelter."

"Lots of babies. Some of them survive."

We made our way back to Debra, and she turned our huge coach toward town. Thirteen miles of road ringed Utqiagvik. We had reached the limit of one of them. Debra apparently knew where Michael lived, for without inquiry she drove us there.

"I'll call you," he said, giving me a brief kiss before he got out.

Now alone in the back of the limo, with Debra smiling at me in the rearview mirror, I wondered like any schoolgirl whether he would.

But he doesn't have my number, I almost blurted aloud. If he wanted it, he could ask Liz.

Why would he call? I sleepily remembered the beautiful young girl who had come into Liz's bathroom. He probably would call her, not me. Even if he did call, when he showed up in the daylight, I wouldn't look like I had in the dark, musical garage with a glass of champagne in my hand. I mustn't expect him to call. Better to just get back to work whenever the hangover was over.

"I'm so glad you had a great birthday," Debra said with a smile, refusing the ten-dollar tip I fished from my purse. "Liz already tipped me."

"Thanks, Debra, for bringing me home."

At least for a few hours, I hadn't worried about the Ipalook double homicide, or how to defend Amos Lane from our office manager—and an entire community who believed he was guilty.

5

For a time, I had to educate this whole community, make them understand the basic meaning of the law . . . [My] five, ten-minute arraignments would turn into half hours or more trying to explain their rights.

SADIE BROWER NEAKOK,
MAGISTRATE IN UTQIAGVIK, 1960–80

I LOOKED UP FROM READING FILES AND FOUND OFFICER Bob Tidwell in his blue-black uniform blocking my office door, a square silhouette beside my morning glories. I recognized him from court. The previous year there was an incident in which he had pursued some juvenile shoplifting suspects on their four-wheelers, but when they headed out on the ice, he gave up the chase. The boys eventually came home for dinner. Their parents turned them in and at the arraignment bawled Tidwell out for not catching the young people and bringing them home earlier. I stood up and said he had done the right thing because chasing the youths farther out on the ice could have had tragic consequences. I wasn't defending the officer but trying to emphasize that the boys had returned on their own and so shouldn't be charged with evading. But Tidwell came up to me afterward and thanked me for "sticking up for him," and I knew I had made a friend.

"Good morning. It's Officer Tidwell, right? Would you like a cup of coffee?" I asked, needing a refill myself.

He shook his head, and his eyes darted around my office as though he feared someone else might be hidden here. I gestured toward my only extra chair. He sat down and drummed his fingertips on the plastic chair seat between his thighs. Tidwell had a ruddy, puffy face and hair so fair he hardly had eyebrows.

"I was the first officer on the scene at the Ipalooks'," he said without preamble, "and I want to talk to you about it before... before it goes any further up the chain of command."

I forgot about coffee, sat back down, and swiveled to face him.

"I'm listening," I said.

"It was Massey and me got the call. Dispatch said it was a possible fatality. We were in one of the Travelalls on the lagoon road, and I had to drive slowly to avoid the kids and dogs playing. Massey asked me whether I had ever responded to a fatality, and I said no, I had just finished my training last year. I couldn't remember where house number 1541 was and said I hated the house numbering system—no street names, just numbers and streets going in all directions. Massey said, 'Town's been here fifteen hundred years. Locals always know where everything is. 1541 is that party house. We get calls from there all the time.'"

Tidwell was talking as though he had repeated this recollection to himself many times and had the sentences memorized.

Suddenly, he looked me in the eye. "Did you know that both the Lindberghs flew here in the 1930s on their way to Tokyo? My wife told me about it. Mrs. Lindbergh liked the nasturtiums blooming in window boxes at the Utqiagvik church. The pastor's wife fixed her a turkey dinner, and she sent two chandeliers for a thank-you gift. You should go see them."

I nodded and wondered whether Officer Tidwell was experiencing some post-traumatic stress.

"Anyway, we see two women waiting on the road in front of 1541. I figured they were relatives. Sweet Jesus, I hope no relative of mine ever has to go through something like that."

Tidwell shot me a glance to see whether I was taking all this in. I felt more like a priest or a psychologist than a lawyer. I didn't want to inhibit him by taking notes, and had focused on being a good listener. Sometimes the less I said, the more they did.

"Massey wanted us to wait for backup, but I thought we had a duty to see if anyone was still alive, especially with the family members there: Old Sara, Bernice's cousin, in her raggedy *atikluk*, and Mary, the ice fisher—I think she was an aunt. Old Sara said no one had seen them in two days, and little Eqalin had been crying for her mama."

This was the first I had heard of either sister being a mother.

"They never locked their door, Mary said, but now it was locked from the outside. Massey and I walked around the place. There was this one window in back that came out on a hinge. Before I really thought about what I was doing, I pried it open and went in headfirst."

I shivered. For all he knew, a murderer was still in there. But he cared about the sisters, and did his best for them.

"I came down on a mattress in the middle of a bunch of old clothes. There wasn't much else in there. I drew my pistol and went in the main room, and that's where I found the first one. Right away, I couldn't hardly see her very well because it was so dark with the blackout curtains. Now I can't stop seeing her."

A crease drew down between his pale brows as though he'd just gotten a sinus headache.

"The pictures in the textbooks, they never show what they really look like. She was all swollen up . . ."

I wished for some way to comfort him, but now I was seeing the scene with him, remembering that room as Joe and I had seen it with the droplight.

"Officer Tidwell, I'd be glad to bring you some coffee," I offered.

This time he nodded. When we were both fortified with steaming mugs, he hurried on with the narrative.

"It wasn't hard to figure out what had happened. She had a hair dryer cord wrapped around her throat, and her jeans were pulled down around her ankles. Then there was this awful pounding, and I almost fired my weapon. But it was backup cutting the lock on the front door. We found another body in the kunnychuck. She was almost naked, with purple bruises on her poor bare breasts. She was bent over to one side like she was trying to sleep on the cold dirt, and there was dried white stuff all over her mouth. Poor little thing. I wanted to put my jacket on her, but we're not supposed to do that."

I waited for him to go on, but he didn't. He shook his head like a man awakening from hypnosis, glad to find the experience over and the lights on. For several moments he studied the morning glories, as though considering what to say next, and whether to say it.

"What's worrying me now is," he said at last, choosing his words carefully, "I don't have any control over what the department does with the case."

I wanted to learn what he thought the Department of Public Safety was going to do and decided to break my silence.

"I know what you mean. I don't have much control over Public Defender policies, either." This comment was not entirely honest. I took pride in the fact that the Alaska Public Defender Agency was less bureaucratic than most state agencies—that HQ did, in fact, listen to input from its outposts. Still, even among us flower children and anarchists, as we were viewed by Public Safety officers, there were times when Anchorage just told us how things were going to be, at least budget- and personnel-wise.

"You and I have both had a couple of run-ins with Ed, our famous lead detective," he said, his voice taking on a bitter tone.

"True story," I said.

"Well, he's got this bright idea that your client didn't do it, that it was the fiancé, John Adams, and he's moving heaven and earth to push that theory."

Here was major news.

At Amos Lane's misdemeanor arraignment, all the knives were out for him. Now Ellingsworth had come up with a different agenda? The head DAs at Fairbanks would listen to him more than they would to Joe Slusser or to an ordinary Public Safety officer like Tidwell. Ellingsworth had been here longer than either of them, had worked on more cases, and talked louder.

"Which one do you think did it?" I asked him.

"Neither one of them."

"Really? Who, then?"

"Listen, Ms. Wright, I know you have some Native contacts." He meant Liz. "I don't, but I'm out on the streets all the time. I see things."

Again, he paused, as if worried he would say too much.

"What things?" I prompted.

"Fourth of July weekend, lots of drug dealers were up from Anchorage. Big players. There's a lot of money in this town, with the huge borough and oil payrolls, and it attracts them. Deals went down. Maybe a deal at the Ipalook house went bad."

"But why would anyone murder them?"

"Them girls was always drunk. I know they come from a good family, the best, but you know how alcohol and drugs get ahold of some people. If the girls tried to hold back a little drug money, thinking no one would bother them because of the family—or they drank it up, or just plain lost it somewhere—they might have been punished. To send a message."

I waited to see whether he had any more information.

He slapped his hands on his knees. "You and I both know that sometimes these guys get drunk and go nuts. They get ahold of some poor Native lady and do whatever they want and figure they won't get caught or, if they do, that nobody will care. Happens all the time."

"Yes, Officer Tidwell, it does," I said.

Suddenly he had said everything he came to say and got to his feet. "Ms. Wright, thanks for listening. I know you won't say anything you don't have to."

"All off the record, Officer Tidwell, and I'm grateful to you."

We shook hands. I watched him go, feeling sorry for him

and the other public safety officers who had to live with these memories.

BUT THERE WASN'T much time for sympathy, and I had to press on with reading the Ipalook files themselves. I opened the brown-and-white file box marked with the sisters' name in heavy ink. Inside were folders of interviews with neighbors and passersby. Right on top were separate pages clipped together that drew my attention because they were not white interview forms but thin yellow copies.

"ADMITTING QUESTIONNAIRE," the heading read. "Alcohol Use History and Survey." On the "Patient's Name" line was written "Amos Lane."

Public Safety was stepping over the line, way over the line. I remembered the little red eye blinking on the hidden tape recorder and got mad all over again. Now they were confiscating material from the alcohol treatment facility where Amos was a patient. It was protected by the treatment privilege of confidentiality, not to mention federal regulations. The facility should have resisted the confiscation, and Judge Jeffery would never have let Public Safety seize this material if given a chance to rule on the issue. The officers had just gone in like Viking raiders, found it, and carried it away. It was up to me to make them regret violating the laws they were supposed to be upholding. I could at least make damn sure the material never reached the eyes or ears of a jury.

Unless it turned out to be favorable, and we wanted it to, of course.

The yellow papers held a series of typed questions, with answers scribbled by Lane himself.

> *At what age did you begin to use alcohol?*
> Around ten or so.
> *At what age did you begin to use marijuana?*

Around ten or so.
What amount did you use?
A normal amount for a kid my age.
Have you ever had any difficulty in relationships because of drinking?
No. All my friends drink.
Have you ever had trouble on the job because of alcohol or drugs?
I have never had a job. I am a hunter.

The violation of confidentiality, and the saddening responses, stressed me out. I set the yellow papers aside for detailed research later. The next item in the file was an interview with Nate Olemaun, a former client and the son of a previous mayor. Nate had appreciated my efforts on his behalf. This, too, I set aside for the time being. I wanted to talk to him in person before reading Public Safety's version of what he might or might not have said.

The next item bore the label "INVENTORY." I drew it out and read "Clothing and property inventory, SATS Substance Abuse Treatment Center." On the dotted line beneath the heading was "Amos Lane, June 15," and these were the entries:

Blue book, "The Big Book of Alcoholics Anonymous"
Leopard-seal skin billfold
$2.32
T-shirts, white, 2
Socks, white, 5
Sweatpants, black
Sweatshirt, black
Leather thong necklace with polar bear claw
Sweatpants, brown, torn
Sweatshirt, white, Pt. Hope on front
Shoes, running, blue and white, size 10
Shirt, plaid flannel, horn buttons, one missing

I read the last item again. "Shirt, plaid flannel, horn buttons, one missing." Then I read the whole list again, and the last item two more times. I put the cover back on the file box and shoved it underneath the well of my desk.

Would Public Safety have found the ripped cloth and horn button in the grease of the Ipalook stove yet? I had no way of finding out without raising questions I didn't want to raise.

Liz came into my office, and I pushed the box further under.

"What are we going to do about Randy?" she asked. "I haven't seen him in a while."

I winced. I had truly meant to seek out Randy in the days since my return, but there had been so much going on with the Ipalook case, and new files that needed a look, that he'd slipped my mind. Sometimes this job was an agony of choosing between priorities. Randy needed attention, but so did other clients, several of whom were in jail wanting bail reviews.

"I don't know," I said, pretty sure she already had something in mind.

"He doesn't have a place to stay. He just flops wherever he happens to be."

"All right, Liz, what should we do?" I asked. "By the way, best birthday I've ever had. You were right about who throws the best parties."

"I know. Put your jacket back on. I want to show you something."

She handed me my jacket, and I followed her down the exit stairway. Outside she led me around the corner to a shiny new vehicle.

"See," she said. "My husband got it for me."

I gaped at the lipstick-red mini SUV Chevrolet Tracker. It was a two-door convertible.

"Jeff spoils you!"

"Yes, he does. Get in."

I climbed aboard and was admiring the console of buttons when she started the car and took off like a dog shot with a peach seed, as my father would have said back in South Carolina. We whizzed up the dam road and turned onto a faint track leading down to the beach.

"Take it easy, Mario!" I hollered.

She braked. "We're here."

I looked around. Other than rocks and ocean, the only thing of note was what looked like two wooden platforms of some sort on nearby walls propped up with two-by-fours. "Where's here?" I asked.

"Hollywood. I'll give you a tour."

Hollywood turned out to be what was left of an old movie set. Liz sat on one of the peeling, teetering platforms and lit a cigarette. I sat on the other.

"What movie was made here?" I asked.

"A vampire movie, years ago. All us kids used to come here in the summer."

"So now Randy does?"

"Probably, but that's not why I brought you."

She stared out over the short, choppy waves of the Arctic Ocean, working up to whatever she wanted to say. I stared at her new car. Liz's husband adored her. Sunday evenings, the two of them had a potluck that I often joined. Jeff cooked and Liz socialized. Jeff was a perfect example of Utqiagvik work ethic and opportunity. Of Polish descent, he had arrived in town broke and found work as a custodian at the high school. Over the years he had learned and demonstrated enough computer expertise to reach his present job as director of computer services for the North Slope Borough School District.

Liz and Jeff both had children from previous relationships, who were in and out all the time, and together had adopted an irritable tortoiseshell cat named Kitty Mae. The household also displayed Liz's collection of Coca-Cola memorabilia, including trays, sets of dishes, clothing, and lighted signs. I had contributed to this collection from airport shops every time my Christmas flight home touched down in Atlanta, the original home of Coke—and I tried to ignore the possibility that the coke Liz favored might not be the fizzy soda.

"I never told you the reason I came to work for the public defender instead of the borough," Liz said.

"Uh-huh."

She drew on her cigarette and threw it away.

"It was back when we were all just kids, playing anywhere we wanted. Day and night were the same. Fishing, wading, riding three-wheelers, picking berries. Sleeping in whatever house we were at when we wore out, eating whatever we could find whenever we got hungry."

I waited.

"I had this one cousin that had a clubfoot, and sometimes he couldn't keep up. I tried to watch out for him."

I could well imagine Liz as a tough little kid, looking out for her cousin.

"There was this other boy, this half *tanik*, half Athabascan. He thought he was a hotshot. He picked on my cousin, knocked him down when he wasn't looking, took his new clothes, whenever he had any, laughed at him."

She closed her eyes, remembering.

"One night, somebody scored some beer, and we brought it out here to Hollywood. We were having a good time until this kid started beating on my cousin. I told him to stop, and he didn't, he just kept on."

I suspected what was coming. Liz now had that light in her eye she sometimes had when she talked to Carol in the office and Carol let slip some particularly annoying put-down of a Native client.

"He took out a knife and was waving it around, and my cousin was so scared he peed in his pants. I grabbed the knife, and the kid lunged for it, and I shoved it in his guts."

"Oh," I said.

"I was only twelve, and they charged me with manslaughter. My public defender worked hard for me and argued I acted in defense of my cousin. I spent a year and a half in detention in Anchorage."

I tried to think of something to say.

"The other kids, they all testified on my behalf. Everyone. Even his cousins."

"Is that all?" I knew she had only been trying to protect her cousin.

Liz looked puzzled. "Isn't that a lot?"

"Well, yeah, it is, but I would have testified for you, too."

"The thing is, maybe that's part of why I want so bad to help Randy. I know how it feels to be a kid that age up here, stressed and confused."

"Yeah," I said. "A teenager shouldn't be left alone to cope with his dying mother, not to mention having to earn most of the money for the family and perform in school and basketball."

Watching terns swoop, one after the other, into an unseen school of small fish, I thought of the stories in the Anchorage papers about the epidemic of Native teen suicides. How could we keep Randy from becoming one of those statistics? The pamphlets in the hospital waiting room explained that suicide could be the ultimate expression of anger, that a young person who is angry at a family member, a school, or a community may use himself as a weapon. Suicide also represented a simple desire to end pain. But for Native kids, there were other issues as well. Some young Inupiat, caught between two cultures, couldn't envision a future that would work for them. I had seen the despair in their faces on the bus in the morning. They wore beautiful fur-and-skin parkas lovingly made for them by grandmothers and aunts—but these kids liked cars and computers more than hunting, and explored drugs instead of the tundra. After school, they watched glittering *taniks* in music videos but knew they didn't fit into that world, either.

"What's the word on Randy's mom?" I asked.

"They're not sure. It may be only a few weeks now. A lot of pain, and she can't talk well anymore."

"You think there's any way to get the dad to come help Randy?"

"Asshole's too busy with his teenage girlfriends and running the chamber of commerce in Anaktuvuk."

"How many hours is Randy working now?"

"Who knows? Every time I go by that garage he's there. There or basketball practice."

"What would be the traditional way to help Randy? The Anglo systems are failing him."

"You mean, what would the Inupiaq community do?"

"Yes."

"Now you're talkin'," she said. "I can find a family who will take him in. Then you'll have to get the social workers to do the paperwork so they can have financial support. And when it's ready, you're going to have to go out and find Randy and get him to go there."

"Me?"

"Yeah, you. You're his lawyer."

"All right. It's a deal."

"Oh, and I forgot to tell you," she said. "He needs a shell."

"A shell?"

"Yeah. I asked him if there was anything his mom would like—flowers or a teddy bear or some music. He said a seashell. She likes seashells. They all went to Hawaii once and she had a good time picking up shells on the beach."

"Okay." The kid wanted a shell for his dying mom. He would have a shell. I had no idea where to get a suitable shell but would figure something out.

If it was up to Liz and me, Randy was going to be all right.

THERE WAS A scattering of snow in the afternoon, and when I got home, I wondered whether I might see boot tracks on the plank walk leading to my door. But the pristine iridescence of the snow was undisturbed.

THAT NIGHT, I was sleeping the sleep of the truly weary on my upstairs futon when a tapping noise woke me up. I thought it must be one of the cats scratching and tried to go back to sleep. The sound persisted. Finally, I made my way barefoot down the stairwell to see whether there was a problem below.

Both cats dozed on the flowered living room sofa beneath the blackout curtains. The refrigerator whirred. The dogs had not bothered to follow me downstairs. What was tapping?

I went to the front door, cold toes curling on the gritty floor, and looked out the security peephole. I could barely make out part of a headband.

It was Michael Nusunginya.

I opened the door and stood there shivering in my pink flannel nightgown, wondering whether I should object to the bizarre hour. Truth was, I was glad to see him.

“Hello,” he said. “I came by the other day on my way out hunting, but you weren’t here. I just got back.”

He unzipped his jacket and pulled me inside it. I smelled the cold tundra air on his neck and felt his hard chest through my soft gown. But he was holding one hand awkwardly away from me, and I drew back to look at it.

“You’re cold,” he said.

“You’re bleeding,” I said.

His right hand oozed dark blood through a bandanna wrapped around it.

“I didn’t get any on you,” he said.

“Come in, come in. What happened?” I drew him inside and closed the door.

“A knife handle split. It’s nothing, but I need to clean it. You got any iodine?” He sat on the coffee table in front of the couch and began to unwrap his hand.

The phone rang. The phone almost never rang at this hour. My eyes still on Michael’s bloody hand, I reached into the stairwell, where the phone sat on the steps. The caller wanted to speak to Michael.

"It's for you. Somebody named Bull." I held out the receiver.

He took the phone with his good hand, smiling at my confusion. "It's all right, Bull. I'm fine. No, I'll clean it here. Really, you don't need to do that. I'm okay here."

My eyebrows rose.

"Let's see. It's around three thirty. I'll be ready at the usual time. Thanks." He handed the receiver back to me.

"Bull is going to pick me up here for work," he explained. "You want a ride? What time do you usually go in? You got anything to eat?"

So many questions for my level of wakefulness.

I tried to remember what was in the refrigerator. Not much. I went to Stuaqpak almost every night on the way home in order to keep my loads small enough to carry on the bus. It was hard to stay stocked with no car, but I have eggs, I thought. Maybe some bacon left over from the last time Anchorage sent an auditor up and she stayed with me for lack of other housing.

"I have to clean my hand first."

I moved into the kitchen and pointed to the bathroom curtain. Michael disappeared behind it. I opened the refrigerator and found there was no bacon.

"All I have is eggs. Do you need any help?"

"I can manage. Eggs and toast?"

"Sure. How many eggs?"

"Six. Where's the iodine?"

Frowning, I put the eggs on the counter, then slipped behind the alcove curtain to rummage in the bottom dresser drawer. Michael was running cold water on his hand and prodding the sliced-open side of his palm.

"Here." I set the iodine down beside the faucets on the sink.

"Mm," he responded.

I returned to the kitchen, and soon the smells of bread toasting and butter melting in the skillet warmed the house. It had been a long time since I cooked for anyone. I seemed to remember there were several things I hadn't done in a long time.

"So where were you hunting?" I called, trying to be hospitable. Hospitality in Utqiagvik might be different from that in South Carolina, but both places were famous for it. Hospitality was a matter of making people feel welcome and comfortable, responding to their needs, being pleasant, I reminded myself.

My guest didn't answer the question. Maybe his hand hurt. Maybe an Inupiaq considered it bad form to talk through a bathroom curtain when one was cooking and the other bleeding. Or maybe it was a stupid question. Maybe all non-*taniks* already knew where hunting was currently going on.

"You got any bandages?" he asked.

"I'm not sure. I'll look."

I put down the spatula and dropped to my hands and knees on the ever-cold floor to search in the kitchen's miscellaneous drawer among discarded tubes of makeup, cat and dog prescription bottles, plant food, and receipts. There were no bandages.

"I don't seem to have any bandages. Maybe something else will work?"

No bacon. No bandages. From the Arctic perspective, I was an inadequate hostess.

"Clean rags? An old sheet?"

"Sure."

I turned down the fire ring under the eggs, ran upstairs, and grabbed a sheet from the closet. Also, my fuzzy pink fleece bathrobe, which I managed to struggle into without falling down the stairs.

"How big should the strips be?"

"Give it here."

I handed it in through the curtain.

"This is a good sheet."

"I've got lots of sheets," I lied, to make up for my lack of bandages and bacon.

The sound of ripping ensued. I took up the spatula and prodded the eggs. I turned on the oven to use for a warmer and put a plate in it. I made a mental list of needed household supplies: bacon and bandages, and maybe I should get some decent lingerie.

Or maybe this was just a friendly après-hunting visit.

Michael emerged with his hand swathed in pieces of ivy-printed white cloth.

"You look like a mummy." I smiled at him as I gave the eggs what I hoped was a professional finishing poke.

"You look like a pink angel," he said, and hugged me at the stove. "Sorry to wake you up. Everybody in Utqiagvik gets a little off schedule in the midnight sun. What time do you need to go in to work in the morning?"

"Oh, uh, eight thirty, I guess," I stammered. "I have a motion I need to get filed."

"Fine. Me and Bull will give you a ride in."

"Oh. Thanks. Were you hunting with Bull?"

"No, he's my brother-in-law," Michael said, by way of complete explanation.

The phone rang again.

"You answer it," I said, since I wasn't expecting any calls. I filled the toaster again.

"Hello? No, it's okay. Four caribou. They're in the truck. Yeah, the first three are dressed, but I couldn't do the last one because of my hand. I can share them out later tomorrow. I don't know. I'll ask her. Listen, would you call Sally and Jer and tell them they can come by Mom's for some meat, so they won't be calling over here? Thanks. See you."

Michael went to the couch in the living room, picked up the remote, and began channel surfing as though he were at home, while I plated the eggs and toast. The hot and high-piled breakfast offering looked appealing, I thought, even though I was out of practice.

I brought him his meal, then retreated behind the bathroom curtain for a quick look at my unadorned and older-than-his face. Not too bad. Sort of dewy from the hours of sleep and an exciting wake-up. I added a touch of peach lipstick and just a hint of eyebrow pencil and returned to the living room.

While Michael ate, we watched a 1930s Cary Grant movie. I wondered whether Cary Grant was popular in Utqiagvik, and then remembered that even the elaborate Utqiagvik cable system offered little to the channel surfer at four in the morning. Michael ate every morsel of egg and wiped the plate with remnants of toast. I felt I had earned at least one gold star.

"That was good," he said. "Oh, I forgot to mention. Sally wants to know if you play softball."

"Softball? Who's Sally?"

"My sister. Her team's short one person, and if they don't field a team, they'll have to forfeit."

"Well, I don't know—I . . . it's been a while."

"And Jer—that's my other sister—wants to know if we can have a barbecue over here Saturday for her husband. It's their anniversary."

"Uh, sure, I guess. How many people do you think will . . . ?"

"Oh, I dunno, he's got a lot of cousins, maybe thirty or forty, maybe more, depending on what else is going on."

"Thirty or forty!"

"Don't worry. They'll all bring food. There'll be so much food you won't have a place to put it. And the men cook, for barbecue. And nobody cares if the house is clean, or what you wear, or none of that *tanik* stuff."

"Oh, okay, well, we can . . ."

Smiling, he drew me toward him. "You need to sleep now, for work."

He put a couch cushion on his lap. I thought about getting up to straighten the kitchen first. I thought about going back upstairs to my futon. I even thought about inviting him up there. Then I decided I wasn't going to worry about any of that *tanik* stuff. I lay down beside him on the couch and made myself comfortable with my head on the pillow. He put his arm over my shoulders to keep me warm. Glancing up at his chin, I was amazed at how familiar he seemed.

"TV bother you?" he asked.

"No, I could sleep through a fireworks display. But aren't you going to sleep?"

"I got a lot of sleep in camp."

I had almost drifted away, feeling cozy, but then had a worrying thought.

"Michael?"

"Yes."

"I haven't played softball in a long time. I'm all out of practice."

"Don't worry. It'll all come back to you."

6

The caribou feeds the wolf, but it is the wolf who makes the caribou strong.

OLD INUIT SAYING FROM THE KIVALLIQ REGION IN NORTHERN CANADA, ACCORDING TO *THE OXFORD DICTIONARY OF PROVERBS* (5TH ED.), QUOTED BY FARLEY MOWAT IN *NEVER CRY WOLF*

FOR ONCE THE STREET IN FRONT OF MY HOUSE WAS no longer empty. Bull waved at us from his shiny blue pickup. I hoped I was dressed okay to meet Michael's relative, in my plaid wool skirt, green sweater-vest, and black high-top running shoes. Almost every Utqiagvik woman wore high-top sneakers in the summer, since they offered a little protection from the gravel streets and weren't as heavy as a boot.

Michael hoisted me and my shoulder bag in beside Bull and climbed in next to me. Bull had a fringe of black hair with a bristling mustache to match and looked extraordinarily vigorous, as though he lived in the fresh air day and night. It was a look that many people who went out on the tundra or on the ice shared. Being in his presence made me momentarily shy and uncertain. I was a *tanik*. Bull knew things about Utqiagvik—about Michael, and about the vast North Slope and its customs—that I would never know. No matter how long I lived here, I would always be an outsider.

"Hi," he said. "I'm Bull."

I smiled and nodded.

Bull stepped on the gas, and we bumped down the street. I could not think of a thing to say, but the ride was noisy with the windows open, so maybe it didn't matter. Instead of heading uphill, as I would have done to reach the bus stop, he turned us toward the ocean, and then at the corner veered left, past the Okpeahas' two-story green-and-white home, along the road that ran parallel to the shore.

"There's a dog out there," I said. Just over the edge of Michael's shoulder, I saw a dog out on the tundra, tethered to what looked like an old rusty car roof rack, iced over, between the road and the shore. The dog was brownish blackish, and husky- or wolf-shaped, with a deep barrel like a Norwegian elkhound. I couldn't tell from a distance whether it was male or female but noticed that no food, water, or shelter was visible. Since I didn't ordinarily go this way, I hadn't seen the dog before and couldn't be sure whether it was new or had been there a long time.

"Polar bear warning," Bull said.

"Really?" I blurted, and then felt like an ignorant *tanik*.

"When the bears come, they usually come in from that side," Michael explained. "Didn't you know that? It's close to your house, and you really should be careful. Crews drag their whales in on that beach, so the bears come there, too."

I knew the site was used by whaling crews. In fact, sometimes I had walked out there and found a hummock from which to watch the crews at work. It was startling, the first time, to witness this ancient hunting spectacle. The men in their home-sewn white canvas anoraks, warmed inside with fur, still went out in fragile-looking skin boats upon that terrifying ice water, and then relatives and neighbors gathered to drag the whale ashore. Some of the crews now used modern boats and power harpoons, but the whaling crew lineages were dynastic and greatly respected.

My heart always ached for the beautiful slaughtered whales,

though I sternly reminded myself that the whales taken were few, especially compared with the legions of butchered cattle and pigs in the Lower 48. The process of obtaining bacon did not differ except in the details.

At one time the International Whaling Commission had attempted to shut down the Arctic hunts, but the Inupiat hired scientific consultants who explained to the commission, with accompanying documentation, that the subsistence hunts did not affect the overall whale population and were tiny compared to commercial whaling. In other words, the Inupiat beat the bureaucrats at their own game.

One thing I had learned from watching the whale crews was that *taniks* who called Natives lazy, because some had difficulty fitting into the nine-to-five office work ethic, had obviously never witnessed the one or two days of arduous round-the-clock labor required to adequately cut up a whale, distribute the parcels of meat, and convey the remains to the landfill.

I watched the tethered dog as long as I could and made a mental note to check on it later. Here sometimes people just forgot their dogs. They didn't mean to be cruel. It was just that dog teams, once so necessary for sled transportation and survival, had been replaced by snow machines and four-wheelers. Dogs were no longer considered valuable enough to be taken care of. I hated seeing lonely dogs on their perpetual tethers and did what I could for some of them, even to the point of trespassing to provide food and a blanket.

Michael and Bull began to discuss which portions of caribou would be shared as Bull turned onto the long swoop of road that ran past the freshwater lagoon toward the main part of Utqiagvik. Technically speaking, I didn't live in Utqiagvik but in its "suburb," Browerville, named after the first *tanik* to settle there, Charles Brower. Brower arrived in the mid-1880s as part of a Yankee whaling crew and stayed to oversee a maintenance and rescue station. He eventually married a first and then, after her death, a second

Inupiaq wife, and many of their descendants populated Browerville today.

We stopped at the door of the court-and-bank building. I thanked Bull for the ride. Michael clambered out so I could exit, and I wondered whether he would kiss me. He didn't. I wondered whether he would return later that night, but he didn't mention the possibility.

"See you," he said, and then they roared off.

Ascending in the elevator to the second floor, I felt a mixture of happiness and confusion. Life in Utqiagvik suddenly seemed more fun. But could I really play team softball and fit thirty or forty people into my house?

"Hey, she made it in," Liz called out when she saw me.

Liz probably knew not only that Michael had shown up at my house but also the number of caribou he had with him and who was going to get which cuts.

"Don't start, Liz. Did I give you a hard time when you got sick in the hall?"

"Yes, you did."

I waved her off for the coffee machine and then my office. I stashed my purse, took a sip of coffee, and settled in to read more on the Ipalook case. I opened the box, and the name Nate Olemaun leaped out at me. Nate was not only a former client but a member of a highly connected political family. He would likely know all about what had happened to Bernice and Wanda. I needed to talk to Nate in person. I took a last sip of coffee, grabbed my purse again, and headed back the way I had just come.

"Somehow I didn't think you'd be here all day!" Liz called after me. "Don't worry about anything—I'll take care of it. At least until two or so."

I half waved in response.

I didn't wait for the elevator but took the utility stairs down to the exhilarating Arctic air. Many people were out on the street, enjoying the summer sun. Native kids in summer parkas and sweatsuits were following a lady carrying plastic bags of groceries down the side of the road, and husky puppies were following the kids. The lady was laughing at the kids, and the kids were laughing at the dogs.

Retracing the lagoon road on foot, I tried to prepare my thoughts for an organized interview with Nate, but they veered to the horn button at the crime scene. Lots of people had horn buttons, I reminded myself. Maybe Amos Lane's missing button was not the one at the crime scene. Even if it was, the fact that he had been there would not in itself mean that he committed a double murder. He could have had a couple of drinks with the ladies and watched TV or played cards and left. Then John Adams came by later and got jealous when he learned Amos had been there. According to Tidwell, that was the lead detective's theory. But Tidwell thought drug dealers had killed the Ipalooks.

Browerville, spread out along the far side of the lagoon, looked almost like suburbs in the Lower 48. Federal housing subsidies had filled it with ranch ramblers. Perhaps some other kind of house would have been easier to insulate and more functional in the Arctic, but local politicians wanted Browerville to look like other American suburbs, so ranch ramblers it was. On stilts, of course, like my house, and surrounded not by lawns and shade trees but by piles of game bones, racks of drying fish, and hummocks of kinnikinnick.

In 1984, I had read, the Barrow Utilities and Electric Cooperative, locally called BUECI (pronounced bee-YOU-see), built the engineering marvel called the utilidor, a 3.2-mile underground tunnel that protects plumbing from the Arctic cold. Homes connected to the utilidor have running water, flush toilets, washing machines, and dishwashers. I had never seen it written anywhere what the utilidor cost to build. Whoever paid the tab must have been afraid to say, or embarrassed about, what all that engineering and jackhammering into the permafrost had cost. But the combination of oil interests, government subsidies, and the Native corporations were a deeper pocket than the utilidor itself.

I recognized Nate's mustard-colored ranch rambler about a block past the video store, and stopped to examine the spotted seal carcass in the driveway, wondering why its torpedolike bulk had not yet been skinned and dressed. I patted the single husky tethered in front, who tried to knock me down with overenthusiastic friendliness.

"It's okay, buddy, it's all right. I'll see you in a bit."

I mounted the warped wooden steps and knocked on the doorframe.

"Come on in, it's open," a familiar voice called.

Nate had been jailed after the grand jury indicted him for second-degree assault. Though he was only eighteen at the time, he had been taken from Fairbanks Correctional Center to a prison near Anchorage and forcibly administered Prozac to make him quit shouting and beating on his cell door. The family and I protested the use of a drug with so many potential side effects on such a young person. The authorities responded that they were acting on the recommendation of the facility's physician, who believed Nate was suicidal. They continued giving him the drug and restraining him, administering it in a way that amounted to torture. The only thing that would trump a doctor's order was the word of another doctor, which the family couldn't afford, and for which obtaining the necessary expert witness fee through the public defender system would have taken several weeks. All I could do to end the Prozac was go to trial early, prepared or unprepared.

In spite of my reasonably good cross-examination of the State's complaining witness, Nate was convicted, and I felt bad about it. Assault charges often had "lesser included offenses" whose definitions overlapped, and often I had been able to persuade juries to reduce the charges to misdemeanor level, but not this time. His drunken attack on a neighbor kid had produced disfiguring injuries the jury was not willing to overlook. Nate tried to console me by telling me he didn't really care how the case came out, he only wanted his *aaka* (grandmother) not to be mad at him anymore about the fight, and she had now forgiven him. His *aaka* attended his sentencing hearing, along with the rest of his family. Nate was transported from Anchorage back to FCC to serve a few more weeks, and then returned to Utqiagvik in time to finish out the basketball season at his high school.

At Nate's invitation, I entered his living room, which was filled with Sears maple-veneer furniture beneath a forest of philodendron vines suspended from cup hooks in the ceiling.

"Hello, Nate," I said. "It's been a while."

He sat in a wingback chair in front of a TV set, which he switched off. On the wall behind him a crowd of family photographs looked down on us: hunters in fur-trimmed white anoraks, standing on whales or beside walruses; aunts and uncles on their wedding days; cousins in basketball tournaments; and nieces and nephews dressed up for birthdays, graduations, and Christmas.

"Hello, Counselor. How about a beer?" Nate didn't seem surprised to see me.

I shook my head, but he ignored me and hollered to his wife. "Kiana, two brews!"

Kiana brought us two damp cans, holding her unbuttoned blouse over where she had been nursing an infant. I recalled seeing pictures of Kiana as Miss Teen Arctic Circle. She had appeared on Anchorage TV with her hair in curly bangs, wearing a beautiful skin parka that did not obscure her curvy figure. If anything, she was prettier now, less curly, more serene. But was that a bruise on her forearm?

"She's a looker, isn't she?" Nate said, following my eyes. "She's cultural, too."

"Cultural?"

"Dances Eskimo dances. Sews skins. When I was in prison, I used to dream of someone like her."

As best I could recall, Nate's dreams on Prozac had not been good ones, but I wouldn't contradict him. I popped the top on my can to be polite, not really intending to indulge. But the beer was so fragrant, and beer itself so rare and precious in Utqiagvik, that I took a sip.

"Have a cookie," Nate said. I noticed a plate of Oreos on the coffee table. "Have two."

"I'll save 'em for later," I said, and put two in my purse. "Thanks. I heard you got married after you got out. Congratulations."

"Doesn't do much dancing now. Stays home, like she's supposed to. You don't have to go to the university to know that, right?"

In order to be agreeable, I nodded, feeling like an undercover agent.

When I had represented Nate only a few short years before, he was a good-looking young man, and the kind who would have been a heroic hunter in the old world, or an energetic businessman in the new. Now his extravagantly long blue-black hair was thinning at the temples, and fat bulged on the compact frame that used to run up and down the basketball court faster than anybody else's.

"You've come about the Ipalook girls, right?"

I ceased my rude appraisal of him, took another sip of beer, and nodded.

"I already talked to Public Safety."

"Yeah, but I know you didn't tell them everything."

Nate grunted and sucked on his beer.

Kiana brought in their child and sat down on the floor beside Nate's chair. The chubby baby curled his fingers on her lapel while she jiggled him on her knee.

"What are you doing in the case?"

"I'll probably be appointed for Amos Lane if he's charged. The

DA hasn't filed anything about the Ipalooks yet. I only represent Amos on some misdemeanors now."

Nate gave a curious wince and dropped his eyes. Kiana put the baby back to her breast. We sat for a while in silence, drinking our beer, while Kiana nursed the child. At last the infant's head lolled back against his mother's arm.

"You don't need to be representing Amos Lane," Nate said.

"Why's that?"

"He's a hound from hell, is why."

I gazed at him in surprise. Utqiagvik, and the North Slope, held several people who could fit that description. Nate was probably cousins with half of them. So why did Amos Lane evoke this response?

"Everybody deserves to be represented."

"You guys always say that, but not everybody."

"They can't just take him out and shoot him."

"Why not?"

I was kidding. Nate was not.

Did I really have to explain due process and the public defender point of view to a former client on whose behalf I had once worked so hard at trial? But my own mother didn't understand them, so I shouldn't be surprised that Nate didn't. I used to think Americans favored the underdog. Perhaps only when the underdog resembled John Wayne.

"Come on, Nate. He deserves a trial, just like you had. Tell me what you know about that night."

Nate looked down at his wife as she swaddled their child in her arms, an Arctic Madonna. Kiana gave a slight expression of assent with her eyes. Nate shrugged his shoulders.

"That weekend, the night that they died . . . Do you remember it?" he said to me. "The first week in August, beautiful weather. Practically the whole town was out in the midnight sun."

"I was out of town."

"Lots of people on the beach. Out on the shooting stations at the Point."

"I'm sorry I missed it."

"Everybody'd been drinking, smoking, since Friday noon. That weekend's a blur. It's sort of hard now, looking back, to be real clear about what happened when."

He shook his head slightly, as if to focus his thoughts, and rested one hand on Kiana's shoulder. I noticed his eyes were bloodshot and his fingernails stained yellow.

"We were at the dugout," Kiana prompted.

Nate shot her a frown, and she bent her head back over the baby.

More silence. I began to feel I was causing a strain between them. I would have asked Kiana herself what happened at the dugout but didn't want to get Nate annoyed at her.

The dugout was part of the town baseball and softball field, excavated with great effort to bedrock. It had steps leading down into it just like the ones in the major leagues, and had become a popular after-hours hangout. Public Safety routinely patrolled the dugout but couldn't be there all the time. I had worked on several cases of assault, either physical or sexual, or theft, or the violent theft that is robbery, that either took place at the dugout or started there and were carried elsewhere.

A wayward thought flitted through my mind. If I played softball with Michael's sister, I would be hanging out at the dugout, too.

"Amos is my cousin, man."

"I thought he was from Point Hope."

"He is, but I've got cousins all over the Slope."

"Tell me about his family in Point Hope." I thought we might approach the subject from a slightly different angle, to get him talking.

"That's a terrible story. That's worse than this one. You sure you want to hear it?"

I nodded and sipped my beer and noticed I was halfway through the can. Liz would smell it the moment I got off the elevator.

"His poor mother, Harriet Lane . . . she was . . . These three guys got her into some cabin. They raped her over and over. She screamed for hours, but nobody came to help. She died the next day."

I realized I was shivering, though it wasn't cold in Nate's sunny living room. Every time I tried to learn about Amos's case, his mother's death seemed to come up.

"Amos was just a teenager then. Only one of the men was ever charged, and he only did a year or so for the rape. Nobody was ever charged for the murder. *Tanik* courts and Public Safety—they don't know what they're doing half the time."

I couldn't disagree.

"We should go back to the old ways," Nate said. "Our own justice. The village always knows what has happened."

"So tell me what happened the night the Ipalooks died, Nate. Tell me what really happened."

"Amos showed up at the dugout," Kiana offered.

I gave her a quick smile of encouragement before she lowered her head again.

"He wanted me to change clothes with him," Nate said.

"Why would he want you to change clothes with him?" A bad fact. Jurors would not like this fact. A fact like this could lead to a negative interpretation of whatever Amos might have done that night.

"I don't know, man. He got all pissed when I wouldn't."

"He threw Nate up against the wall," Kiana said.

"He what?"

The story was coming out now, and Nate began to speak rapidly.

"That guy is stronger than four bears. I fell to the ground. The next thing I knew he had grabbed Kiana by the hand and was dragging her off. I got up and jumped on his back. Everybody in the dugout—there were ten or fifteen of us—we all piled on him. He shook us off like we was puppies."

I held my breath a moment before asking, "What happened then?"

But Nate stopped talking. He drained his beer. Kiana got up to get him another, and brought one to me, as well, but I didn't touch it.

I was disturbed by what Nate had told me, and my face probably showed it, but I could see why Nate hadn't told Public Safety all this. They hadn't believed him in his own case, when he voluntarily came in and tried to explain that the so-called victim had pushed his grandmother down the day before and taken her bag of groceries. The officers knew Nate was a felon and possibly an addict. They would jump to the conclusion that he must have been drunk or high that night and was exaggerating what was a simple fight over a girl.

Nate laid his hand on Kiana's head and caressed her hair. The baby, fat and happy, awoke, and grabbed at his daddy's hand.

"Nate, one of the most important parts of this whole case is the time. Can you tell me exactly when you saw Amos?"

"Why does it matter so much?"

"The girls probably had lots of visitors that evening. It was the last one that killed them. I'm trying to figure out who was there when."

"Don't know, man. Can't say. I was smashed that whole weekend, starting Friday. For you, I would tell you, but I really don't remember."

Kiana shot me a brief glance. "There's more," she said.

I waited.

Nate picked up the TV remote, then put it down again. I felt he was waiting for me to leave. I had almost gotten to my feet when Kiana spoke again.

"Amos had gone by the dugout a little earlier. That time he was on a three-wheeler," she said.

She had my complete attention.

"He was following Bernice and Wanda up the road. They were drunk. They were always drunk. Laughing and shouting. Bernice got on behind him."

Nate sat forward, leaning between me and Kiana, and took the baby from her. She stopped speaking.

I had heard enough and figured it was time for me to go. I told them what a beautiful baby and home they had and thanked them for the visit and their hospitality.

Nate got up and followed me to the door, still holding his plump son.

"I don't want to testify," he told me. "I got my wife and baby now. I never want to go near that court again."

I nodded.

He gave me a one-armed hug and shut the door after me.

I tossed my Oreos to the husky and headed to the courthouse, glad to be out of Nate's overheated living room. I had to wonder what drugs had cycled through Nate's brain since the Prozac, and so would an Utqiagvik jury. But people would listen to Kiana. If Public Safety ever talked to her, her testimony, plus the missing horn button—if Public Safety ever found it—could get Amos indicted. It was time for me to go see Amos at the jail to try to clarify his whereabouts the night Bernice and Wanda died.

7

To me, the beauty of what became known as Inupiat Ilitqusiat—Inupiat Values—was the fact that they were not material. They were deeply entrenched in the mind and heart and spirit, and entirely transportable.

WILLIE IGGIAGRUK HENSLEY, INUPIAQ STATE LEGISLATOR FROM KOTZEBUE

I PUT TWO HUGE PRIME-RIB ROASTS IN THE OVEN TO bake slowly for hours. I washed, pared, and diced an entire sack of potatoes to boil in the one kettle I had that was big enough. I put out frozen bread dough to rise, hoping the thirty or forty people coming for the barbecue wouldn't notice I had cheated by using store-bought dough instead of making a batch from scratch.

Michael returned from the airport with cases of beer. Utqiagvik was a "damp" town, which meant residents could order shipments of booze from Anchorage or Fairbanks but could not buy it locally. He put the beer in my shower and packed it in ice he picked up at the grocery store. Then, out back, he set up a flimsy grill he had borrowed from a sister and began to broil pieces of chicken.

Around one o'clock, people started calling to verify the place and time, to offer to bring anything we needed, or to ask Michael to come help transport pots and extra children.

"I can't," I heard him say. "We're cooking."

I looked out my kitchen window at the tundra between me and the backs of people's ranch ramblers nearby. Other families were out grilling, too, this Saturday afternoon, just like people in the Lower 48. Today was the first time in the four years I had been here that barbecue smoke floated up over my place. I felt warmer than the weather. Liz was right. I had worked too hard too long.

Around two, the Bull himself arrived, with much admonishing of children and handing about of covered dishes. He rushed into the kitchen, ignoring the potato masher in my hand, and enfolded me in an embrace that lifted me to my toes and made me fear for my ribs.

"Michael saved my life once," he said into my ear. "On the ice. Did you know that?"

I couldn't think of anything appropriate to say, and just hugged him back.

"This is Angela," Michael said.

A toddler wearing a hand-me-down pink windbreaker that reached to her ankles maneuvered her way into the kitchen by clutching at counter knobs. Swaying on her feet, her pointed chin barely clearing the oversize collar, she broke into a smile like the rising of dawn over snowfields.

Angela thawed my *tanik* stiffness. I put down the potato masher and held out my hands to her. She toddled forward, raising her arms. I picked her up and held her astride one hip. She smelled of fresh air on sweat.

"Stacy," Michael said.

A slender, serious-faced girl came in carrying a doll and looking back over her shoulder at another child, plump and bustling, who nudged her to proceed.

"And Mary."

Next came a solemn five- or six-year-old boy whose eyes flew over me in curiosity. His mother accompanied him, carrying a newborn baby swathed in covers.

"Ranger, Danielle, and my sister, Sally."

"Do you have a Humvee?" Ranger inquired.

"Ranger thinks you're a rich *tanik*," Sally explained.

"Sorry to disappoint him!"

"Do you have any juice?" Ranger asked.

"Ranger!" his mom chided, settling herself into a chair at the kitchen table and preparing to breastfeed Danielle.

"Well, let's see what there is," I said, hoping that the refrigerator contained something Ranger considered drinkable.

"7UP!" he cried.

It crossed my mind that parents might not think 7UP an appropriate drink for a child, but nobody was paying any attention because Jer and her family now entered the kitchen. I handed the can to Ranger, who literally jumped for joy.

Jer brought a huge pot of caribou stew. I carefully traded Angela for the stew, put it on the stove beside the potatoes, and ceased to worry about whether there would be enough food. Jer was a sturdy woman who barked orders at her nearest relatives about the placing of wraps and additional dishes. Her teenage children eyed me with brief appraisal and then took up the darts and began a highly competitive game with Bull at the wall target in the living room. One began to climb the stairs.

"Don't go up there," Bull commanded the ascending child.

"It's all right," I said from the stove. "Really. There's nothing up there that they can hurt or that can hurt them." I was only hoping they wouldn't open the door to the walk-in closet where the dogs were cooped. The cats, I knew, had hidden themselves by now.

The young person did not listen to either of us and continued upward. Michael appeared at the back door requesting another beer and a plate, and a pretty blond child asked whether she could use the computer on the kitchen table.

"Sure, honey."

"Are you and Uncle Michael going to get married?" she asked. "He said you were very pretty."

"Not as pretty as you," I said.

"My daddy needs a beer," Ranger called from the living room.

I hugged the computer operator, extracted two cans of beer from the tub in the shower, gave one to Ranger for his dad, and carried the other and a plate out to Michael, who rewarded me with a kiss that tasted like beer. For just a moment I wished we had the house to ourselves, but when I looked up at him, I could see that he was pleased with the occasion, and with me, and so I returned to my cooking, warmed in spite of the wind.

When I got back to the kitchen, it held five more adults I didn't know. These were, Sally explained, cousins Jacob and Jack, who waved and smirked, and their girlfriends, Della and Flossie, who shyly offered damp hands.

And in the middle of the linoleum, there stood Mamie, the matriarch, mother of Michael, Sally, and Jer; mother-in-law of Bull; aunt of Jacob and Jack; and grandmother of the maybe fifteen children swarming through my house.

Did I have mashed potato on my sweater or jeans? Did I look older than this lady, whose son's kiss I could still feel on my mouth?

I went to the stove and clutched at the potato masher as though the potatoes had to be done right away. Mamie took her time looking me over.

She was a petite woman clad in stirrup pants and a cherry-colored satin baseball jacket with matching cap from which spilled abundant gray curls. She had Angela's pointed chin and Michael's almond eyes, now reflecting the dignity of her years. I could tell by the energy she brought into the room that she was a force to be reckoned with. With her bright complexion and regular features, she must have been, at one time, irresistibly lovely.

I made myself put down my potato-masher crutch and turned to try to offer her a proper smile and words of greeting, in spite of the timidity I felt. The kitchen fell silent except for the running TV football commentary someone had turned on in the living room.

"I brought some earrings," Mamie said. "I hadn't really decided whether to give them to you or not, but now I will."

I felt Sally and Jer and half a dozen children watching. Mamie took two small roses carved from ivory, set on silver hoops, from the pocket of her windbreaker. I pulled back my hair, and she put them on for me, and we embraced.

"Now I'm going to win some money from Bull at darts," she announced, and walked into the living room.

"Go get 'em, Mama," Sally said.

"Yay!" Jer cried.

I finished mashing the potatoes and then made gravy, wishing for the encouragement and instructions of my own mother, a much-admired South Carolina cook.

The mashed potatoes turned out fine. The rolls were a little tough but tasty, and Sally's stew and my roasts were excellent, but I have to admit I couldn't eat much of the vegetables cooked in seal oil. My gravy disappeared almost immediately. By the time every family member, including second cousins, great-aunts, and adopted siblings, plus girlfriends, in-laws, neighbors, and coworkers, had eaten barbecue, watched football, played darts, tried the computer, and chased children, few leftovers remained.

People sat or stood around in the living room half stupefied, while Michael scanned in vain for another football game. I had begun to wonder whether people were still having a good time when Mamie took from her purse a Rolling Stones tape and directed the nearest child to put it in my boom box. Then she brought out a deck of cards and a bag of poker chips and stared commandingly around the room.

"It's going to be a good night!" she announced.

Michael set his plate of bones and bread crusts on the floor beside the couch. With a glance he invited me to his side. But I felt shy about joining the game with Michael's family members.

"I wanna sit by Michael," Ranger declared, squirming onto the couch. Michael kissed the top of his head but lifted him over beside Mamie's chair while she was clearing a place for the cards and chips on my cedar chest that served as a coffee table. Would-be players and spectators gathered around. Surprised, the boy climbed onto his grandmother's comfortable lap.

"Sit here, Rebecca," Michael said, patting the flowered couch beside him.

Hesitantly, I sat, thinking that I had not heard him say my name before. He pronounced it "Reb-ec-KAH," with a slight guttural semi-emphasis on the last syllable.

Mamie shuffled the cards as others carried in kitchen chairs. Some dragged boxes from my stacks of supplies in the hallway to use as stools. I ordered in bulk from the barges that came in during the summer, when the sea was free of ice. Kitty litter and canned goods were much cheaper that way.

Jer settled a sleeping baby on the couch beside Michael and me. Other children went outside or upstairs, and two teens found leashes and took the dogs for a walk. Michael gazed around the table at the faces of his friends and relatives. Then, with deliberation, he settled a hard hand on my knee.

A silence fell over the room except for the Stones lamenting "Ruby Tuesday." I did not dare look up for fear someone's skeptical gaze would ruin my pleasure in the moment.

"They're cute together," I heard Sally whisper.

Were we? I regarded his tan hand on my knee and saw the shine of scars. Gazing about, I realized that in spite of my *tanik* agendas and anxieties, I felt warmly included within this gathering. The clan had absorbed me, perhaps not permanently, but at least, for Michael's sake, for the occasion.

"Ante up!" Mamie commanded.

"Omigosh, I'm going to lose all my money," I said, and everybody laughed.

We played poker for hours and played it fast. The deal changed with each hand, and every new dealer called out which style of poker they wanted, how many cards to draw, and the different values of cards. Stud, draw, Texas hold'em, lowball, highball, roll your own, and several styles I didn't catch the names of. Michael, who was a very good poker player, but not as good as his mother, kept up a running undertone of instructions for me, but I could barely follow the play. Mamie ignored everything but the cards. She consistently won. They both put away an amazing number of cans of beer, and around ten o'clock switched to a bottle of Jack Daniel's I didn't even know we had, yet their skill was not affected.

By midnight, though the poker continued, the children had fallen asleep—some of them upstairs, some of them on the corners of furniture or on parents' laps or on coats on the floor. The teenagers had disappeared to wherever teenagers go. The tape was switched from rock to R & B.

By two, most of the parents had peeled off for home. Several pots and pans and not a few blankets, sweaters, and shoes had been left behind, and I wondered vaguely how people were going to come collect them while I was at work tomorrow. I was determined to go to the office as usual on Sunday. The Ipalook case needed work, and so did the rest of my caseload. No matter what, I couldn't afford to fall behind.

To my surprise, there came more knocks at the door, and a different crowd began to gather.

"Dancing?" a pretty young newcomer inquired. From the sleeve of her jacket, she produced a fifth of vodka. The bottle, innocent of wrap or tags, did not look like part of a shipment to the airfield, but I felt no duty to ask where it came from. She was probably one of my bootlegging clients, either customer or vendor.

"I've won enough," Mamie announced. She collected her cards, the chips, and most of the money on the table. "Michael, where's my coat? Call me a cab. Everybody that's not going to dance, go home."

At the door, Mamie hugged me before going out into the cold Utqiagvik sun dazzle.

"Treat her right," she instructed Michael.

Her command gave me pause instead of reassurance. Why would she need to tell him that?

Then he put on a tape of Percy Sledge's "When a Man Loves a Woman," and we danced in the middle of my small living room, surrounded by his friends and cousins. I decided to set aside my *tanik* worry. When the crowd had thinned to only a few asleep on the couch, Michael and I went upstairs together, and I did forget to worry, at least for a while.

8

He who has been bitten by a bear will never again find life so sweet.
INUIT PROVERB

PUBLIC SAFETY'S GRUBBY LOBBY, WITH ITS TABLE-armed chairs for driver's license testing, was empty on Sunday, except for the receptionist behind the smoked and chicken-wired glass. I felt oddly uneasy about talking with Amos, and the hangover didn't help. Utqiagvik's small jail facility lacked an attorney visiting room with a glass barrier between counsel and client. You either talked with your client in the middle of the dayroom, where the inmates were watching TV and there was no privacy, or you sat on the edge of their bunk and interviewed them face-to-face.

I wasn't afraid of him, exactly, though I knew that a client could do considerable damage to your eye with a pencil before a guard could stop him. You couldn't always predict who might try. With Amos, it wasn't fear that I felt but an odd uncertainty. He had told me nothing. Public Safety apparently had found a new suspect, but Nate Olemaun, and Liz, believed Amos had killed Bernice and Wanda. The midnight sun had confused the witnesses. The case wasn't a matter of fitting the puzzle pieces together. Some of the pieces were missing.

"Hi. Public Defender," I said to the Public Safety receptionist.

The receptionist, who looked as weary as I, called upstairs to let the jail know I was on the way. When the security door buzzed, I dragged it open and headed up the dark, smelly stairs. At the top, the guard was waiting for me with his ring of keys.

"Afternoon, Ms. Wright. How's business?"

This guard was a short, slight Filipino who was still recovering from bruises one of my clients had inflicted on a night when he was the only guard on duty. He had been unable to reach the alarm button and was saved from even worse injury by the assistance of another client, who either felt sorry for the guard or hated the other inmate.

"Afternoon, Sergeant Rosas. Lots of business—I have total job security. Are you still having much pain? I worry about you."

"It's getting better. You here to see your star client, the famous Amos Lane?"

"I never can fool you, Emiliano. Did you get his autograph yet?"

The guard made a moue of disgust and motioned me toward cell 5.

I knocked politely on the partially opened heavy gray door.

"It ain't locked," a voice responded with a wry tone.

The cell had beige carpet on the lower half of the walls, for the head bangers, and a floor of seamless yellow poured vinyl. A structural shelf ran the width of the far wall, on which rested a pad that served as a bed. There was the usual stainless steel combination sink and rimless toilet, with a polished piece of metal glued to the wall above for a mirror. Above us, the ceiling camera, a ceiling light, and a fire-extinguishing sprinkler were enclosed in a protective cage.

Though the cells were designed to resist inmate vandalism, the toilet was still vulnerable. From time to time an inmate would stuff clothing into it and, by repeated flushing, manage to flood the floor. I had never understood why anyone not entirely nuts would want to make a damp, stinky mess of his own living quarters. Out of anger, I suppose.

A few of Lane's personal items were scattered around: a hairbrush, paperback books, court papers, a toothbrush and toothpaste. Lane was lying on the mattress pad in a green jumpsuit and green plastic sandals with black socks, reading a Bible. His hair was tied back at the nape of his neck, and he looked younger than he had in the courtroom.

Maybe he read the Bible all the time. Maybe he had just heard me come in.

"Isaiah 54:17," I said to him, closing the door behind me.

He turned pages to find the verse and read it to me. "'You will refute every accusation that is raised in court against you.' I like that, Counselor."

"How about Deuteronomy 16:20?"

I removed my coat and placed it on the floor, which was cleaner than most bathtubs, free labor being plentiful in the jail, and motioned for permission to sit on the end of his bed. There wasn't any other place to sit. He nodded while searching for the second passage.

I recited for him my favorite verse: "Justice, justice shalt thou pursue." I didn't give him the citation of the verse that I always carried with me into jury trials, Proverbs 21:31: "The horse is made ready for the day of battle, but victory rests with the Lord."

Lane sat up and closed the Good Book. His eyes roamed over my jeans and sweater, and I wished I had left my coat on. I studied him in return. He seemed calm. Apparently, he had learned during previous lockups to do "good time," to behave well enough to avoid losing privileges because of disciplinary write-ups.

"I like that, too," he said. I wasn't sure whether he meant the verse or my sweater.

"We need to talk about your case," I said.

He shrugged.

"The problem is, we don't know yet how much they know."

"Meaning what, Counselor?"

"I have a name, you know. You can call me Ms. Wright. You can call me Rebecca, if you want. Lord knows we will be spending a lot of time together before this case is over."

Once again he smirked. "Sounds good to me."

"Amos, listen to me. You need to think hard about your demeanor between now and when we're in front of a jury. People notice everything. They're not stupid."

He got up. He paced to the door and back. I could imagine him doing that a lot while cooped up in here. When he sat down again, his face had the same stony look he had worn during the arraignment, which was worse than his smirk.

I sighed. A mistake to bring up trial. We had a long way to go before then.

"The reason I came to see you now is . . . well, the case is in an odd posture, and we need to talk about strategy."

"Yeah?"

"No one has been charged. The investigation is still going on. They have given me some information, but they're not going to give anybody all of it until the grand jury decides who to indict."

"Okay. So?"

"So that makes it harder to decide."

"Decide what?"

"The State is offering to dismiss those misdemeanor cases, all of them, in exchange for you telling them who you visited—your relatives, or whoever, if you did visit anyone—the night the girls died. And what time."

"Yeah, but those cases are all bullshit."

"Right, but I was thinking we might make them a counteroffer."

"Like what?"

"You're not the only fish in the barrel. They're looking hard at John Adams."

"The boyfriend? Yeah, I know him."

"We know there were people partying at the girls' house that night. Maybe Adams was there. Maybe you were there. That doesn't mean either of you killed them. The question is who left while the women were still alive, and who left last, after he killed them."

"Who knows? It was the midnight sun. Everybody was everywhere."

"So, if you could testify truthfully that, yes, you were partying with Wanda and Bernice, so maybe Adams got jealous when he heard about it and went over there later—well, then the State might offer you immunity in exchange for your testimony against him."

"Immunity."

Yes, it was a lovely word. Immunity.

"Immunity means you could never be prosecuted in this case. You could never be charged with the murders."

"But I'd have to get up and say I was there with them?"

"Well, yeah, but you'd be safe from prosecution."

He sat silent, staring down at his socks and plastic-sandaled feet. I noticed with a start that at the end of one ankle, there was only a stub of about six inches, and on the other, about a quarter of the foot lengthwise was missing. Sympathy stirred in my heart for him. What an awful human condition, to be alone and pursued by armed strangers, and then, in spite of your own strength and your best skill and greatest courage, to be overwhelmed by the cold and never to reach home. No wonder he was surly at times.

I wanted to reach over and pat him on the knee. That gesture, though, was both too feeble to be of comfort and too dangerously subject to misinterpretation. This was the kind of case that would likely be reviewed in the future by various watchdogs using film from the camera in the ceiling. I had watched enough conduct-of-counsel videos to know that scenes could look very different when viewed later by third parties tasked with investigating some inmate's or guard's allegation of improper conduct.

"Nobody expects you to say you hurt the sisters," I told him. "It's just that if you saw them at all, even to play cards and watch

TV—that testimony would be useful to the State if they charge Adams. On the other hand, without some kind of deal in place, with your record, if they can prove you were there, you're at terrible risk yourself of being charged."

"What do you think?" he asked me.

Was he asking whether I thought he had killed the girls? I didn't know whether he had or not, and it didn't matter what I thought. It mattered what a jury thought. Or did he want my considered legal opinion on what his best option was? If he wanted my blessing to lie to the court, he thought wrong. Like all attorneys, I was an officer of the court, and one of my ethical duties was not to deceive the tribunal.

Strategy was okay, deception was not.

"There's one other choice. If you and Adams are both indicted, and he goes to trial first and you are subpoenaed to testify, you can take the Fifth and refuse to answer anything they ask you. For you to admit only that you were in town that night is potentially incriminating, and Judge Jeffery would not force you to answer."

"That sounds good. I like that. Let's do that."

"Problem with that choice is that if you go to trial first, Adams will probably be testifying at your trial instead of the other way around. He could get a good deal by blaming you."

"So it's who screws who first?"

"Pretty much. But if we offer testimony against Adams now and the State offers you immunity, you can never be indicted."

"I walk?"

"Yes, you walk. You've already done enough time to cover sentences for any of those misdemeanors we can't get dismissed or beat at trial. I know you don't trust the court or Public Safety, or me, for that matter, but it's unusual to have a chance at immunity, and if it's offered, you should take it." There was no point in treating Amos to a lecture on legal theory and practice, but the truth was that district attorneys did not like the concept of immunity. They wanted to prosecute all involved in a case. Immunity was like a get-out-of-jail-free card, and the DAs agreed to it only in those rare situations when they needed the testimony of the grantee more than they disliked letting them off. The *Gonzalez* case enlarged the scope of immunity in Alaska. Before *Gonzalez*, immunity meant only that the immunized's testimony could not be used against them. Now it meant that the recipient could not be prosecuted at all in that particular case.

I had to wonder, though, since the Alaska Supreme Court had recently made new law in the area, new law that had not yet been tried by any challenges or appeals, how it would play out in actual practice. Would the grant of immunity become even rarer? Would the State find ways to skirt the new interpretation, perhaps by charging the witness with some other crime, like perjury, to attempt to claw back the immunity it had offered? I didn't know.

Amos sat there for a long time without moving or speaking, as though he had not heard me. He covered his face with his large hands and then rubbed his temples. He reached back to the rubber band at his neck and pulled it off and shook his hair down. Reddish in cast and crimped at the ends, it fell to his shoulders and hid the side of his face.

Why did he hesitate? If he had been there, if that was, in fact, his button on the stovetop, all he had to do was say so, not that he had hurt anybody. The immunity plan seemed great to me, but I was not someone whose life experiences had trained me over and over to never trust *tanik* authority of any kind. And I was not someone who was scarred for life because my mother had been had been tortured to death when I was fourteen. Who knew what was twisted up inside him, what nightmares drove him, or what he was capable of. I waited in silence, thinking that if Amos was granted immunity on this case and then went on to live a peaceable life, perhaps the elders would be persuaded that he was not responsible for the sisters' deaths but deserving of compassion for the loss of his mother, and he could once again have a respected place in the community.

"That reminds me, Amos. You'll get out, sooner or later, one way or another." There was no point in speculating on what sentence he might serve if convicted. The average murder convict served less than twenty years. This case was not an average case, of course, but, with the alcohol factors involved, he would likely be returned to society at some point, even if as an old man. "What do you want to do then? Go back to your family in Point Hope? Move to a new place?"

"Ivory carving is what I want to do. It's harder for me to hunt now, with my feet."

"What kind of carving?"

"Seals and birds and bears—walrus ivory, Dall sheep horn, polar bear teeth, and baleen. I made some money at it before. I want to open a shop in Anchorage."

I was impressed. This plan sounded not only admirable but doable. The prices for ivory went up all the time, while the number of skilled Native carvers dwindled.

Now I did pat his knee. Briefly. "Amos, that sounds great. I will buy from you."

It was time for me to go. Jails were like airplanes: There was never enough real fresh air in them. As casually as I could, I reached for my coat. Some clients suffered severe separation anxiety and acted out when you began to leave.

"What do you want me to say to them?"

He shrugged. "Don't say nothing to them. Let 'em come after me. We'll fight it out."

"It's your case. We'll do it your way. I won't mention immunity to the DA unless you decide you want to go for it."

I struggled into my coat and waved to Rosas behind his counter to let me through the security door. Out and down the stairs to the blessed, clean Arctic air that I inhaled deep like the huskies did—fresh air that was denied to Amos Lane.

9

Our creation myths say that Raven is the creator. Some say that the creative force took the form of the Raven to make the world so that the Yupiaq will never think they are above the creatures of the earth.

ANGAYUQAQ OSCAR KAWAGLEY

SATURDAY I WAS GLAD TO SEE SLEET SLIDING OFF THE neighbors' roofs because it meant the softball game would be canceled.

"We can't play when it's sleeting, right?"

Michael sat at the kitchen table, cleaning a rifle.

"You sound like a *tanik*," he said. "Here we play unless it's snowing too hard to see, or blowing too hard to stand up, or the ice is coming in."

"I *am* a *tanik*. What do you mean, 'coming in'? When does the ice come in?"

"Not often. Usually you have time to leave. Unless it happens at night, of course, when everybody's asleep."

"Are you kidding me? Does the ice really come in? What makes it come in?"

"Earthquake on the other side of the world. You need to get dressed for the game. What are you wearing?"

"Uh, jeans, I guess."

"Jeans are not warm enough, unless you put on two pairs."

"If I wear two pairs of jeans, I won't be able to run."

"Don't you have any warm underwear?"

"I don't know about this. I haven't played softball since—"

"Do you remember the rules?"

"Yeah, I guess. So, really, how often does the ice come in?"

"The ice is not coming. Go get dressed."

"But how often does the ice come?"

"About once every three generations, little Miss Tanik. Get dressed. Go!"

I stomped up the stairs, trying to remember whether I had actually agreed to play or had been volunteered. Now I would get to make a fool of myself in front of Michael's entire family and probably half my clients. I thought of stomping back downstairs to yell, Hell, no, I won't go! But then I remembered little Angela toddling into the kitchen, and Bull's rib-endangering hug, and the warm society of the poker game. All right, I would play, and try to remember the game was about the team, not my *tanik* self.

I pulled on a pair of thermal long johns and then jeans and searched in my closet for the roomiest pair of running shoes that might allow for two pairs of socks. I didn't have a sports bra, so I notched my regular bra tighter. I put on a thermal top and a plush shirt. The layers were so tight they restricted breathing, and I hoped they would loosen with some action. I waddled downstairs, trying not to look as uneager as I felt.

"Not bad," Michael said. I could tell he was trying not to laugh. "But you need a rain slicker. You can't get wet down your neck, or you'll have to come in. And something for your head."

We rummaged among the clothing and gear hanging on the kunnychuck wall. My rain jacket fit over the two layers I was already wearing, if snugly. Michael tied a fine wool scarf around my head.

"That's gonna get wet," I warned him, like I knew all about proper Arctic clothing.

"When it's sleeting like this and you're out on the field, your head is going to get wet no matter what you do. This is good wool, and wool stays a little warm even when it's wet."

I whimpered when he pulled the scarf tight, but he persisted.

"The trick for staying warm is to keep the wind out, to keep wind from getting into your neck and wrists. A zipper is better than buttons, anorak pullover better than a zipper."

"Mittens or knit gloves?"

"Neither. You can't catch a wet ball with mittens or gloves. Put your hands in your pockets whenever you're not using them."

"Thank you for the mitt." I had found a fielder's mitt lying on the coffee table when I got home the night before.

"Thank you for helping out my sister's team."

He kissed me on the forehead, and we went out to his truck.

Driving toward the ball field, we passed that dog again, still staked out on the tundra with no shelter and no food bowl. Now it was getting sleeted on and curled into its tail so the droplets would roll off its fur. Maybe the dog could stand the conditions, but I couldn't stand seeing it in them. I resolved to help this dog even if my neighbors got mad at me for interfering.

My heart sank when I saw all the cars pulled up alongside the field, so people could watch the game in comfort. Maybe they wouldn't recognize me in my strange outfit. They were used to seeing me in court suits, in the quiet court atmosphere, not blimped out in three layers of clothing, toddling around a ball field.

Michael stopped the truck beside the dugout.

"See you later. Good luck," he said.

"What? Aren't you staying for the game?"

"I'm going to city hall. They let me come in on weekends to study for my electrician's license."

Involuntarily, my lower lip pouted within my tight wool headscarf.

"You volunteer me to play and you aren't even going to watch?"

"This is my only time to study for the license."

"Electrician's license? I didn't know you were doing that."

"I've been working on it for a while."

I got the impression that Michael was making an effort to be offhand about something that was important to him.

"That's great, Michael. You could have your own business."

He glanced away, but I saw a small smile. I wondered if our relationship might encourage him to study hard, and felt a little warmer inside my three layers of clothing but did not want to embarrass him by gushing about it, so I climbed out into the sleet. Perhaps it was just as well he wouldn't be there to see me if I fell face down in the slush.

When I plodded down the slick cement steps of the dugout, all eyes turned in my direction, just like in the courtroom. For a moment I flashed on the memory of Nate and Kiana telling me about their confrontation with Amos in this place, how Amos had grabbed Kiana and thrown Nate off like a puppy, but I tried to push those thoughts out of my mind.

"It's my lawyer," a voice at the far end said.

So much for incognito.

"Hello, Celestine," I said.

Celestine wore a real baseball jersey that bore the name of our sponsor, British Petroleum, and a matching hat and sweatpants, plus shoes with cleats. She looked cute, while I looked like a walking yard sale. A huge first base mitt dwarfed her diminutive hand. She's Inupiaq, I told myself. She's used to the cold. Though I suspected that she probably also had on a pair of expensive long johns.

Michael's sister Sally came to me, holding Angela sound asleep in her arms.

"Thanks for coming. You're late. We had to tell the officials you would be here for sure or forfeit. Here, hold her—I'm up."

I took the limp child. Maybe I could be the official baby- and benchwarmer. The ladies scooted down to make room for me, and I settled Angela in my lap without arousing more than a nose twitch from the little sleeper. I gazed down into her small, exquisite face. My son and daughter were away at school, and I had forgotten the beauty and wonder of children.

The lady beside me had two scarves tied around her head.

"My first game," I whispered to her. "Do you have any idea what position I'm supposed to play?"

"Just go wherever's not covered."

I nodded.

"You Michael's girlfriend?" my new teammate asked.

"Uh, we're friends," I said, feeling oddly flattered.

"You met Mamie yet?"

The lady sounded half dubious, half curious.

"Yes, she came over to the house for a barbecue last weekend."

"Mamie have sad history," she said. "She comes from Atqasuk, where the TB and the measles hit everybody hard."

"Oh," I said.

"Her father and mother die in front of her, when she was only a little girl, seven or eight or so."

"Good heavens," I blurted out.

"I don't know how long she was there, sick herself, with them dead, and finally somebody found her."

I looked again at Angela's peaceful countenance. Somehow Mamie had survived and was now making sure that Angela's life was easier than her own.

"I can't even imagine how hard that was," I said.

"Her husband some *tanik* in Fairbanks, but he—"

I didn't want to hear any more of Mamie's history. I bent over Angela as though her nose needed attention.

Sally got to first base on an error. We sent up two more batters but went out without score, and then Jer summoned a girl from a car to hold Angela while our BP team took the field. Celestine took a long lead away from covering first base, and Sally played shortstop. They looked like they knew what they were doing. I trotted out toward the empty left field.

Frozen granules of sleet had collected in the lace holes of my sneakers. I didn't know whether my feet were wet or dry inside because I couldn't feel them anymore. The only thing I could feel was the sleet needling my forehead. Per Michael's direction, I put my left hand in my pocket but kept my right ready in its glove. Concentrate, I told myself. If you keep your eyes on the ball, you will be ready if it comes to you. They won't yell at you when you screw up if they think you were at least trying.

There came the sharp crack of the bat connecting, but the ball popped up, and our catcher caught it. The next batter was walked, and she and Celestine started dancing back and forth at first. The following batter got a base hit with a bouncing grounder that took Sally a while to trap.

"Come on, you guys," Celestine called to us. "Talk it up—I wanna hear some chatter."

"Easy out, easy out," I hollered as their next batter strode to the plate. "Heads up, this is it!"

The batter hit a line drive to right field, but our right fielder was ready. She caught it on a bounce and fired it to first. Celestine leaped high for the catch. Descending to tag the plate, she pivoted in midair to land in perfect planted stance for the double play to second.

"Way to go, Celestine!" I screamed, hopping up and down in a puddle like a frog, like every girl on the BP team was doing. "BP number one! BP number one!"

Sally was laughing at me and pointing toward the road, where a gray tourist bus had paused, every window holding a moonfaced *tanik* staring in astonishment at us Inupiaq ladies jumping up and down and yelling on the baseball field in the sleet. For the moment I was not an outsider, and almost as proudly Native as my teammates. BP won the game, 5–4. Victory was sweet, but what for me was even sweeter, I told Michael later, was holding little Angela and having the *tanik* tourists gawk at us.

Still in my wet clothes, I hovered around the kunnychuck.

"Where are you going?" he asked. He was deboning a bird at the sink for dinner.

"Nowhere . . . I'm just . . . ah, I'll be right back."

Moving around the corner, where he wouldn't see me, I ladled dog food into a white plastic grocery sack, grabbed an empty milk jug and a knife, and headed out the door.

The dog saw me coming. I saw she was female, was neatly made, a pretty dog with tapering legs and waist, heavily pelted from being outdoors all the time, and a wolflike head and yellow eyes. She was that indeterminate breed usually called a sled dog: mostly husky, some shepherd, and a good bit of Norwegian elkhound.

She got to her feet, and the tip of her tail quivered with hopeful anticipation. I stamped out a little hollow among the tundra plants and poured the kibbles into it. She ate so quickly she seemed to inhale the food. I carved the jug in half and found a patch of water in the always-soggy ground, and scooped some into it for her, hoping she would drink before it got spilled.

I looked around to see whether anyone was watching. She was somebody else's dog, and I had no business meddling with her. Alaska was not a glorious, wide-open frontier from a dog's point of view. Rabies was such a threat in outlying communities that leash and inoculation laws were strict. You do not see stray dogs in Native villages. Dogs are either caged, housed, tethered, or shot. For all I knew, Michael might object to my helping her as well. I was going to feed the dog regardless, but there was no need to advertise the fact.

Once I had noticed a small Native boy throwing rocks at a crippled duck that was swimming back and forth in the lagoon. I had no authority to tell him to stop, so I offered him a dollar to go get a treat instead of worrying the wounded animal. The hunter-child was incorruptible and refused the dollar.

"Going to eat the duck," he said.

I trudged back to the house, thinking that these sets of values differed as much as the Anglo and Inupiaq systems of justice. One tried to be content with small efforts: At least I was able to feed this dog, and it was nice that commercial oil interests supported ladies' softball.

10

Strange things done in the midnight sun . . .
The Arctic trails have their secret tales
That would make your blood run cold.
ROBERT W. SERVICE

CAROL WAS IN COURT, LIZ WAS ON THE PHONE WITH some cousin in a village, and I finally had a window of time in which to sit and study the Ipalook file. Public Safety had conducted many interviews of neighbors and people who'd encountered the sisters that weekend. Somewhere in the file, there was also the interview with John Adams, Bernice's fiancé.

Ron Ahgeak told Public Safety Officer Marten he was walking home from an after-bingo party on Friday when he thought he heard women screaming. But he wasn't absolutely sure it was screaming. It could have been just kids playing on the beach. He wasn't exactly positive about the time, either. He had gone to bingo on both Friday and Saturday. He was pretty sure that on Friday he took a cab home because he had won a little money, but on Saturday, he walked because afterward he went to a poker game and lost a little. But it could have been the other way around.

Officer Larry Hinken interviewed Craig A. Jackson, who lived at the nearby Barrow Apartments. Jackson related that the

Ipalook sisters' house was known as a party house. He often saw people coming out of the house stumbling drunk. Everyone at the Barrow Apartments knew of this house and called it the "crack house," because it was a spot to buy and sell drugs and bootlegged alcohol. Jackson also said that he went to work at five in the morning and didn't even bother looking out the window anymore when he heard yelling and screaming.

Doria Koonaloak, who worked for the City of Utqiagvik as a clerk and lived directly in front of the Ipalook home, was one of the several neighbors interviewed by another officer, Ted Barnett. Koonaloak told him, "I was home Friday night. I was tired from work, and I slept all night and didn't hear anything. Saturday, I cooked all day, making caribou stew and some cakes for a feast. I didn't hear anything or see anybody over there all day. I figured they were asleep. Saturday night I take the food to my daughter's house in Browerville. Bernice and John have been engaged for a while. They get along good, take good care of their little girl, little Eqalin."

Nayuk and Isabel Nungasuk, elders, lived beside the Ipalooks on the east side. They said: "Our son and his wife were in Hawaii all week, so we had our grandchildren. Mornings usually the kids watch TV, then afternoon we go to store or to visit. We don't drink. We try to stay out of the way of Bernice and Wanda Ipalook, because we don't like our grandkids to see people real drunk. Kids turn TV up loud, run around and holler, so we don't much notice noise coming from over there. No, nothing special about that weekend. If we hear screaming, we call Public Safety."

The neighbor on the west, a cab driver from Pakistan who did not wish to give his name, told the officer that he drove nights and slept days and didn't know the Ipalooks. He said he hadn't heard or seen anything unusual and wouldn't tell Public Safety if he had.

Officer Dolph Olson took a statement from Alfred Maleak. "I never saw nothing that night. I never heard nothing. They was all right, the sisters. They were nice. I'm sorry they got hurt, but I don't know nothing about it."

Officer Olson also talked to Florence Okpeaha, who said: "I went to school with both of them. Wanda used to be really good at the basketball. She was a great player. Everybody thought she would go to the U with her basketball, but she got to drinking and dropped out. Happens to a lot of kids here. Happened to my nephew. He eventually went back, but Wanda never did. I had gone to the store that weekend. Not the big store, Stuaqpak, but the little store in Browerville, and when I came out, they was walking toward me. I guess they were going to get a video or something. They were already drunk. They were really loud. They kept calling out to whoever went by, especially the guys, hollering, 'Give us a ride, sweetie' and 'What you got in your sleeve, honey,' and stuff like that. I crossed the street 'cause I didn't want to talk to them. I used to try to talk to Wanda whenever I ran into her, to invite her over when I could, but after a while I quit. The way they lived was just too rough."

Then I found the interview that Sergeant Rick Staley conducted with Bernice's fiancé, John Adams.

> At 1:55 p.m. Investigator Larry Paul and myself went to the John Adams residence at house number 5288 in Browerville to speak with him. Upon entering the residence, we met with John Adams, who was bent over suffering from stomach cramps. We drove him to PHS Hospital at his request along with Lloyd Paningonna. I explained to Paningonna that I would like to speak with John Adams when he was through with the hospital and we would be able to pick him up. About 2:36 p.m. myself and Paul picked up Lloyd Paningonna and Adams from the PHS Hospital and took them to the Department of Public Safety where

I and Investigator Paul interviewed John Adams. Attached is his signed statement:

I live at House No. 5288 with Bernice Ipalook and my children. I work at Utpeagvik Inupiat Corporation Construction on the weatherization project. Last week Bernice and I were down in Anchorage where my son had tubes put in his ears. We came back here to my house. We were drinking here at the house. Bernice and Wanda went out in a cab a couple of different times. Elizabeth Ahgeak and Allen Kaleak, Jr., were over here that evening as well. Also Dorcas Hugo from Anaktuvuk Pass was here. On Sunday I stayed home with the kids. I didn't go out looking for Bernice. Dorcas called looking for Bernice and I said she hadn't come home yet. She called on Monday and said that she was over at Wanda's and the door was locked. Usually they'll go to Wanda's house if they're going to party. I stayed home all day on Sunday. Sheryl Neakok came in the morning and then Lloyd Stine came by in the afternoon. I don't have an ATV or a car. I only have a snow machine for winter time. Wanda doesn't have a phone at her place. We used to stay over there about a year ago and we had a padlock that you use a key to open and I think that's the one that Wanda used to lock her house. Bernice and I just got engaged to get married. I bought her this ring and then she got mad and threw it at me. I don't know why but she just got mad. She threw it at me Saturday night and my sister was there when it happened. I don't have any idea who might have done something like this to her. I don't think she was seeing anybody else, and she never told me she was seeing anybody else. I didn't call anybody looking for Bernice. I don't have anything over at 1541 which is Wanda's house. The last time I was over

> at Wanda's was over a month ago. We had stopped by and got some mail for Bernice. Neither Bernice or Wanda said anything about anybody bothering them or being afraid of anybody or being mad at anybody. Bernice never talked about any harassing phone calls that she received at the Borough or anything like that. The last time I saw Bernice and Wanda was about two o'clock in the morning on Sunday. I was drinking Southern Comfort. Bernice and Wanda went out two times during the night and came back and they were drinking at the time. The first time they went out Dorcas went with them. The last time I saw them Bernice said to her sister, "Let's go back to your place."

I set aside the interview with fiancé John Adams for further study. I had thought that Bernice and Wanda lived together in the little house where their bodies were found, but Bernice's fiancé said that she lived with him and their daughter. For the hundredth time I reminded myself not to jump to conclusions. Bernice and John had been a family, and now their little girl was without a mother, and her daddy was in jail. This case got harder and harder, and sadder and sadder.

Ed Ellingsworth had taken a statement from their neighbor Wiley Ungarook, who told him the same story I had heard from Officer Marten, that Wanda came over to Ungarook's place to borrow a cigarette. He vividly remembered her coming over because she ended up taking half a pack and he was annoyed. But when Ed pressed him about the time of her visit, he couldn't be sure whether she came over Saturday morning or Sunday morning.

I removed Wiley's file from the pile and placed it with the John Adams file to look at again. If interviewed once more, Ungarook might remember more clearly, especially if he talked to someone other than Public Safety.

Ed also spoke with Harry Sovalik, a bus driver. Sovalik said that John Adams, who was his second cousin, had boarded his bus on the last run, around eleven o'clock on Saturday night. Sovalik said that Adams didn't say hello like he usually did and appeared to be upset. He said that Adams sat there in the front seat of the bus staring down at his little finger. When he kept staring at it the whole ride, Sovalik tried to see what was on his finger. It looked like some kind of fancy ring, like an engagement ring with a diamond.

So here was what Ellingsworth was basing his theory on. At first everybody had pointed fingers at Amos Lane because he had a record and was in town, but Adams was the one who had argued with Bernice that night and got a ring thrown in his face. I withdrew Sovalik's page, highlighted it with a big check mark, and laid it with Wiley Ungarook's and the John Adams interview. Maybe my client Amos Lane was not the devil from hell everyone thought.

SHOPPING IN UTQIAGVIK was an art form. In the summer, ships and barges supplied the Arctic, but for most of the year, groceries had to come in by plane, and prices were elevated as a result. The first Thursday evening in September, I made my daily stop at Stuaqpak, the Alaska Commercial Company grocery store, and had selected a package of hot dogs for $12 and some oranges for $8.50, and was staring forlornly at a bag of wilted romaine when a hand fell on my shoulder. I turned and looked into the grinning eyes of Ed Ellingsworth.

"Evening, Miss Becky," he said jovially. "Any decent lettuce today?"

"Actually, I was checking it for tape recorders."

"Sorry about that. We got a little carried away. I have good news for you and your client."

I retreated behind my shopping cart. Perhaps he had accepted a job in Flagstaff and was moving away?

"I mean it, hon. Ordinarily, I wouldn't come after you in the produce section, but I just called your office and got the answering machine, so I figured you were here."

I gave him a questioning look.

"We, uh, know your habits," he said.

I sighed.

"Get used to it, Miss Becky. You're an important person."

I rolled my eyes.

"Actually, we know everyone's habits. It's our job."

I wondered whether there was any other person anywhere as irritating as this detective.

"The heat's off your client," he said.

"How do you mean?"

"We know who murdered the girls, and it wasn't him."

He had my attention, but I asked myself why he would be so eager to tell me this news that he'd tracked me to the lettuce bin.

"Good for you. I'm sure the whole community will be relieved." I picked up a head of iceberg lettuce. The outside leaf hung down limply, and the inside leaves looked shriveled. I put it back in the bin. "Are you going to be putting out a press release?"

"We need to set up a conference with you and your client. A little cooperation from him and we can present the case against John Adams, Bernice's fiancé, to the special grand jury. It's set for the 20th."

"Conference about what? I thought you said you knew who did it."

"Oh, we know. Just trying to clarify some timelines. We can prove they were both there, Amos and John, that night. Question is, Who left last? We think it was Adams. And he was mad because Lane had been there. We have another witness who says Bernice and John argued that night and she threw her ring in his face."

Ellingsworth's countenance reverted from forced friendliness to the wolfish expression I found more familiar.

"And nobody is saying Amos Lane was there, anyway," I added.

"We know he was there. He left his DNA on Wanda."

"You couldn't possibly have DNA results this quick. Plus, I don't think they have enough Eskimo population samples to get a reliable reading on Eskimo DNA."

"Miss Becky, you told us you had the names of other places he was that night besides the murder house."

There wasn't any point in asking him not to call me Miss Becky. He wouldn't honor the request, and asking him would only encourage him to say it even more often to annoy me.

"I never said any such thing. And I know you have exactly what I said on tape. Until Adams is indicted, I don't see how much is changed."

"What has changed is that Adams has confessed."

"John Adams confessed?" Ed had a reputation for being a ferocious interrogator, but surely even he could not browbeat a person into confessing to a double murder he hadn't done. I tried hard to keep a poker face. The fact that Public Safety had moved its laser eye of suspicion from Amos to John was great news for our side. So why did I feel uneasy? Was I allowing my dislike of Ellingsworth to make me doubt his judgment? No, it was my own intuition, my own hunch, my own gut instinct, that would not be stilled. Something was off about this case, and about the State's sudden change of course, and I didn't want Amos and me to be ambushed if the State changed its collective mind yet again. "So why do you need a conference with us if Adams confessed?"

"To make the timelines crystal clear. And also for motive."

"Motive?"

"You're a little slow today, Counselor. Maybe you eat too much lettuce." Ellingsworth was drawling again, always a bad sign. "Lane was at the Ipalooks'. He had sex with one of the sisters, maybe both of them. We've got the DNA to prove it. Adams found out about it and argued with Bernice. She threw the ring in his face. He flew into a jealous rage and killed her. It's the oldest story in the world. The sister was a witness, so he killed her, too."

I didn't know what to say. I picked up a head of lettuce without looking at it and put it in my cart. Granted, a fiancé or boyfriend is the usual suspect and often does turn out to be the perpetrator, but it sounded to me like Public Safety had been under so much pressure to solve the case that they were pinning the tail on the nearest donkey and then asking for help from the also-ran. Perhaps they'd pushed harder on poor grieving Adams than he could bear. If he had, in fact, confessed, he would not be the first Native who had told the officers what they wanted to hear.

"I've already talked to Amos, and he doesn't want to work with you. Sorry."

The detective tamped his lips into a grim line and appeared to be struggling with the desire to smack me. He and I had long ago assumed the basic positions of cops and robbers, cats and hounds, and it was hard for us to communicate in any useful way.

"When you really do get your DNA results, maybe we can talk again. But then it will probably have to be in court."

"Oh, there's more."

"Like what?"

"Ask your client where he lost the grommet to the key to the three-wheeler he borrowed that night. Ask him . . . Well, I'm going to save that one for later."

Grommet? What the hell was a grommet? Whatever it was, why had I not heard of it before? Above all else in criminal defense, I hated surprise. Cornered in the produce, the only thing I could do was fight back.

"Maybe there are some things we'd like to ask you, too," I said. "About time."

"For instance."

"When exactly did the sisters die? Does the State even know?"

"If certain defense counsel cooperated a little more—if they weren't so damn pigheaded—we could make a lot more progress in this case."

"Like on Theo Johnson?" I bit my lip. I really hadn't meant to bring Theo up again.

"Yes, like on Theo Johnson. Damned cop shooter."

"There were no deaths in that case, no thanks to you. If you'd just left Theo alone, let him pass out in peace, nobody would have gotten hurt. But you couldn't miss a chance to get all dressed up in SWAT gear and storm the house."

"Never mind a little detail like the judge's children having to be on lockdown at the school because Theo's house was within a thousand yards."

"The whole town is within a thousand yards!"

Two little kids in grubby blue nylon parkas were staring at us, round eyed, while their mother tried to shepherd them past. I wheeled my cart away and left Ellingsworth standing among the lettuces.

I cruised up two aisles and sought asylum in canned goods.

"Can I help you?" a uniformed clerk asked. She was looking at me with an odd expression.

"I, uh . . . I'm just browsing."

The shelves of canned goods were a blur, and I rolled on into the bread section. What was it I was missing about this case? Something did not add up. First they wanted to hang Amos. Now the posse had passed him by and was galloping after John Adams. I don't claim to be the greatest defense attorney ever, but I do have an instinct for criminal law. It has boundaries of legalities, and cases have timelines of facts. Once you learn them, you can do your job with a certain degree of confidence. But this case had no factual timeline. The testimony of witnesses wandered all over the clock. And the State had blurred legal boundaries with its own lawless activities, illegal tape recordings and misappropriated treatment records.

On impulse, I trundled the cart onward to my favorite part of the store, the back room, a quiet, dusty corner where a few beaded gloves, skin-sewn dolls, and carved ivory seals, whales, and birds were displayed. The artistry of Native ivory carvers never failed to awe and delight me. For generations their forebears watched the seals, hunted the whales, and caught the birds, until they knew every behavior, every movement and look and line of them all. The creatures they freed from the ivory were the essences of their kind, now preserved for other generations and other peoples to appreciate.

Life in Utqiagvik was sometimes hard, and this job, harder. Too hard, on occasion. But no matter how difficult the case, or how far I lived from family, or how much I missed the presence of trees, the beauty of the carvings reminded me I was still glad to be in this unique place at the top of the world, and I wanted to do the best I could for my clients, including Amos Lane.

Smiling, I returned to the search for salad. Natives ate the linings of caribou stomachs in order to have vegetables. I could make do with some elderly cabbage.

11

If you are afraid, change your ways.
INUIT PROVERB

RANDY WAS WAITING IN MY OFFICE IN MORE THAN usually rumpled jeans and his usual red basketball jacket. I was happy to see him, but the minute I took off my jacket and sat down to visit, Carol stuck her head in the door and told me Amos was holding on the phone with an emergency and Liz hadn't made into work. Worried now about Liz as well as Randy, I picked up the receiver. Randy, to my dismay, retreated to the outer office.

"The trooper brought me this here subpoena. I have to come to court to give . . . evidence before the Special Grand Jury, it says."

"For when?" I asked.

"Today," Amos said.

"Today!"

"I don't care what they do to me, I ain't gonna say a word," he said.

"Amos, listen to me. Remember when we talked about immunity?"

"Yeah."

"Do you want to go that route?"

"Tell me it again."

"It boils down to this. Yes, you would have to testify, but no, they could never prosecute you."

"Never?"

"You could never be charged with the Ipalook murders."

There came a pause that lengthened into silence. I peered through my office door to see whether Randy was still there. Thankfully, I saw basketball shoes on the other side of Liz's desk.

"Yeah, I want to be immune."

"You'll have to testify."

"All right. I can do it."

"Okay. I'll file a motion to quash. Bye."

"What's that? But what if—"

I hung up on him. I had no time to explain to the client what I needed to do for him, I had to go do it. But first I needed to talk to Randy before he gave up and went away. I brought him by the hand into my office, where he sat down and stared out through the morning glories toward the Arctic Ocean. Sometimes in the summer you could see gray whales from this window, which, although only on the third floor, was one of the highest in Utqiagvik. A client had once explained to me that gray whales liked to swim near shore to scratch their bellies on the gravel.

"Randy! I'm so glad to see you. How is your . . . ?"

When I got a good look at his face, the words died in my throat. Today he looked as sad and worn as any grown-up cancer caretaker ever did. There was something about this kid that went right to my heart. Liz's too. When I met him at his first children's court hearing, he had looked like such a healthy young person—fit and bright-eyed—that I hoped he could be a happy one, too. But his mother's cancer was gutting him as well as her, and his dad's indifferent absence made everything worse. Plus there were the piled-on pressures of school and being the mainstay of the basketball team, as well as keeping up what was practically a full-time job at the car repair.

I wheeled my desk chair closer to him and impulsively took his hand again and then, embarrassed, put the hand on his knee and patted it.

"Is she not doing well?"

He shook his head, and I could see in his face the effort not to cry.

"Has your dad come in?"

He shook his head again.

So his dad still refused to quit his fun-filled Anaktuvuk aerie and left his teenage son to cope with one of the toughest circumstances that life could inflict. I had to swallow hard to avoid cussing him out in front of Randy.

"I'm so sorry. What is happening?"

"Sometimes she doesn't know me. She's all doped up for the pain."

"Oh, dear. Randy, tell me what I can do. Should I get a letter from the doctor so you can take off from school? How many hours are you putting in at the shop?"

"Can you talk to my dad again?"

"Of course I will," I said, not expecting a phone call would make any difference. "Liz and I will both talk to him."

For a moment it crossed my mind to offer to take Randy to breakfast or to accompany him on a visit to the hospital, but the special grand jury and Amos Lane's motion to quash had hijacked my day.

"Thanks," he said. He got up. At the door, he turned and added, "See you."

"See you."

Randy had an even more crowded schedule than I did and probably wouldn't have had time for breakfast, anyway. But the fact that he had at least spoken of his pain to another person might be a hopeful sign.

Mechanically, I switched mental gears from Randy's situation to Amos Lane's. There wasn't much time in which to get a motion filed and heard. Everything had to be done now.

Since the Fifth Amendment of the United States Constitution guaranteed to Amos the right not to be compelled to incriminate himself, the State would have to grant him immunity from prosecution in order to question him about a double homicide in front of a grand jury. This meant full immunity in terms of *State v. Gonzalez*, the Alaska Supreme Court case that had just crossed my desk. *Gonzalez* had been published only two months before the Ipalooks died, on June 4, 1993.

Some people, like Liz, said I worked too hard and that I could do a better job if I concentrated on basics and quit worrying about details—but if I'd followed that philosophy, I would never have read *State v. Gonzalez* in time for it to help Amos Lane. Our office received copies of all the criminal appellate decisions as they were issued. No matter how far behind I fell, I always looked at the new opinions and skimmed enough of their headnotes to know what they were about, and then shoved them into a loose-leaf notebook under general headings such as "Search and Seizure," "*Miranda*," "Sixth Amendment Right to Counsel," "Probable Cause," "Evidentiary Rulings," and so on. I never had time to read the entire opinion, but because of this crude filing system, I was aware of *Gonzalez* in time to use it to help Amos.

The computer whirred into its semi-life, and I browsed my inventory of motions. I had to edit an existing template for the motion to quash subpoena and get the new document printed, served, and filed, along with a motion for expedited hearing and affidavits supporting them both, within the hour, or Amos Lane would be dragged unprepared and unrepresented before the grand jury.

Carol came in. "Amos Lane on 2."

"Please tell him I'm working right now on the motion to quash and will call him after it's filed."

"He wants to know what a motion to quash is."

"Could you please help me out and explain it to him?"

I hadn't taken my eyes off the computer but could feel her standing there, hesitating.

"I don't know much about it myself," she said.

"Tell him I'll call him later, okay?"

It was on the tip of my tongue to say to her, Couldn't you just this once, in an emergency, try to pitch in and help a bit? But I bit my tongue and didn't. I tried to smile at her, hoping she wouldn't make another complaint to Anchorage that I was uptight and hard to work with.

"When are we going to get somebody that can really help us?"

"What do you mean?" I asked, still typing. I knew very well what she meant.

"Liz isn't here half the time."

Maybe so, but any time Liz spent with us, plus her knowing everybody in town and being related to half of them, helped more than Carol had the sense to realize. I didn't say that, either. I also didn't say that I was well aware that Liz's frequent absences and late arrivals might signal that she, too, used one or more of the illegal substances that were all too common in Utqiagvik. Carol hadn't been in town long enough to understand certain things about the place. One was the sacred rite of the hangover. I never saw it codified in anyone's personnel regulations, but local employers tacitly acknowledged that Utqiagvik was often a difficult place in which to work and live, that sometimes people needed a respite from the midnight sun or the polar night or the claustrophobia of being indoors so much. If an individual relieved stress with alcohol or something else and duly called in sick, well, they were entitled to the day off and would not be disturbed. Better this method than having them quit and leave town.

"I hope she isn't sick," I said.

I pressed on with the motion and sensed rather than saw that Carol disappeared from the doorway.

"I am counsel of record for Amos Lane," I typed. "Mr. Lane

has been a focus of investigation into the recent deaths of Bernice and Wanda Ipalook. Virtually anything he can say, even just to confirm that he was present in Utqiagvik on the evening they died, has the potential of being viewed as incriminating by the Special Grand Jury now convened in the case. This morning Mr. Lane was served with a subpoena to give testimony before the Special Grand Jury. Mr. Lane respectfully asks the Court to review his situation in terms of the recent Alaska Supreme Court Case of *State v. Gonzalez*, a copy of which is appended, and to quash the subpoena until and unless the State grants him immunity from prosecution in the case."

I set this motion to print and scanned the index for my motion for expedited consideration.

"Rebecca!" a friendly voice called at my door.

I took my eyes off the computer screen long enough to say, "Della, how nice to see you!"

Della breezed in with her long blond hair draped attractively over the hood of her rickrack-trimmed summer parka and handed me a white paper sack. Della was an acquaintance from community meetings and task forces who had become a semi-friend. We went to lunch occasionally and shared stories of joys and hassles. Her community liaison job was easier than mine, but her commitment to service was similar.

"How about lunch? I just got back from my vacation in Palau, and I brought you the seashell you wanted."

Seashell. Seashell! Randy's seashell. I had to admit I hadn't made any progress in finding the seashell Randy had said his mother might enjoy, hadn't even mentioned it to him today, and had forgotten my half-serious request to Della. Weeks ago, when she told me she was going to Palau and asked if I wanted a postcard, I'd said, "No, no postcard—bring me a nice shell!" God bless this lady—she had remembered, and had brought one from thousands of miles away. I took my hands and my attention from the computer, opened the sack, and found an exquisite chambered nautilus, a natural work of art. I traced its smooth coils with my fingertips.

For a moment, then, in spite of the motion to quash and the stress of Della's well-meant intrusion, the hair prickled on the back of my neck as I contemplated the shell. Here, literally, was a gift from the sea, like Mrs. Lindbergh, herself a visitor to Utqiagvik sixty years earlier, had written about. But the shell most brought to mind the stories of what shamans had once wrought in the winds and waves. Only a few years earlier, archaeologists dug up near Utqiagvik a sod home that had been buried long ago by a movement of the earth. Utqiagvik elders had seen baleen effigies within it. Baleen is the material in the mouths of some whale species, such as bowheads, that strains the krill and plankton they eat from seawater. Natives used baleen for special items like tiny baskets, sled fastenings—and shamanic effigies. The elders respectfully asked the scientists to re-cover the dwelling and leave it alone because it had belonged to a shaman. The Anglo experts refused. Within days a great storm arose and washed the entire site into the ocean, along with a couple of neighboring houses.

Perhaps forces far more powerful than Liz and me also cared about Randy and his mother. For a moment I wondered whether Randy was subject to, or a part of, these forces. Then I shook my head, placed the shell on the desk, and tried hard to greet Della.

"Welcome back, Della—you will never, ever know how glad I am to see this shell! It is absolutely gorgeous. Soon we will have lunch, and I will explain it all to you. But right now, I have this awful emergency and there just isn't any time," I said, trying to smile.

"Surely you have time for lunch! Everybody has to eat."

There are plenty of days that no, not everybody has time to eat, I wanted to answer but said only, "It's the Ipalook case. I have to get this motion filed within an hour."

"Oh. I understand. Big case. I've come at the wrong time." Della gazed at me for a moment with a look half mournful, half reproachful, and then removed the exquisite shell from my lap and placed it on the windowsill. "For later," she said.

"It's so beautiful! I'll call you," I murmured.

Della disappeared. I knew she didn't understand at all and would say to others that I was working too hard.

I was adding Amos's personal details to the order for expedited hearing when Carol reappeared.

"The court called. They want to know why you're late for the Okpeaha children's hearing. They're all waiting for you."

"Oh, shit. Shit. Shit," I said. After talking to Amos first thing upon walking in the door, I hadn't even looked at my daily calendar.

"Shall I tell them that?"

"Carol, this is an awful emergency. Could you please help me make copies of these pleadings and get them down to the court for filing—and keep calling the clerks until we get a hearing set before noon? It's about the Ipalook case."

"Everybody says your client killed those women. He should fry."

Since when had Carol tuned into the tundra drums?

"That's just gossip, Carol."

She was glaring at me from the doorway, hands on hips. No doubt later in the week I would get one of those "How are things going up in Utqiagvik?" phone calls from Anchorage, after she complained to them, again, but that was not the worry now.

"How come I have to do part of your work? I've got enough of my own."

I bit my lip so hard I feared I would give myself a blood blister but managed to say with relative calm, "Okay. You go do the children's hearing, and I'll get the motion filed. It's called working in a law office, Carol."

Carol heaved one of her patented sighs but turned and headed to the printer to receive the newly hatched pleadings for copying. I dug out my Okpeaha children's case file and charged out the door, almost knocking down my client, Bertha Okpeaha, the children's mother, waiting in the hallway. Bertha was large and round and had seal-shiny black hair streaming down her back.

In the past two years Bertha had set an informal courthouse record for receiving the most minor-in-consumption-of-alcohol charges. Now, thankfully, she had turned twenty-one and was no longer eligible to commit that particular crime. She could drink legally, but the problem now was that one drink often led to many, and by the time she was too drunk to care for her children, it was too late to arrange for a babysitter. Bertha loved her children dearly and wanted them back from where the State had placed them, with relatives in a distant village. Today it was up to Bertha and me to explain to Judge Jeffery that she had learned her lesson and would be more responsible, and would at least plan to get a babysitter before she ever took that first drink.

"Just one minute, Bertha!" I said.

As a practical matter, I had to run to the ladies' room across the hall. I could tell that this day was going to be one of those in which bathroom breaks were hard to find, so before heading to court I should take the opportunity.

The second-floor bathroom in this modern court-and-bank building was indistinguishable from business office bathrooms in the Lower 48—white tile floors, steel stalls, porcelain sinks. I was washing my hands and checking the mirror to see whether I looked tired when one of the social workers in Bertha's hearing walked in. She was a Native lady with permed gray hair and a chubby face and freckles, usually friendly and cheerful, but today unaccountably haggard.

"Ila, what is it?" I blurted out.

She put a hand on my forearm as if to steady herself, then leaned back on the metal partition. I waited for her to tell me.

"My daughter," she said. "They found her."

I had not heard of anyone being lost. "What . . . ?"

"In Anchorage. They say she is going to be all right, but . . ."

I moved to her side and placed my arm around her shoulder.

"She was buried alive. Somebody dragged her into the woods and . . . and when they were done, they dumped dirt all over her."

Ila began to weep, and I took her into my arms. I don't know how long we stood there, rocking slightly back and forth, before one of the other social workers came in, bustling with nervous purpose.

"Ila—we've got your ticket made. Come on—I'll go home with you to pack, and the flight's at one."

She hustled Ila out the door, but I remained staring at myself in the mirror, frozen with shock at this new horror. I thought of my own daughter, of daughters everywhere, of the Ipalook sisters and other sisters, of the mother of Amos, another victim, and of Ila, the mother of a victim—all so precious, all so vulnerable. I splashed water on my cheeks but still saw those faces.

The bathroom door opened slightly, and Bertha peeked in.

"You okay, Ms. Wright? What happened to Ila?"

Bertha brought me a paper towel, and I dried my face.

"Thank you, Bertha," I said. "We're a little late, and we'd better go to court now."

While we listened to the DA's opening statement, I did some deep breathing, reread some of the Bible verses scribbled in my trial notebook, and was able to return to normal function. Bertha behaved with tearful dignity during the two-hour hearing, and I was proud of her, even during the testimony of the social worker who had found the two toddlers crawling, dirty and hungry, upon their mother while she was out cold.

At the close of the inquiry, Judge Jeffery continued the State's emergency custody of the children for an additional ninety days to give Bertha a chance to consolidate changes to her lifestyle, but he also ordered that the children be returned from the outlying village to the Utqiagvik children's home where their mother could visit them daily while attending parenting classes.

Bertha looked up at the judge in his black robe, elevated upon the bench. I wondered whether he appeared superhuman to her. Sometimes judges looked that way to me.

"Thank you. Now I can see my babies again," she said.

Judge Jeffery had served in Utqiagvik a long time, first as Legal Services attorney, then as judge. Before he came to the Arctic, because of injuries in an automobile accident, he had spent healing time in an ashram in India. He was a thin and graying man not really much older than me, who had a beatific smile and a courteous word for everyone. In spite of his frail appearance, he always conscientiously, and sometimes maddeningly, did his duty, however much time and scholarly research it might require.

Once, during the second week of a murder trial, news came that a relative of the judge had suffered a medical emergency and had been medevaced to Anchorage. The DA and I came to court the next morning expecting to be told that the judge was unavailable and we were probably looking at a mistrial and then a do-over of ten days of agonized testimony by three generations of prosecution and defense witnesses. I was staring down at my schedule in despair of finding a date for the new trial when a familiar voice said, "Good morning, Counsel. Any preliminary matters to take up before the jury returns?"

He had stayed at his post.

I loved the man, in a distant and respectful way.

Bertha hugged me and left the courtroom. I silently prayed that Bertha and her children would be safer than Ila's daughter, the Ipalooks, and Harriet Lane. I was gathering up my file papers when Judge Jeffery said, "Counsel, the Amos Lane matter is set for today at 11:30 a.m."

"Thank you, Your Honor." Carol had done her duty and filed the papers. The clerks had done theirs and brought them to the court's attention, even while Judge Jeffery was on the bench hearing Bertha's case. We were all doing our duty, and Amos would get his hearing.

The judge went to his chambers. I crossed the well of the

courtroom and mounted the dais to reach the clerk's phone and tell the jail to bring Amos over at eleven thirty. I didn't have the authority to give such a direction, but the jail knew I wouldn't make it unless appropriate. Then I took the copy of *State v. Gonzalez*, which I had managed to slip into the Okpeaha file, and went down the inner stairs to the chilly rear exit of the courthouse, where I could review it without interruption. And smoke a cigarette.

Sometimes a raven joined me in that courtyard-like space between the walls of two buildings. He scavenged what he could from the trash of the Mexican restaurant next door and would answer with a croak if I spoke to him. He was not there today.

According to some Native lore, ravens roamed the earth as messengers between beings of earth and those not of earth. I wondered whether Randy knew any ravens.

Then I immediately wondered whether Liz was right. I had been working too hard.

I read: "Article I, section 9 of the Alaska Constitution states that '[n]o person shall be compelled in any criminal proceeding to be a witness against himself.'"

A previous case had pointed out that a person could, in fact, be compelled to give testimony if "the State has taken measures to remove the hazard of self-incrimination." The State could compel the testimony but could not use that specific testimony against that particular witness. Then, the State could still prosecute that same witness if other evidence in the case pointed at him. This practice was called "use and derivative use immunity."

Gonzalez declared:

> We now reach the question at the center of this case: does a grant of use and derivative use immunity remove the hazard of incrimination? We do not doubt that, in theory, strict application of use and derivative use immunity would remove the hazard of immunity.

> *See* Kastigar v. United States, 486 U.S. 468 (1972) (Marshall, Jr., dissenting). In a perfect world, one could theoretically trace every piece of evidence to its source and accurately police the derivative use of compelled testimony. In our imperfect world, however, the question arises whether the judicial process can develop safeguards to prevent derivative use of compelled testimony that satisfy Article I, section 9. Because we doubt that workaday measures can, in practice, protect adequately against use and derivative use, we ultimately hold that AS 12.50.101 impermissibly dilutes the protection of article I, section 9.

Now, it wasn't enough for the State to promise that the testimony would not be used against the suspect who gave it. The State had to provide complete immunity from prosecution in the case if they wished the individual to testify.

Thinking over *Gonzalez* and taking deep breaths of the lemony-cool air and my cigarette, I contemplated the little patch of tundra that remained between the side of the courthouse and Pepe's North of the Border restaurant next door, making sure my purse was in place so the door wouldn't latch; otherwise, I would be locked out in the cold with no coat. The raven strutted into view from between the pilings on which the buildings rested. The bird shot me a penetrating gaze and cocked its head toward me, as if waiting for me to speak. I didn't have any more time for the raven than I'd had for Della. The big oily-black bird continued its search for restaurant garbage.

From the defense standpoint, the complete immunity conferred by *Gonzalez* was a great opportunity. Amos Lane would be fortunate if the State wanted his testimony enough to offer him immunity to get it. So why did I feel uneasy?

Some attorneys confine their entire practice to lower courts where only misdemeanors are handled because mistakes made there are easily corrected. Circuit is different, and this case was a good example of how and why. If the State conferred immunity upon Amos and he agreed to testify, once Judge Jeffery entered this deal on the record, it became permanent and binding. It could not be undone. Amos could never be prosecuted.

If I felt uneasy, if my stomach churned, perhaps it was only because the case was unpredictable and hadn't followed the usual pattern of investigation and resolution. There was no reason to deny my client this choice if offered. In fact, I had a duty to pursue it. But what if Ellingsworth was wrong? What if Liz and Nate were right? It was possible Amos murdered the sisters, and that by doing my job and pursuing immunity I was helping ensure that Bernice and Wanda's killer would go free.

Due process, I said to myself. Amos was entitled to due process. For the first time, the words sounded in my head more like "bureaucratic process." In any case to which I was appointed, it was my job to defend, the DA's to prosecute, the judge's to referee, and the jury's to sort the facts. This system, in which I had been trained and in which I believed, provided justice only if all played their roles well. It wasn't my role to jump the rails and determine right from wrong, guilty from innocent.

Only once before had this issue been presented to me so directly. Several years earlier I had represented a polite and articulate young man accused of hitting his girlfriend's baby so hard that the infant received a concussion. Hoping to clear himself, and against my advice, the client took a lie detector test. Any defense counsel will tell you that lie detector test results are inadmissable in court because they are unreliable, and they are often used to induce suspects to make admissions during the warm-up questions. This client failed the test. I presented the DA with all the articles declaring lie detector tests to be useless, and an affidavit from the operator who administered the test stating that he had his own doubts about the results in this instance. The young man got a sentence of probation.

The following year he hit another child.

I almost hung up my license after that one, I was so appalled that I had helped keep this guy on the streets.

So, now, was I an advocate for due process—or a bureaucratic cog acting without choice or responsibility? The answer to that question no longer seemed as clear to me as it should. Ellingsworth wasn't troubled by such questions. He didn't listen to the Native community. Perhaps I had listened too much.

I RETURNED TO a visibly nervous Amos Lane in the courtroom. Amos, his trooper escort, and the clerk and I sat in silence, waiting on the assistant district attorney, who was tied up assisting the Fairbanks DA in the special grand jury proceedings now meeting on the floor below us. Finally, Joe Slusser entered the courtroom, looking paler, blonder, and more distracted than usual and holding in his hand the copies of my motions that Carol would have provided to his office. The clerk dialed the judge's chambers and simultaneously called out, "All rise."

Joe stood at his table, reading my motions, while Amos and I got to our feet, and the judge entered, bearing a single law book. *State v. Gonzalez* was so new it couldn't already be included in the bound volume, but each set of lawbooks received monthly or weekly updates, called pocket parts, which were slip opinions of new cases. These lived in a parchment sleeve in the back of the book until the information they contained was included in a hardbound volume.

"Please be seated," the judge said.

We sat.

"We are here regarding a special grand jury that is convened today. Mr. Amos Lane has received a subpoena to testify in these proceedings now taking place in Utqiagvik concerning the deaths of Bernice and Wanda Ipalook earlier this year. Present are Mr. Lane; the trooper, since Lane is in custody pursuant to other cases; his attorney, Rebecca Wright from the public defender's office; and for the State, Assistant District Attorney Joe Slusser. Defense counsel has filed a motion to quash the subpoena. Ms. Wright?"

"Yes, Your Honor. Thank you for the expedited scheduling."

I stood up. I could feel Amos trembling at my side.

"Your Honor, Mr. Lane was an immediate suspect in the Ipalook case simply because he has a prior conviction and he happened to be in Utqiagvik the weekend of these tragic deaths. Virtually anything he might say to the grand jury has the potential of incriminating him. Anything—that he walked down the street, or called a cab, or visited a home in the vicinity of the Ipalook residence. We therefore ask that the court quash this subpoena pursuant to his Fifth Amendment right to be free of compelled self-incrimination, or, in the alternative, pursuant to *State v. Gonzalez*, which is attached to our motion, that the State grant him immunity."

I sat.

"Mr. Slusser?"

"Your Honor, the State is prepared to grant Mr. Lane use immunity."

"Ms. Wright?"

Back to my feet. "Your Honor, Mr. Lane and I rely on the recent Alaska Supreme Court case of *State v. Gonzalez*, with which I know the court is familiar."

Judge Jeffery took up the tan, red, and gold volume he had brought to the bench, opened its back cover, and withdrew some tissuey pages.

"Mr. Slusser, I realize you have been in grand jury proceedings all morning and have had no opportunity to respond to the defense's motion, and probably not even had time to read it through. Nevertheless, the question before us must be answered now. I should advise you that pursuant to *State v. Gonzalez*, which was only decided on June 4, that use immunity no longer exists in the State of Alaska."

A silence followed, one of those courtroom silences in which even the clerk and the trooper paid close attention.

Poor Joe turned even paler. My heart went out to him. Usually, it was defense counsel who got blindsided with some development that the State in its infinite resources could bring to bear, but this time it was a decent guy who tried to be a decent DA but was too busy running after the Fairbanks DAs to adequately respond to the most important issue in the double homicide they were struggling to bring to court.

A mistake to feel sorry for DAs. Like football teams, they had a way of coming back off the bench and stomping you into the mud.

The holding in *Gonzalez* was only basic fair play. The State should not be able to go after Adams, the fiancé, and then, if that prosecution didn't work out, go after the guy whom they had called to testify against him. Like the old gambling slogan said, you had to call your shot and place your bet. You paid your money and you made your choice.

Judge Jeffery said to Joe in his always-courteous manner, "Would you like a recess in which to review the motion further? It would have to be fairly brief."

"Yes, Your Honor."

"Fine. We will be in recess until 12:45 p.m." It was almost noon. Joe would have less than an hour to explain *Gonzalez* to the Fairbanks DA, who probably hadn't read it, either, and to decide the trajectory of the double homicide investigation.

We rose again.

The judge left, the clerk left, and Joe left. It was just Amos, me, and the trooper amid all the expensive blue carpeting and blond wood of the superior courtroom.

"What's going on?" Lane said.

I ignored this question. Amos was far from dumb. He knew the score well enough by now and only wanted hand-holding. I was in no mood for hand-holding.

"What did the judge say?"

"The judge said that if they want you to testify to the grand jury, they can never charge you with the deaths of the Ipalook sisters. Never. Nothing. Ever. Is that clear?" I probably sounded irritated. I was. Amos and I had been over this ground more than once. But did my irritation arise from fatigue—or from suspicion? I told myself that securing immunity for a suspect in a double homicide case counted as a coup for defense counsel. I reminded myself that I was merely proposing immunity, an appropriate defense, and it was up to the DA and the court whether that offer was accepted. I tried not to think about that other case, the one of the child with a concussion, and how ill I became when I learned about the second injured child. It was part of my job to maintain a professional composure, to not let personal emotion disrupt the process—and I had been well schooled in the job by years of intense experience.

The trooper, who was almost always in good humor because of the fortune he reaped in overtime pay transporting prisoners back and forth between Fairbanks and Utqiagvik, had pulled a pamphlet from his pocket and was reading it on his stool near the bench. It was probably about resorts in Cabo San Lucas.

I waited grimly for the action to resume. Lane glanced at my face, shut his own, and commandeered my legal pad for doodling. I did not know any convicts who did not doodle. They have the time to practice, and some go beyond the clichés of roses and puppies to make some art. Amos, I thought, was improving. He had completed the outline of a descending dove with an olive branch in its beak, and underneath it a scroll bearing the single word *Peace*, when the courtroom door whooshed open and Joe returned. I turned toward him with a sympathetic look, but it was not an occasion to offer small talk. Again, he did not sit down.

Judge Jeffery and the clerk joined us, and we went back on the record.

"Your Honor, I have conferred with my colleagues from Fairbanks. The State is prepared to grant Amos Lane full transactional immunity in this case. We will be calling him to testify to the special grand jury this afternoon."

"Ms. Wright."

This was it. The State was accepting defense's proposal. Once the deal of immunity was approved by Judge Jeffery and entered into the court record, Amos could never in the future be prosecuted for the deaths of Bernice and Wanda. "Yes, Your Honor, we understand, and we accept."

"Ms. Wright, I'm going to ask your client to stand, and with your permission, I will be asking him some questions for the record."

"Yes, sir." I motioned to Amos, and he rose.

"Mr. Lane, since Alaska law has recently changed in this area, I want to go over some of the issues with you just to make sure everything is clear. Have you and your lawyer talked over the subject of immunity?"

"Yes, Your Honor. My counsel came to see me at the jail, and we talked about it."

I glanced at Amos in surprise. He was no longer the sullen, indifferent client but was presenting to the court a respectful, attentive, humble version of himself.

"You've scoped it out?" the judge continued.

"Yes, sir. She told me what my choices are."

"So you understand that you will be called to the grand jury this afternoon, and you will not be able to take the Fifth Amendment. You will be expected to testify truthfully."

"Yes, sir, I understand."

Amos was telling the court that he understood immunity and that he wanted to give up his Fifth Amendment right not to testify at all in exchange for it. Gazing at his extraordinarily calm countenance, I wondered what he truly had in mind. Amos had been unwilling to confide in me, his own counsel, any details of his whereabouts the night the sisters died. Did he suddenly now trust the State enough to tell an entire grand jury the whole story of that evening? Did he truly believe he would never be prosecuted even if he told the grand jurors that yes, he was with Bernice and Wanda that evening? Or was he just taking what seemed to be the easiest route at this time, while still planning to use his own judgment on what to say or not to say?

No doubt time would tell. In a way, that result was what I feared most. This case was far from over, and I had a feeling that the consequences of today's work would take a long time to reach their end.

The judge nodded at us and we sat, and he took up the same issues with Joe. He asked Joe even more questions than he had put to Amos. *Gonzalez* had laid down new law, and Judge Jeffery was making sure the State followed it. For the State, there would be no going back. In five minutes, the court had engraved upon its record in the case a deal of immunity that could withstand air attack. Whatever might happen in the future—even if he admitted on the witness stand to committing the murders—Amos Lane was now and forever after immune from prosecution for the deaths of Bernice and Wanda Ipalook.

THE NEXT DAY, the Sitka public defender's office faxed me an article from the *Daily Sitka Sentinel*:

> John Adams of Utkiagvik has been indicted in the recent strangulation deaths of his fiancé, Bernice Ipalook, and her sister, Wanda Ipalook. The sisters were found in their residence on Tuesday, August 3rd. They are the grand-daughters of Fred Ipalook, the first Inupiat Eskimo school principal, for whom the Utkiagvik elementary school, believed to be the northernmost grade school in the world, and one of the largest elementary school buildings in the United States, is named.

> Some fifty witnesses testified before the Special Grand Jury convened to look into the case. Medical Examiner Michael Probst of Harborview Hospital in Seattle testified that the bodies of the sisters had been moved some time after their death and before they were found.
>
> Adams has a DUI conviction on his record, and is employed by UIC construction in Utkiagvik. He and Bernice have one child who was not at home at the time.

The Fairbanks PD sent me a piece from the *Fairbanks Daily News-Miner*:

> Authorities in Barrow have arrested a 29-year-old man in the strangulation deaths of two sisters. The North Slope Borough Department of Public Safety said in a news release Monday that John F. Adams was indicted late last week on two counts of first-degree murder. Wanda and Bernice Ipalook were found dead at their residence August 3. Borough police said the two women were strangled and that there was evidence of sexual contact with at least one of the victims. Adams was arrested without incident and is being held at the Borough jail on $50,000 bail, Borough police said.

Perhaps someone shared those articles with Amos, for he called again with a note of desperation in his voice, and I tried to explain to him in detail the function of the grand jury. No, the proceedings were not a trial, though it was called a jury. The trial jury was actually a petit jury, but no one used that term any more. Some states had done away with grand juries altogether, and the DAs simply filed any charges they thought they could prove.

Alaska and many other states still relied on the grand jury to serve as a buffer between prosecutors and citizenry, to screen cases in order to decide whether they should proceed—that is, whether the suspect should be indicted or whether they thought the DA was full of it. It was a quick and sometimes dirty process, an up-and-down, yes-or-no vote, and the result was rendered and published right away.

The public was not admitted to grand jury proceedings. There was no judge and no defense counsel there, either, just one or more DAs and the jurors themselves. In most states, the proceedings remained secret, but in Alaska, counsel for whatever defendants were indicted would receive copies of the pertinent grand jury tapes. Since Amos was not indicted, he and I would receive no such tape, but whoever represented John Adams would get one.

Amos still didn't seem to understand—and I didn't get why he was so concerned about the process. After all, he had received his immunity. Whatever was said in the grand jury didn't affect him any longer—nor did whatever happened, or didn't happen, in John Adams's case. Amos Lane could now never be prosecuted for the murders of Bernice and Wanda Ipalook.

"Don't worry about it, Amos. It's not your problem any longer." Then I hung up.

Perhaps I should have asked Joe to send me a copy of the grand jury tape as a favor, even though we were not entitled to it in the discovery rules. Perhaps I should have found out then what Amos said, or didn't say, to the grand jurors—and whether, in fact, he had actually testified, or whether the State, with their dozens of witnesses and Adams's confession, had decided they could get an indictment without Amos's help. But I had other clients to worry about besides Amos Lane and now needed to devote some time to them.

12

Respect for elders, for nature, for the community, for each other, and for ourselves.

THE INUPIAT ILITQUSIAT

THE BRIEF ARCTIC SUMMER WANED AROUND US. THE days changed from perpetual noon to lingering dawns and twilights. Shorebirds and land birds gathered in flocks and flew off to warmer areas of the world. This part of Arctic life, when the birds left, made me uneasy. Soon the only remaining birds would be the ravens who overwintered in the landfill. I had been told that the leaving of the birds was not a function of the cold but of the food supply. Still, when it happened, I wondered what the birds knew that I didn't. The winter would be silent without them. Once the full darkness fell, people turned on their Christmas lights, and neighbors went into winter mutual-helping mode, I would be okay. Plus, the stupendous spectacle of the aurora, great glowing pipe organs of undulating green and blue and white, made the darkness worthwhile. It was just the transition that was disorienting.

Our softball team finished the season 3–3. Celestine was disappointed, but I was proud. My skills had improved. I practiced catching with Michael in the dust and gravel in front of my house and batted okay, though I never could throw worth a darn.

I fed the dog every day. She watched for me, and I couldn't let her down. I wondered whether the owners had forgotten about the dog they'd left staked out, while the tundra turned to ice beneath her. Sometimes I spent a little time with her, smoothing her apple-domed head and telling her what a fine dog she was. More than once I came near to slipping her tether, even though, if someone complained, the Anchorage office might decide I was better suited for some less controversial posting and transfer me to Ketchikan or Juneau, and I didn't want to leave my cases, and the Arctic, and Michael.

Most afternoons when I got off the bus, I saw Michael's beat-up turquoise-and-white pickup parked in front of my little cube of a house. Often, he was inside cooking dinner. But one Friday in October he was waiting for me at the door.

"Come on," he said. "Tuna's crew got a whale."

I switched from court suit to sweatsuit, and we drove out onto the tundra.

A prism of moisture hung in the air, and the low angle of the sun created a double rainbow that split ahead of us as we rode toward Point Barrow, the northernmost point of land in the United States. Land's End. End of the earth. The Top of the World. I thought of how this place looked on a map. Alaska was on top of the United States, Utqiagvik was at the top of Alaska, and Point Barrow was the last bump on the shoreline. For all its austerity, on a golden fall afternoon like this one, Utqiagvik was the most beautiful place in the world, and the snowy owls circled above us like cosmic escorts.

I laid a comfortable hand on Michael's knee. He switched on the radio station KBRW and found Seismic Isaac rebroadcasting hymns from last Sunday's service at the Presbyterian church.

"Michael, I have to tell you something."

"What's that?"

"As much as I respect and admire your people for their courage and their sharing . . ."

"What?"

"They're terrible singers."

"They sing all right. It's just different, and you're not used to it."

I changed the subject.

"I have a question that nobody seems to be able to answer."

"What is it?"

"It's about the land bridge."

"The land bridge?"

"You know how the *tanik* archaeologists have a theory that people migrated here from Siberia eons ago when Siberia and Alaska were connected by land? They say the migration ended when the land bridge submerged."

Michael laughed. "That's bullshit. I could walk from Nome to Siberia anytime I wanted."

"You mean during the winter."

"Of course during the winter. The ice is a better highway than the land. There's no land under the pole anyway. It's just floating ice."

"I didn't know that. But everybody seems to overlook those facts."

"It's because they've never been here. And then there're all those stupid stories about people living in ice igloos. Ice shelters are just for emergencies if somebody gets stuck out on the ice during a storm. Nobody here ever lived in them full-time. Maybe someplace else they did, but not here."

"So how do you think stories like that got started?"

"Some of the elders told stories like that to be funny, and some of them told stories to throw people off the track."

"Why would they do that?"

"They wanted to keep the truth to themselves. More private. Safer."

We passed ravens wheeling over the landfill and neared the

Quonset huts and metal-gridded airfield of what used to be the Naval Arctic Research Facility, called NARL by taxi drivers. Here scientists studied everything Arctic but never mastered the topic. To this day things crawl up out of the sea at Point Barrow that astonish and mystify all observers.

"Who is that, the old man walking by the road? I see him all the time."

"Joshua Ahvakana. He's a whaling captain, one of the best. His crew almost always gets a whale. But he hasn't gone out for the last few seasons."

"Is he too old now?"

"They never get too old. They go out in their seventies and eighties. He has his reasons. You could say he was one of your client's victims, too."

"Which client?"

"You know who I mean. There've been other dead women found in other villages, and your client was always around. But Ahvakana's grandson, Jens Paningonna, was convicted for one of them."

"That's nothing but gossip."

He looked sideways at me, the Inupiaq confronting the *tanik*. "You should get off that case."

"You know I can't. It's my job. Everybody is entitled to a defense."

"No, not everybody. We have our own justice."

"In your justice, what would happen to him?"

"He would be cast out. He could never go back home or to any other village. It's been done before. Sometimes people are left on islands, sometimes they have to live out on the tundra alone."

Alone. In the cold. Forever. Liz had mentioned banishment, too. Somehow it seemed worse than prison.

"Should we go back and give Mr. Ahvakana a ride?"

"He has his own truck. Newer than mine. He likes to walk."

"Where does he walk to?" I asked, gazing around at the endless tundra beside the infinite ocean.

"Every day he goes to the bluffs and climbs down to the beach and predicts the weather."

"How?"

"He looks at the clouds, the winds, the currents and wave patterns, the color of the water and the temperature, the behavior of birds and animals—even the tundra plants open or close and can turn over depending on what weather's coming."

"I'm impressed. That's a lot of knowledge."

He patted my knee. "Most *taniks* never notice the elders, how they are always watching out for the community, trying to help people be safe, trying to help the kids grow up good. It's like your Greatest Generation, only we always have one with us."

We approached the bowhead whale, dragged up on the shore with great cables. Trucks and SUVs and four-wheelers lined the road nearby. Men with machete-like flensing knives cut the blubber from the giant carcass in great slabs, while others hacked at what was called the "bloody meat" inside, and a third team loaded sledges that would be pulled to Utqiagvik for sharing. Onlookers stood three and four deep around the workers, congratulating the crew members, comparing this whale to others and happily contemplating winter feasts to come. When we parked and got out, Tuna ran over to give me a hug. He offered us a share, even though Michael was not on a crew.

"Think of it as another birthday present," he said, winking at me.

Michael went with him to get some bloody meat and muktuk, but I got back into the truck to be away from the wind. I was glad that Michael and his mom and sisters and their families would get a share, but I had never acquired the taste myself.

Two girls I remembered from Liz's party came over to the truck, and I rolled down my window.

"Hey, how are you—when are you having another birthday?" they chorused, giggling.

"Hey, you have birthdays, too . . ." I said.

"So do you think it's true?"

"Is what true?"

"You know . . . you and Michael . . . what they say . . ."

I was beginning to figure out what they meant and remembered Liz telling me in the ladies' room that parties were not the only thing Eskimos were best at.

"We think so! *Tanik* men are so shy," the taller girl with the curly perm told me. "It takes them forever to dance or come over or—"

"Yes, and when they finally do, they're all embarrassed and it's like they don't know how . . ." the other, short and plump, cut in.

"And then I'm disappointed if they're all pudgy and . . . it's like they sit at a desk all day long and never go hunting or out on the ice or—"

I had opened my mouth to try to say something, anything, but Michael, bless his heart, came up and the girls ran off, laughing and waving at him.

"What was that all about?" he asked when he had stashed the meat in the truck bed and slid into the driver's seat.

"Oh . . . just girl talk."

"It's cold in here," he said, rolling up the window and starting the truck. "You should have a jacket. It's colder than it looks."

I pulled up an old blanket from behind the seat back. The light had faded, and the Arctic shore and the ice limning the horizon beyond it had begun to look less glorious and more perilous. No wonder the Inuit, in another part of the Arctic, raised stone Ebenezers like people in the Old Testament, to show wandering souls that another human had passed that way, and encourage those who got lost.

"Rebe-KAH," Michael suddenly said.

"Yes?" Startled, I sat up a bit straighter.

"You must never walk out on the road like Joshua Ahvakana."

I tried to follow his train of thought. Inupiaq people said a lot of things I did not understand. Sometimes language or my own brain failed me.

"Why not?" A person had to get a little fresh air and exercise to be healthy, particularly a person with a job like mine, and the roads were a lot easier to walk on than the bumpy and lumpy tundra.

"Especially in the spring and fall." He looked sideways at me, waiting for me to get it, but I only stared back in bewilderment. "I told you this before. Don't you remember? Those are the whaling seasons." His voice had taken on a patient tone, as though I were a three-year-old.

I blinked at him.

"The whales attract the bears."

"Oh," I said, recognition dawning.

"The crews take the leftover scraps to the landfill, but they always miss a few. The bears come to get them. Then, if they're still hungry, they come into town."

I had read accounts in the paper and heard stories from my clients about the bears. A few years earlier, Carl Stalker was walking with his pregnant girlfriend on the edge of Point Lay when a bear came up. He told his lady to go on home and stood to face the bear with a pocketknife. When she ran screaming into town, all the hunters turned out to find the bear. They shot it, cut it open, and found pieces of Stalker's arms and legs.

In another one of the outlying villages, a grandmother was berry picking with her grandchild when a bear appeared. She also sent her loved one home and waved at the bear to get his attention. The child made it home safe, but all that was ever found of her was her broken eyeglasses.

I had seen the eight-foot-tall stuffed white bear in the glass case at the Fairbanks airport. I knew they were incredibly fast, overwhelmingly powerful—and not uncommon in these parts. Still, they seemed as exotic to me as Bengal tigers or African elephants, and the only way I could imagine seeing one was in a zoo.

"Even at your house, be careful," Michael said. "Your house is near the shore. They come there."

"At my house?"

"They've come into town before, and you're right on the edge. That's why at Halloween the kids go out with guards."

"I'll be careful," I said. "Especially in the spring and fall." But I was wondering how I would avoid going on the road when I had to walk a block to catch the bus, and sometimes the dogs and I walked out a bit when it was sunny. I filed Michael's warning away, along with all the other warnings, admonishments, and complaints I had received in the years I had been in Utqiagvik.

Michael did not head directly back to town but turned inland on the road that was called Cakeeater. He grew quiet and did not switch on the radio. I assumed we were just driving around for a while and snuggled into the blanket, watching the dimming tundra for touches of scarlet and yellow in the ground willows and creepers.

We passed the natural gas works, with its network of cement platforms and pipes; waved at the helmeted fellow on duty, who was, of course, a friend of Michael's, and drove on. I had never been out this far. Now it was almost impossible to see anything of Utqiagvik except a few dark outlines on a small part of the horizon. There was just tundra, sky, and us.

Then I glimpsed some movement. Craning my neck as we went by, I made out a family of Arctic foxes, already pelting up in white, romping on a hillock many yards off road, two adults and three semi-grown kits, rolling and tumbling in the low bushes.

All at once Michael stopped the truck. He seemed intent on some thought. I waited for him to speak, but the wait grew long.

"This used to be my land," he said at last.

"Oh? I didn't know that you had—"

"This used to be my allotment."

We sat there looking at what to me was indistinguishable from any other place on the tundra. The word *allotment* triggered memories of orientation lectures at the Anchorage public defender's office, and I struggled to remember what we had been taught. At the time, it was just general information about Alaska history and politics. Now, I could see how it all intimately affected people I cared about. Alaska did not become a state until 1959, and that year was when questions of land ownership, legal jurisdiction, and Native sovereignty came to the fore. Neither the Yupiks in the west nor the Inupiat in the north had ever organized into tribes, in the Lower 48 sense of the word, but the federal government was used to dealing with tribes. The federal government did not want the Arctic land, per se. It was only tundra, after all, but the government was interested in what might be found beneath it.

When oil was discovered in 1968, suddenly everybody was interested in the North. Just three years later, the Alaska Native Claims Settlement Act was signed into law by President Nixon, in spite of the fact that the people of the North Slope had voted against its adoption. The act extinguished all Aboriginal land claims and transferred title to twelve Alaska Native regional corporations and many local village corporations. Native allotments under previous laws that were designated as home sites were preserved. Michael's land must have been one of these.

For the only person in the group of new attorneys who was headed for the Slope, me, one additional fact was stressed. Though some of the new Native corporations foundered, the Arctic Slope Regional Corporation had prospered under the new law, and so had the Inupiat, who were all shareholders. Not only oil revenues but good management of investments and diversification served the corporation well. It netted $3.7 billion in 2022. I had seen the resulting prosperity in Inupiaq homes that featured interior gardens and personal spas. A family in which adults worked for either the Arctic Slope Regional Corporation or the Ukpeagvik Inupiat Corporation could bring home around $250,000 a year. They were not the downtrodden minority citizens familiar to public defenders in the Lower 48.

I was trying to think of something to say to Michael about his allotment when he spoke again.

"I smoked it up," he said. "I sold my land for cocaine. And when that was gone, I used my girlfriend's Permanent Fund Dividend check. And our little boy's. Each year. Until she moved back to White Mountain and took him with her."

The Permanent Fund checks were dividends from the oil revenue, which were distributed each year to all Alaska residents. I got one myself.

I sat there trying to register this information and waited to see whether there was anything else.

Finally, he said, "I don't do as much as I used to."

In an effort at honesty, Michael was letting me know that he had a coke habit. He was not saying he planned to give it up.

His black hair fell over the collar of his windbreaker like a raven's wing, and I saw only enough of his face to catch in his eyes an expression of simultaneous defeat and defiance, while his mouth registered a quiet pain. Maybe he wished he could tell me he was going to give it up, but he just wasn't and couldn't.

If he thought I might say, It's okay, don't worry about it, he was to be as disappointed as I was. I had visited too many addicts in jails and prisons to be okay with cocaine. I wished miserably for a piece of useful wisdom to share but couldn't think of anything at all.

"I see," I finally said.

We sat there awhile, dusk falling around us, and then he turned the truck around and we headed back to Utqiagvik. The double rainbow had disappeared, and the tundra looked black and empty. I was thinking that Michael was not some client that I could exhort to get treatment, and I knew enough from dealing with clients that the exhortations did no good, anyway, until people wanted to recover for their own sake. I wasn't a family member entitled to advise him. I wasn't even a long-term girlfriend. Maybe I wasn't even a good prospect for becoming a long-term girlfriend.

And what about his child?

I watched the dark tundra slide by as Utqiagvik's rooftops grew larger, remembering Liz's attempt to tell me about Michael at my beautiful birthday party. I guess what she was trying to say was not that I was too old for him but that he was too illegal for me.

I couldn't let him slip away so easily, like a dollar bill on the pavement when the wind blows. The time with him was sweet. Something might happen, and he might decide to change. I had known a few clients who did, even ones who had been to treatment so often that everybody had given up on them. Some finally made a decision to put that life behind them forever. After a year or so of Alcoholics Anonymous, these clients had jobs, they had families, they had cars. The others didn't. The others ended up dead or in prison.

Of course, the drug users I had represented were in jail for overdoing the habit, usually by selling to others to support their own needs. As far as I knew, Michael had avoided legal consequences. Yes, he had "smoked up" his own precious land, surely a serious sign, but perhaps he had reached a point where his use could be considered controlled and not obsessive. I knew there were some individuals for whom cocaine was merely a weekend diversion, like alcohol was for me. Time would tell. I was going to give him that time.

Any way I looked at it, though, cocaine was illegal, and I had a legal job. Time would also tell whether I was wishfully thinking in order to stay in the relationship. Just like time would tell if Ellingsworth made the right call to prosecute Adams instead of Lane. Time seemed to have an agency of its own up here on the Slope, as we teetered between the midnight sun and the polar night.

"Thank you for telling me," I said at last.

I pulled the dirty blanket up around my shoulders and wished we had never driven out on Cakeeater Road.

13

Commercial chicken eggs, tasteless by comparison, have replaced wild bird eggs. Grandma died and took her stories with her. Spring camps are a thing of the past. BB guns have antiquated Grandpa's bows and arrow. TV, the VCR, and "Super Mario" have become more interesting than "storyknifing."

LUCY NUQARRLUK DANIELS, YUPIK WRITER

SINCE THE FOCUS WAS NOW ON JOHN ADAMS, AND Amos was immune from prosecution for the murders, I decided it was time to try to get my client out of jail. Unable to post the $500 bail, he was still being held on the two odd misdemeanors. I filed a motion for bail review in both.

The State responded to my bail review motion with the offer of a deal. In exchange for a guilty plea on either, the other would be dismissed. His sentence would be a year's probation with one special condition: that he remain in the SATS treatment facility until the Adams trial. After his truthful testimony in the Adams trial, pursuant to his immunity deal, he could finish the rest of his probation at large.

The special condition had a special condition. SATS would not release him on any more weekend furloughs such as he had been on when the sisters were murdered. It was obvious to me that this deal represented the State's plan to keep as tight a leash on Amos as possible, until he did what they wanted.

The State declared that if he refused this deal, they would try each misdemeanor case to a jury, one after the other, and argue for jail time of a full year on each conviction.

I didn't like the deal. I thought both the cases were trumped up and that after we had tried the first case and won it, the State would throw in the towel on the other.

Amos seemed oddly skittish about going to trial, and he said he didn't mind staying in SATS for a while. The decision was his to make, not mine, and so we agreed with the State that he would plead to the case involving the theft of ivory, and that the case involving assault on Harold Killbear would be dismissed.

As it turned out, on the day set for Amos to change his plea, the magistrate was on vacation, and so the misdemeanor docket was set in Judge Jeffery's court. Waiting for court to convene beside Amos at the defense table, I realized with a start that the trooper was leading John Adams into the jury box. Why was Adams in court? He would already have been arraigned on the double homicide indictment. Obviously, the public defender's office could not represent him, since we were working with one of the main witnesses against him. When there was a conflict of interest with the public defender, usually an attorney from the Office of Public Advocacy would be appointed. But I had heard that Adams had planned to hire his own attorney, and so the Office of Public Advocacy was not yet involved.

Amos and John locked gazes. John leaned forward and placed both handcuffed hands on the rail of the jury box as though preparing to vault over it. Amos half rose out of his chair. The trooper, more alert than usual, leaned on John's shoulders to push him back into the seat.

Judge Jeffery swept into the courtroom, followed by his clerk. The bailiff left his position in front of the judge's bench to take a stand between the two defendants.

Sizing up the situation, Judge Jeffery declared: "We will first go on record in cause number 4BA-S93-734, *State of Alaska versus John Adams*, since Mr. Adams requires the presence of the trooper.

Mr. Adams, I understood that you wished to hire your own attorney. Is that correct?"

Adams made some inaudible response.

"Trooper, Mr. Adams is a long way from a microphone. Can you bring him to the witness chair?"

"Yes, Judge."

The trooper raised Adams to his feet, revealing that both hands were shackled to a leather belt around his waist and his ankles were hobbled. The poor guy could barely shuffle. Accustomed to the problem, the trooper assisted him down from the jury box and up into the witness stand.

"Thank you," Judge Jeffery said. "Now, Mr. Adams, please say for the record if you have been able to hire your own attorney."

Adams mumbled a no.

Amos remained rigidly tense at my side, but I forgot about him in my concern for John Adams. He appeared so tired, so sad, so overwhelmed with stress. Though wiry, he was not a big guy like Amos. FCC had not provided him a haircut, and his black hair straggling over his sallow forehead gave him a wild look.

Here was a man who needed defending, for sure.

"You have not been able to hire counsel of your own choosing, is that correct? You have contacted several attorneys?"

Adams said he had. Heaven only knew what fees he had been quoted for defending a double homicide in a far-flung jurisdiction.

"Very well," the judge went on. "It's my understanding that you have already completed an affidavit of indigency and that it is on file with the court."

"Yes, sir."

"Fine. Madam Clerk, are we ready on the call to the Office of Public Advocacy in Fairbanks?"

Obviously, this procedure had been carefully preplanned.

"Yes, Your Honor," the earnest young woman said, fiddling with the phone console in front of her. The speakers in the courtroom came to life, and we could hear someone on a distant microphone shuffling papers. Alaska being such a huge landmass, telephonic court appearances were routinely allowed.

"Do we have the Office of Public Advocacy on the line?" the judge asked.

"Yes, this is Nelson Traverso, Judge."

"Good morning, Mr. Traverso. We are in court today with Mr. John Adams. Mr. Adams has been indicted and arraigned on two murder charges. He has a conflict with the public defender office and has been unable to hire private counsel. Are you available for appointment on this case?"

"Yes, Your Honor."

"Very well. I am signing an order appointing you to represent John Adams in cause number 4BA-S93-734, with a copy to the district attorney's office so you can receive discovery. A trial date of December 5 has already been set. Do you have any issues for us this morning?"

"Yes, Your Honor. I would like to inquire as to what bail has been set for Mr. Adams."

"Mr. Adams is presently being held without bail. If you wish to file a motion for bail to be considered, we will schedule a hearing. Anything else?"

"Your Honor, we will be asking for him to have a psych eval. We will also be asking the court to approve calling an expert witness on the subject of involuntary confessions, and an investigator to look into the background of Amos Lane."

"We will consider those matters as they are filed. Thank you for being available this morning."

"Thank you, Judge. Mr. Adams, I will come to see you when you return to FCC."

Traverso and the distant microphone fell silent. Adams once again drilled Amos with his eyes. In them I saw pure hate. Amos winced perceptibly.

While the trooper and Adams left the courtroom, I considered what I had just seen. Did John Adams hate my client out of jealousy? Did he think Amos Lane had gone to house number 1541 that deadly weekend and been intimate with Bernice? Perhaps he now hated Amos for causing what he himself had done. This scenario was what Ellingsworth was banking on.

Or did Adams hate Lane because he believed it was Lane who strangled his fiancé and her sister? Liz, Michael, and Nate thought so.

Judge Jeffery now took Amos through the standard recitations that were required for entering a plea agreement on the record. The trooper returned from putting Adams in the holding cell and escorted my client to the jail, where he would bundle his personal items for transfer to the SATS treatment facility.

I was glad Nelson Traverso had been appointed for John Adams. He was a good advocate. I hoped his investigator could shed some light on the case, especially the question of time. Knowing when the sisters died, and who was with them last, could incriminate one man and exonerate the other.

AFTERWARD, I HAD hoped for a chance to catch up on returning messages and reading files, but Liz cornered me in the morning glories.

"I know what you're going to say," she said, "you're too busy with the caseload plus the Ipalooks, but there's something that can't be put off any longer. You've got to go to Anaktuvuk Pass and talk to Randy's asshole father. A phone call won't work."

I sighed. I knew she was right. But how was I going to come up with two whole days away from the caseload?

"And then you can go straight on to Fairbanks to see Bobby Nashookpuk at FCC."

"Liz, you're a nag."

"I don't nag as much as Bobby Nashookpuk. He calls three times a week, every week."

"I didn't know he was calling."

"I don't always tell you who calls because I know you can't always go. But now you need to go."

"When is his release date?"

"2060," she said.

"2060! What on earth did he do?"

She shrugged. "Maybe he didn't do it. That's what you always say."

"Liz, the post-conviction cases are hard. There aren't many ways to even get a case back into court once a conviction is entered and an appeal heard."

"So. All the cases are hard."

"The Ipalook trial starts a month from now. I've got to make sure Amos is ready. If the State doesn't like Amos's testimony, they might indict him for some other charge, like perjury."

There was also the ghostly, haunting specter of a chance that the State would conclude that Amos didn't live up to his end of the bargain and attempt to weasel out of the immunity deal, ironclad though it appeared. I didn't think the State would abort the immunity; however, I knew better than to predict outcomes. Anything could happen when the stakes were as high as accountability for the brutal murder of beloved daughters of the community. Amos might yet be dragged into the dock.

"Fuck Amos Lane."

I was startled at Liz's tone.

"Everybody knows he did it. Not that poor slob John Adams."

"That's not what the State thinks."

"Fuck what the State thinks. The Anglo courts don't even belong here. We have our own system. Yours is just an add-on."

"I'm behind in all my other cases," I whined. I was weakening, and she knew it.

"There's something about Bobby you need to know."

"What's that?"

"He's the best ivory artist to ever come out of the Slope."

I was silent a moment. Then I said, "You win, Liz. You always win."

She doubled down.

"Oh. I forgot to tell you. You remember Wiley Ungarook? The one the Ipalooks borrowed cigarettes from, but he couldn't remember when? He's at FCC now, too. He got charged with something in Fairbanks. You can go see him when you see Bobby. There's also about five other current clients you need to talk to."

Liz had pleaded and maneuvered on behalf of Randy and Bobby Nashookpuk like she wouldn't do for herself if she were dying in a ditch. She would have her reasons, which I had come to trust without explanation. For a moment, I reflected on the prospect of a public defender's office without Liz. No more local goodwill. No more trial-witness locator. No more jury consultant who knew the entire venire personally.

No more birthday present?

"I'll go to Anaktuvuk and FCC, but you'll have to make all the arrangements by Wednesday, and when I get back, I don't want to hear any more about how I shouldn't represent Amos Lane. It's my job. I don't judge them; I just represent them as best I can."

A brief silence. I could see the gears turning behind her slightly almond-shaped brown eyes. Then, in a happier mood, she turned on her heel and got on the phone to Alaska Airlines and Era Aviation.

TWO DAYS LATER I was crunching through the gravel airport parking lot toward the small hangar of Era Aviation, hoping to be told the flight had been canceled because of the fog nestling around the edges of the runway.

"Hello?"

A heavyset Native girl ceased weighing luggage behind a plywood partition and came out to the counter to greet me.

"Checking in for the flight to Anaktuvuk."

"Yes. Four people on charter. We usually don't go there."

"You don't?"

"Yes. Charter for funeral. Very sad. Girl my age."

I waited for her to tell me what had happened, but she didn't. She consulted the Mickey Mouse watch on her wrist. "Leaving in forty-five minutes. Maximum carry-on ten pounds."

"Ten pounds!"

She grew round eyed at my tone. If I had known about the weight limit, I wouldn't have brought a duffel but just stuffed a few things into my shoulder bag. An elderly couple and one young woman, all in *atikluks*, summer parkas, sat against the wall on yellow plastic chairs, drinking pop out of cans. They politely pretended not to notice my rude exclamation.

"Can I just leave this bag with you?" I asked. "Sorry. I should have called ahead." She gave me a forgiving smile and accepted my bag after I had off-loaded parts of it into my shoulder purse.

It turned out that "forty-five minutes" actually meant two and a half hours, because two more people signed on for Anaktuvuk. The increase in the passenger list caused the pilot to decide to take the Beaver instead of the Cessna, so the larger plane had to be unblocked and rolled out and serviced. Then the pilot had to call for a weather check more current than the one he had previously ordered.

"Anaktuvuk bad for flying," I heard someone whisper. "Too many mountains, not much runway."

It's for Randy, I told myself. Remember Randy.

Finally the girl called to us, and we trudged out to board. Buckling myself into the left front of six seats, I noticed that the fog now covered the end of the runway and that the pilot looked to be about twelve. Wisps of blond hair stuck out from his Yankees baseball cap, worn backward, and he had acne.

He trundled the plane out to the end of the tarmac routinely enough, but at the end whirled us around like we were a dune buggy. I glanced in alarm at the elder lady sitting opposite me and wished fervently I had told Liz to go to hell. I wanted to ask the lady, Why is life so hard? She gave me a beatific smile.

The revving roar of the plane enveloped my senses like when a nurse tightens the blood pressure cuff. Our teenage pilot let something loose, and we thudded at breakneck speed down the runway and then struggled upward but could not seem to escape the ground. I opened my mouth and was about to yell, "Appendicitis, appendicitis!"—any excuse to get me back on the ground—when all at once we lurched skyward. I thought for a moment we were falling because suddenly the world became much quieter, and then I realized we were leveling off in the air and I had been holding my breath.

The engine settled into a steady drone. We flew just below a dense layer of fog. Underneath us the tundra went by in a ribbony blur of plants, water, and stones.

"We're only about a hundred feet off the ground!" I hollered at my neighbor.

"Nothing down there stick up that far," she hollered back. "Not till the Brooks Range."

I don't believe law school lasted as long as this particular flight. We were so close to earth that if the pilot nodded off, we would hit the ground before he opened his eyes. The anxiety of monitoring the back of his head must have finally exhausted me enough to doze off, for when my eyes snapped back into position, we were in the middle of the fog and climbing. Perversely, I wished to be back down where I could see my doom. The pilot perhaps felt my eyes boring into his head, for he called to us, "We're at the Brooks Range. We'll have to go in a little higher than usual because of the fog."

Oh, good. This teenager was going to get higher than usual. We burrowed upward like a seal through ice water and erupted into the sunlight among great shining ramparts of ice, the Brooks Range. Now it was my companion who looked perturbed.

"Not good to come in high at Anaktuvuk," she told me,

forming the words with exaggerated movements of her creased lips. "Airport in narrow pass. Lots of crashes. Lots of dead people."

Soon I saw what she meant. When we cleared the peaks, the pilot had to tack from one mountain to another as he sought to work us down to the elevation of Anaktuvuk airfield in its namesake pass at a lower elevation. I flashed on a movie I had seen about the singer Patsy Cline. Portraying her death by plane crash, the camera showed the pilot's windshield view of emerging through fog into a sheer rock face. We now acted out that scene over and over, zooming toward one invisible side of the granite bowl, sideswiping just as it came into view and skimming away toward another, and with each trajectory sinking lower.

I regretted my bad thoughts of the pilot, who now held all our lives in his nail-bitten hands. That heroic young man was providing my first experience of personal, no-instruments, no-directions-from-the-tower, little-visibility flying. Was this what they called *seat-of-the-pants?*

Suddenly the fog parted, and I glimpsed the village of Anaktuvuk Pass nestled in a mountain sanctuary like an Arctic Machu Picchu or Brigadoon. Not a bad place to die if die we had to. We descended so fast that I groped the wall for handholds. What was that sound? Was someone vomiting? Had some baggage come loose, or was the plane coming apart? We plummeted on. We leveled slightly. We banked a little as pressure surged in my ears, and we fell even farther into the hands of God.

"Hold on, folks," the pilot called. There was joy in his voice. He was having a wonderful time.

Our rear thunked on something. Rock? Ice? Tarmac? We bounced, slightly off center. My bowels went into jumping jacks, and I closed my eyes. For just the teeniest instant, the aircraft considered cartwheeling to the right on a wing. Then the front touched down, and again the rear. We careened madly forward, faster than the pilot could control, but at least it was now the ground we plowed and not the unknowable air. We fishtailed.

Rebecca in new parka, with neighbor's dog, Spirit. *(Olan Mills)*

The house Rebecca rented from the Utpeagvik Inupiat Corporation, her home for seven years. *(Courtesy of the author)*

Elizabeth Kanayurak at her desk in the public defender's office. *(Courtesy of the author)*

The North Slope Borough Police Station, now the Department of Public Safety, where Amos Lane was housed in the jail. *(Daniel Lang / Alamy)*

Inupiat hunters haul in their "umiaq," or skin boat, from the Arctic Ocean off Point Barrow, near Utqiagvik. The flag identifies this captain and crew. *(Kevin G. Smith / Alamy)*

Rebecca at the high-priced "work camp" in Anaktuvuk Pass. *(Courtesy of the author)*

President Obama tries Alaska Native dancing with schoolchildren and an elder during his 2015 trip to Alaska. The little girls in front are wearing their "atikluks," or summer parkas. *(White House Photo / Alamy)*

An Inupiat mother prepares geese in the kitchen while her son works at his computer. *(Alamy / Caroline Penn)*

Rebecca with local celebrity, DJ "Seismic" Isaac Tuckfield. *(Elizabeth Kanayurak)*

Qutliiraq, a unique and fragrant spring flower that blooms in rocks and frost. The roots can be eaten raw, boiled, or fried, though too many will make you sleepy. In English it's called the "woolly lousewort." *(Alamy / Arndt Sven-Erik)*

A perk of living in the Arctic: you get to see snowy owls all the time. *(Richard Mittelman / Alamy)*

“Homage and Respect for the Spirit World of the Seals,” by Bobby Nashookpuk. *(Angie Tabb, with permission of the artist)*

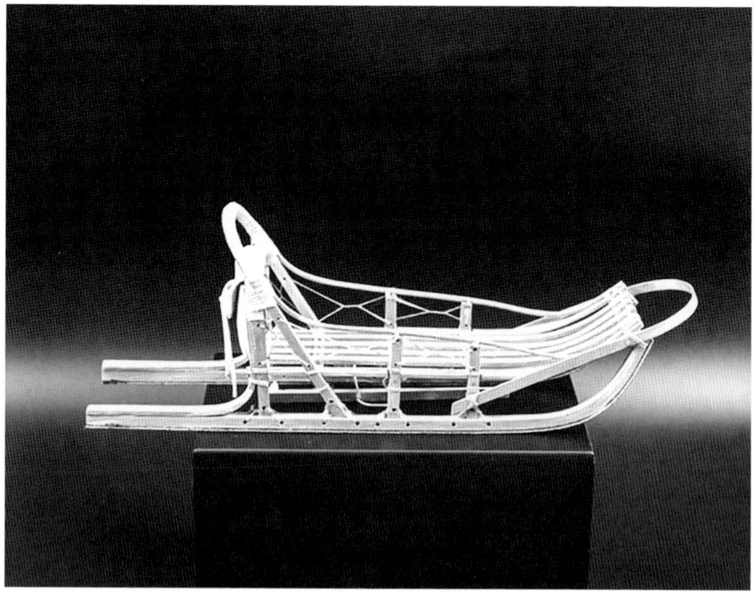

Miniature basket sled of molded and dried willow, attributed to Amos Lane. *(Angie Tabb. The artwork was a gift to the author.)*

TOP TO BOTTOM:

Funeral program for Amos Lane. *(Prepared by the family of Amos Lane and reprinted with permission of Amos's sister, Kiimiiraq Lane)*

Grave of a whaler in Utqiagvik. *(Peregrine / Alamy)*

Courthouse in Utqiagvik as it appeared when John Adams was tried in 1994. *(Jet Lowe / Library of Congress)*

Utqiagvik, Alaska. *(Chris Boswell / Alamy)*

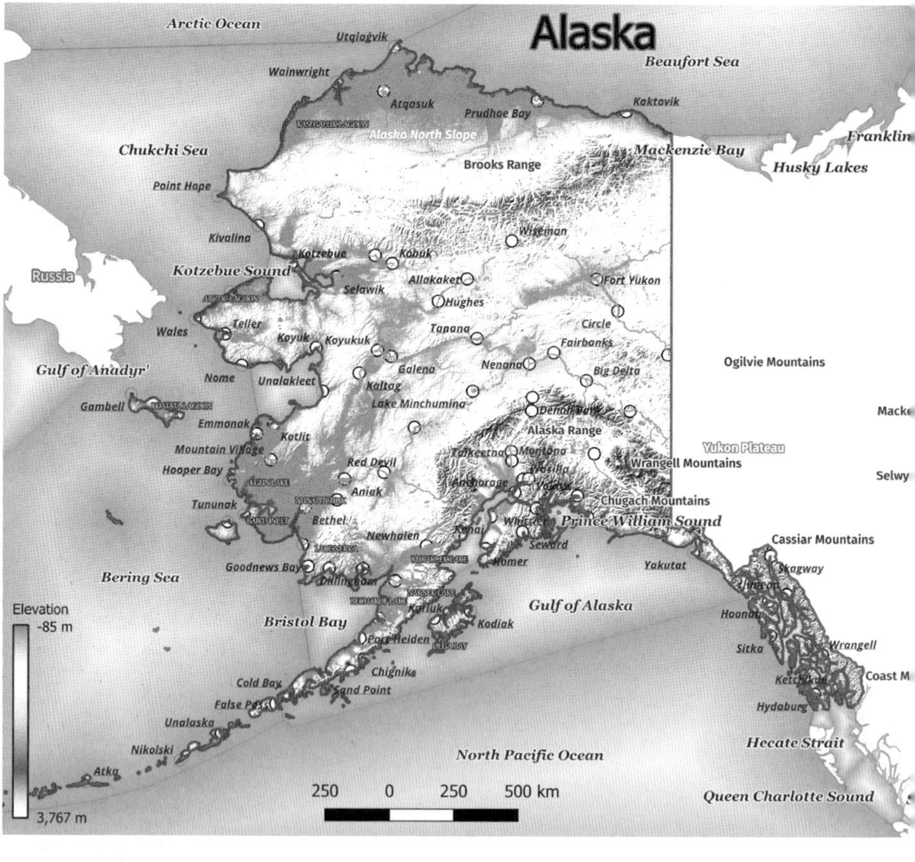

Map of Alaska showing Utqiagvik, the North Slope, and the Brooks Range. *(M & M Baciu / Alamy)*

I wondered how much runway remained. I opened my eyes. We were indeed on the ground. There was no fog here. I could see buildings. I could look up at mountains rather than directly into their pectorals. We slowed a little, and I knew the pilot was winning.

"Great job!" I screamed.

"Welcome to Anaktuvuk Pass, the queen of the Brooks Range," he called, and with a flourish turned the plane at just exactly the edge of the blacktop. We motored sedately toward the air shack.

Once we had all scrambled out the small kidney-shaped door, I threw off the airborne nightmare, just as one forgets seasickness, and looked around with interest. Welcomers had come out to meet us brave fliers. A different Arctic here. Utqiagvik encompassed three or four miles at its widest point. Here the diameter of the whole inhabited area looked to be half a mile. In Utqiagvik you saw quite a bit of grass. In Anaktuvuk your eye fell everywhere on rock. In Utqiagvik you stood at the end of land, between the great flat sea and the arching sky. Here, rock ramparts rimmed you in. But the same gravel underfoot in both.

"The funeral is delayed until tonight because there's one more plane coming up from Anchorage," someone told my former seatmate, during a hug.

"God help them," I murmured.

I followed the small crowd through the chain-link gates of the airfield and up a sloping gravel road.

"Work camp?" I asked an elder trudging nearby. "Can you please tell me where the work camp is?"

Wordlessly he pointed to a tar-papered structure fifty feet in front of us on the right. I couldn't see any kind of a sign on it. I rock-hopped the string of pallets in front and entered the dirtiest, scroungiest, most rancid and stinking hovel I'd ever seen or smelled. If Robert W. Service had come here first, he would never have stayed in Alaska long enough to write about Dan McGrew.

On the left, buckling card tables crowded underneath a

television set, while to the right, I saw more than I wanted of a grease-pit kitchen. On the serving counter between sat a sagging plastic sack of yellow-tinted lard, beside a plate piled with saltine crackers.

"Can I help you?"

A thin, middle-aged *tanik* in shirtsleeves emerged from the hall ahead.

"I need a room," I said without enthusiasm.

"No reservation?"

My eyebrows went up.

"Big job going on over at the jade quarry, and we're pretty full," he explained.

"Oh, I see," I said, humbled. I did need a room, any room, even here.

"Come in for the funeral?"

"Uh, not really. I'm here to see a client. Uh, the family member of a client."

"Legal Services?"

"Public defender." I was going to object to any more questions, but then he said, "We'll try to squeeze you in. That'll be a hundred and eighty in advance."

"A hundred and eighty dollars!" I had never paid that much for a room anywhere.

"Cor-rect. Check is fine." He lowered his eyes to the sign-in log on a shelf under the TV. To hide his amusement, I guess. "Includes dinner," he added.

"Oh, great," I said, fishing in my shoulder bag for my checkbook and wondering whether the price also included a lunch of crackers spread with some of that nice butter. I paid the man, anticipating all the paperwork Liz would have to do to get me reimbursed.

"Luggage?" he asked, looking to either side of my feet.

"Just my carry-on."

"Better no luggage than the wrong kind," he commented

jovially, and eyed me and my bag as if expecting me to open it to show I had no contraband.

I ignored this comment and waited for him to take me to my room. As we walked deeper into the camp, I had to wonder just who was making money out of this dump. The borough no doubt subsidized it initially, just to have some housing available for visiting contractors. Travelers were a captive population, and innkeepers could extract from them what they pleased. I wished I had thought of the scheme first.

He opened a door in the wall, handed me a key, and waited until I had shut myself inside. It was about eight by ten and stunningly cold because the window had a hole in it. There was a portable electric heater in one corner, but I couldn't figure out how to use it in such close quarters without setting fire to the bed. For a moment I wondered whether any of my clients slept as miserably as this. I doubted they did. Most of them had more sense. I took the bedspread off and folded it against the opening in the window. Very gently, I slid the bed diagonally so that I could position the heater at the farthest point from it. If there had been any other furniture in the room, my plan would not have worked.

Even with the chill, the bed looked appealing, but first I had work to do. I off-loaded several items to lighten my burden and went back out, carefully locking the door behind me.

I discovered that the unnumbered door in the hall was a lavatory, and freshened up as best I could while standing on a pallet whose greenish color I did not think was due to paint. I went out the way I had come and tried to avoid eye contact with my fellow boarders, all *taniks*, eating crackers in front of the TV and looking like they would be more comfortable roaring through North Dakota on Harleys than cooped up in a tiny Arctic clip joint.

Heading downward on the gravel instead of up, I passed a newish structure with one of those molded roofs that resemble rubber tiles, which bore a sign that said "North Slope Borough Clinic, Anaktuvuk Pass." Then the Nunamiut School, which was even newer and had more and brighter molding. Obviously, huge amounts of money had been directed into the welfare of this community.

A banner in front of the school proclaimed "Congratulations, Graduates."

There were very few vehicles about and lots of pedestrians. I stopped a young man in a blue-and-gold Nunamiut windbreaker and asked as politely as I could where the city offices might be.

"Funeral at six," he said.

"Oh. Yes. Before then I need to . . . find, uh . . ."

"You a tourist?"

"Uh, I . . ."

"Two main things to see. Old Catholic church," he said, pointing in the direction of a peak looming over us, where a small log building with a simple cross on top of it rested halfway up the slope. "Funeral there."

"Yes," I said.

"And one of the homes of the old ones." Now he pointed at the opposite side of the bowl, toward something that at a distance resembled a Kansas pioneer's sod home, subsiding into the earth. A few ancient timbers shored up the sides, and in one corner an intact pane of glass peeped out at a crazy angle.

"Warm and cozy," he said. "You'd be surprised."

I nodded, uncertain how to pursue my request.

Puzzled at my apparent incomprehension, he added, "Anaktuvuk famous for caribou herds using the pass. Thousands. Just like in Africa."

Involuntarily, I looked around.

"None here now," he said patiently. "Wrong season. In spring, it's like drive-up caribou steak."

I said, "Yes, I see! Thank you so much—my first trip here, and I appreciate your hospitality. Uh, could you also please direct me to the city offices? I'm looking for Marvin Ahtanguarak."

Recognition lit his youthful face, and he asked, "Randy's dad?"

"Exactly."

"Is Randy with you?"

"No."

"I thought sure Randy would be here for the funeral. We were all friends together."

"Oh. I see. Maybe he'll come on another flight."

"There are no other flights, except from Anchorage. How is Randy's mom doing?"

"That's why I'm here," I said, trying not to say more than I really should.

"Okay, I take you to his dad."

He motioned to a cement block structure only a few dozen yards away. "Is Randy okay? He's going to school in Utqiagvik, right?"

"Yes, he is," I said, struggling to keep up with him on the shifting gravel. "He works so hard. I . . . I worry about him." It occurred to me that I might obtain some useful information from this young man, who apparently knew Randy.

"I miss him," the young man said. "We were always in school together until his mom had to go in for treatment."

"When did you talk to him last?"

"Last summer sometime. I thought Randy would stay here with his dad because he always loved the mountains so much, but I guess she needed him. How much longer does she have? Maybe Randy will come back here. We need him on the basketball team. It's not like him not to come for the funeral."

Everybody needed Randy. That was his problem.

"I'll be sure to tell him you asked after him."

"Yes, tell him Tarzan said hi—he'll know who that is—and tell him she mentioned him in the note."

"What?"

"The note. Didn't you know? She left a note."

"No, I, uh, I'm sorry. What happened?"

"I thought you knew. She shot herself."

My head jerked back as though he had slapped me, and images flashed behind my eyes of Liz insisting I come here—she must have known—and of Randy the last time I talked to him, when he was weary, confused, and despondent, and then of reading statistics in the *Anchorage Daily News* about teen suicides in Alaska, teen suicides on the Slope, an epidemic of teen suicides, and of myself, fixated on my own fears during the flight, surrounded by the grief of everyone else, probably the young girl's relatives, maybe her own grandparents. Oh, no, I thought. People can survive anything but losing their beloved young ones.

"Saturday night. Out behind the school. They heard her puppy yapping and found her."

We had reached our destination, and I stood staring into the young man's face, grappling with his words.

"You all right?" he asked me.

"I'm all right. It was a . . . long plane flight, is all."

"I'm late for practice. Hall on left. Second door. See you tonight."

I nodded, and he loped off down the gravel.

"Thank you," I said to his retreating form. He waved over his shoulder.

Shell-shocked, I marched inside and, as directed, turned left into a hallway toward the second door. There, lounging in an upholstered swivel chair while he talked on the phone with his feet up on a bare desk, was Randy's dad, whom I remembered from meetings with the whole family in our office when the case first began. I caught his eye. He sat up straight and took his feet down but didn't seem to recognize me. I waited while he went on with his conversation.

"That might work, but we'll have to take it to the Board . . . I don't know. They've tried that before, but the mayor nixed it. No, the same. Well, it won't hurt to try. Maybe you can talk to the shop heads to see if . . ."

I returned to the front room and looked at school lunch menus posted on the wall—they seemed to serve a lot of Tater Tots—until I heard him conclude his conversation and hang up the phone. He came out of the hallway with his hand extended.

"I know we have met, but right now I'm not remembering . . ."

"Wright. Rebecca Wright. I'm Randy's guardian ad litem in his children's case."

"Yes, of course. Won't you come in? I am so sorry I have been hard to reach . . . and I was planning to call you today . . ."

He settled back into his swivel chair, and I sat in the straight-backed metal chair in front of his desk, glancing around at his plaques and service awards. A framed picture of Randy in a basketball uniform sat by the phone, dark brown hair falling to his shoulders, his hands competently gripping the basketball.

"Can I get you some coffee? What brings you to Anaktuvuk? Have you found a place to stay? Don't stay at that wretched work camp. We could probably put you in the community center somewhere."

I tried to compose my face into a smile despite the anger I felt toward this man. He didn't look like a scoundrel. He was trim and well-dressed in jeans and a white shirt, with salt-and-pepper hair modishly cut to spike just a little on top and give him a tousle-headed-boy look, gold-rimmed spectacles, and an easy smile. But he had a habit of looking surreptitiously out of the side of his face, as though constantly checking whether the image was projecting well, though perhaps only my critical imagination saw it so.

"Coffee would be very nice," I said.

He bustled off. I sat there trying to come up with the right words to tell him, courteously, and within the boundaries of appropriate legal representation, that I thought he was a snake and that his habit of using his wife's illness to manipulate Randy into making money for him while he was still in school was appalling, and that he was driving Randy toward the same path his young friend had recently taken.

"Thank you so much," I said when he handed me a paper cup

of black liquid that resembled diesel oil. I took as small a sip as possible and set the cup on the edge of his desk.

"What brings you to Anaktuvuk?" he asked again. "Did you come for the funeral? Was she a client?"

"Actually, I've come to talk about Randy."

"Is Randy in trouble?"

I tried to smile instead of grimace. "I almost wish he were. No, he never gets in trouble. Always polite. Good grades. Athlete. In spite of the fact that he puts in thirty, forty hours a week or more at the auto repair."

"Exactly. I've never understood why some anonymous tattle-teller called the Office of Children's Services when Randy is obviously doing so well—"

Probably a caring teacher, I thought to myself, who can't bear to see a great kid worn down.

"—or why OCS even took the case. I mean it's not like anybody is being beat up or abused or anything like that. So what business is it of theirs, anyway?"

I said carefully, "I think some people are worried that maybe he's working a little too hard, that maybe there might be too much burden on him—working, going to school, sports, and then taking care of his dying mom on top of all that. He's only sixteen, you know. Not supposed to be a breadwinner."

"Well, as you know—or maybe you didn't know—it's always hard to tell how much a *tanik* knows about the community, or understands about a family—"

I could feel my forehead furrowing.

"—but ever since my beautiful wife, Maggie—"

Yeah, the beautiful wife whom, according to Liz, you've betrayed with every willing teenager you could find.

"—ever since she was diagnosed with pancreatic cancer—"

And here he pulled a long face, swiveled sideways in his chair, and folded his hands in his lap as though in a paroxysm of grief.

"—you just can't imagine how the expenses mount up and up unless you've been through something like that yourself."

Now I squirmed in my own chair. This particular *tanik* might not know everything about the community or about each family, but I did know that no Native person was going to be out a single dime for medical care in any facility on the Slope. I also knew a bit about grief, as a widow, and couldn't see it in his handsome face. I wanted to yell at him, You're crucifying your own kid, you self-centered bastard! If you keep it up, he's probably going to check out like this Anaktuvuk child has done. I was tempted to smack him right in his chamber-of-commerce countenance.

Since he apparently had run out of hypocritical remarks for the time being, and I couldn't trust myself to say anything, we went through an interval of silence. I could hear children's voices from a nearby playground. Farther down the hall, a Native female voice was talking to someone on the phone. A whistle tooted, like at a factory, though I doubted there were any factories here.

"Mr. Ahtanguarak, I wouldn't have come this far if I weren't concerned. I don't know if you have seen Randy recently, but he appears . . . to be under a great strain. I'm not a social worker or a psychologist, but I can tell he's troubled, and I was wondering if the family might—"

"If he's having a problem, why didn't they give him a real attorney?"

"A guardian ad litem is an attorney. It's just the name given to a lawyer who the court appoints to look out for somebody's interests during litigation."

"Oh. I thought you were a public defender."

"Public defenders are lawyers who specialize in criminal law." Here I looked directly at him and let my opinion of him show in my eyes. "The reason the case was opened is that Randy has more than he can deal with. Frankly, he's a suicide risk. For starters, it's against child labor laws for a sixteen-year-old to put in that many hours, even if it is 'informal' or 'voluntary,' after everybody else goes home. And he's too young to be the main caregiver for a mother dying of cancer. Is there any way at all you could come to Utqiagvik to help with her care? It won't be long now. Or are there other family members who could help?"

I felt I had said about as much as I could say. He was correct that there were, indeed, limits on how far an outsider, even a court-appointed outsider, could reach inside a Native family. Often the cases revealed that arrangements were the best the family could make under whatever circumstances they were facing. But in Randy's situation, Liz and I saw the boy withering and warping before our eyes. He couldn't stumble along much further under the burdens he had. His dad, hiding in the mountains, needed to emerge from his lair to help him.

"Tell you what," Mr. Ahtanguarak said, getting to his feet. "I'm going to call Randy right now and see how I think he's doing. Ask him what he wants, you know. Then you and I can talk again."

He was terminating the conversation and stood there waiting for me to leave. I felt uncertain whether to acquiesce in ending the interview. Did he not believe Randy was hurting? Was he brushing me off with complete indifference, or would he really call his son to inquire? I would rather he had yelled at me when I mentioned that terrifying word, *suicide*, than brush me off. I couldn't tell whether he had even listened to me or was simply applying his corporate skills of disengagement. A long trip for an inconclusive five-minute meeting, but I doubted I had the authority to insist he talk to me further. At least my coming might get his attention, might remind him people in Utqiagvik, in the borough, were watching, and that if Randy killed himself, his father might stink in front of his other relatives, as well as lose a source of income. I got to my feet.

"See you at the funeral tonight. By then I will have talked to Randy and will have a plan to tell you," he said.

I took a minute more to study his face before I shook his hand, thanked him for the still-full cup of coffee, and turned to go.

These damned children's cases drive me crazy, I thought, plodding out the way I had come. In criminal cases the possibilities, the parameters, the time frames, are usually clear. You can do certain things; you can't do others. You can try to push the envelope, and the court will let you know whether you have gone too far. And if not that court, then a higher court. But the children's cases hemmed and hawed, yinned and yanged all over the place. The few guidelines were usually honored mostly in the breach, and the cases did not take place between the accustomed poles of prosecution and defense but with the added third-party participation of a huge social service network that was not truly accountable to anyone, and the issues were confused by the vagaries of people's families. Randy's dad was right to be surprised that Children's Services had even gotten involved, since Randy had not been beaten or abused. Probably only because some social worker had cared, just like Randy's teachers and his mother's nurses and Liz and I cared.

I went back to the work camp and lay down to rest without taking off my parka, thinking that if I woke up in time, since I was here, I owed it to Randy to attend the funeral so I could carry to him greetings from his friends, and to hear what else his dad might say.

AHTANGUARAK WAS WAITING for me where the path leading upward upon the mountain split off from the main gravel road. I was still trying to digest the warmed-up canned chili I had eaten for dinner because it was included in my $180, and was not happy to see him. We trudged uphill in silence among such a throng of people that I doubted we would be able to enter the church.

When we reached the door, however, friends of his and former clients of mine motioned to us. A way opened in the crowd, and places for two were found among elders in the second row, all of whom wore fortunes in furs. I did not notice the slight fragrance of fish or seal oil in this place as in Utqiagvik. Here there was a different scent, that of smoky sage. I had read that many peoples in the circumpolar world, including the Mongols and Cossacks on the other side of the globe where the tundra became the steppes, burned wild sage as an insect repellent, just as the citizens of Anaktuvuk did.

The little log church looked like many another frontier chapel except for the altar cloth on the communion table. It was a beautiful example of skin sewing in the checkerboard pattern of small squares of cowskin in white, brown, and black that often adorned mukluk boots and house slippers. Local skin sewers had found cowhide easier to work with than seal or caribou, and ordered it up from supply houses in Anchorage, since as far as was known there had never been live cows on the Slope.

The pews were so packed I feared soon we wouldn't have enough of the thin mountain air to breathe. Native families and *tanik* teachers, borough officials and staffers, plus students, crowded so closely together that everybody's shoulders were cramped forward. Toward the front were folding chairs set within a roped box, and I wondered whether these might be for a choir.

At the altar, a smallish closed coffin rested on benches, surrounded by displays of flowers both plastic or silk and real. A large easel held a collage of photographs of a slight young girl with pulled-back hair holding a softball bat at age eight or nine, praying in a white communion dress, walking arm in arm with classmates, and smiling at the world in a prom gown.

I noticed the distracting sound of jackhammering or heavy construction equipment in use close by.

"Can't they stop that noise for the service?" I whispered to my escort.

"They're digging the grave," he said, "in the permafrost."

Finally the choir filed in, wailing "Nearer, My God, to Thee," accompanied by an elder lady who sat at a small portable organ that looked very old. A pastor came forward, and to my surprise it was not a priest but the minister from the Presbyterian church in Utqiagvik. I knew this lady, a stout *tanik* in purple robes with fair fluffy hair, from the Bible classes I had attended on those Sundays when the caseload that week was less overwhelming than usual. In a time when female pastors were still a rarity, Pastor Willa Roghair had not been called to any church except the arguably difficult one in Utqiagvik. The Lower 48 lost out, and Utqiagvik gained a star. Pastor Roghair was a gifted linguist, a cellist, and a poet. She loved God and she loved the people of her flock, and she was not afraid to go up against any power—secular or spiritual—that threatened either.

Now she tried to smile at the family members packed into the first two pews. "I remember when Eqalin was a little girl in Sunday school," she began, and told of their first meeting.

A white-haired gentleman sitting by the front aisle lowered his face into his hands, and his shoulders heaved. His neighbors patted whatever parts of him they could reach.

Tears in her own eyes, Pastor Roghair said that now we would have the "specials."

I knew from other occasions that a "special" was a contribution to the funeral program by someone other than church staff. For this one, several kids who looked to be members of the young girl's high school class made their way through the crowd to the front of the church. From a cardboard box beside the altar, each took a rose that had probably arrived that afternoon in the charter of mourners from Anchorage. The flowers were a little wilted and needed support from both hands to keep from lopping over. On a pitch pipe cue, the young people looked toward an elder in the middle of the congregation, who rose in place to direct them. They sang, a cappella, "The Rose."

After they had finished and filed back to their seats, laying their flowers one by one on top of the casket, nobody made much of an effort anymore to keep from crying.

A half dozen other young people came forward to stand beside the casket. As a veteran of many interviews with many young people, I noticed, in the open necks of their jackets and *atikluks*, the same brands and logos that *tanik* kids wore in Fairbanks and Anchorage. For this occasion, the kids had put over them the parkas that their mothers and grandmothers had lovingly hand-sewn for them.

A lanky kid of about fourteen with a fervent pain in his eyes drew a much-creased piece of notepaper from his jeans and began to read.

> Dear Ayla Eqalin, I wish you hadn't gone without saying goodbye. All night long I looked for you everywhere. I wish I could go with you to make sure you don't get cold and afraid like that time we climbed the peak looking for birds' eggs and the wind came up, but I can't come because of my little brothers and sisters. Promise me one thing, that you will find a place that's safe and warm and out of the wind and wait for me. It won't seem like so long for you as it will for me. When I get there we'll play in the creek like we used to when we were little kids. Forever.

He turned his back to the congregation while he replaced the paper in his jeans, and a lady in the front row got up and went outside. I probably would have joined her except that I would have had to step on people's laps to get out.

I was startled to recall that the daughter of Bernice Ipalook and John Adams was also called Eqalin. Officer Tidwell, the first responder to the murder scene, had mentioned the child, and one of the neighbors had told Public Safety that Bernice and John took good care of their little girl. The child was now half orphaned, and her father was in jail. Babies on the Slope were often named for cousins, uncles, or grandmothers, but this duplication seemed to me eerie, almost inauspicious. I was already praying for the grieving congregation; I added a prayer that young, surviving Eqalin might never enter the awful cycles of addiction or violence or abuse that had destroyed her mother and probably her namesake. But her innocence was already impacted by tragedy.

A very young Native girl was reciting, "Dear sister, I miss you. You always made the best pancakes. I'm so sorry I broke your new necklace you got for Christmas, and I promise I will take good care of your puppy . . ."

I did not see how these people could bear this pain. Almost anything was bearable except the senseless loss of one's own flesh and blood future. What possible words of comfort, what hope of consolation, what hearts' ease, could Pastor Roghair offer? But when the young people sat down and she stepped to the pulpit, her tone was angry, not consoling.

"Who among us has truly fought evil?" she asked.

Ahtanguarak and I both startled slightly.

"Which of us who has met evil has resisted it unto death?"

People ahead of us and beside us ceased to employ their handkerchiefs and raised their eyes to her.

"In the fourteen years I have served here, I have not spoken on some subjects. But I have to now."

All coughing and rustling of clothing ceased.

"Some of you have wanted to go back to the old ways. Some of you have wanted me to close the church and leave. Some still believe that the war the shamans conducted between good and evil was closer to the truth of the world than is the sweet love of Jesus. They believe that following Jesus weakened them for the struggle, and that the church, like the school and the hospital and the court, was for *taniks*, and not for you."

I stared hard at the pastor. She looked pale from strain and haggard from lack of sleep, but she didn't look crazy.

"I am not here to argue those issues. I can only try to offer Jesus's love to you, and then each soul must make its own choice."

I found myself confused about her entire meaning. Was it suicide that was the evil, or drugs, or violence, or some abuse within the girl's own family? Perhaps local residents knew, but I did not. I remembered how Pastor Roghair told me once in her study, before the others came for a Bible lesson, that a longtime resident of Utqiagvik had advised her not to oppose the shamans but to join their ancient spiritual practices with her own.

"I can't," she had told that person. "Some of the shamans are good and seek the welfare of the community, but some are evil, and some are both."

No doubt she understood shamanism better than I did. Its mysteries were beyond my ken. Natives acknowledged its existence and power but did not talk freely about shamans, at least not to *taniks*. Whenever the unknowable shamanic presence was manifested, people fell silent and kept a distance. Inside my coat in that small, crowded chapel, elbow to elbow with fur, I shivered.

"Remember this. Whatever you choose, we are each responsible not only for ourselves but to the others in the village. Even more than in other places, here we are all responsible for each other."

Was she speaking now from Christian theology or Inupiaq culture? I could not tell. I could see, though, that apparently she had struck a chord with some in the congregation. A few nodded. Some conferred in low whispers. One young man stood up and with difficulty made his way through the crush to a wall, where he whispered with an elder standing there.

Now she stepped down from the lectern to stand beside the coffin. "Goodbye, sweet child," she said. "You were the light of our long-distance-telephone Sunday school, and we will all miss you for the rest of our lives. May Jesus keep you in utter peace and love and safety for eternity."

We then sat in silence so long that the organist began to fidget.

Finally she took up her hymnal and selected a page, and an elder stepped forward to lead us in "Amazing Grace" while the pastor quietly left the church through a back door.

The murmur of people standing, struggling with their clothing, and comforting their neighbors arose around us. By the time Ahtanguarak and I had cleared the church, I had framed a question for him.

"I would be grateful if you would explain to me what evil she meant," I asked in as straightforward a manner as I could, no longer as attorney and client's father, or *tanik* and Native, but simply person to person, I hoped.

"We need to have a talk," he answered.

Along with the crowd, we dispersed down the hill toward the center of the village. I worked at not falling on the loose gravel and almost tripped when someone grabbed the sleeve of my jacket. Turning, I saw Randy's friend who had given me directions earlier, still in his blue-and-gold windbreaker.

"Randy did," he whispered.

"What?"

"Randy did what she said," he persisted.

We stepped out of the way of other funeral-goers, and I motioned to Ahtanguarak to go on.

"What do you mean?" I asked.

The young man waited until most of the crowd had passed us. Then he said, "I thought you knew."

"No, I don't know," I said, "and I want to know. Please tell me."

"Some of the kids thought Randy was a shaman," he said, in a voice so low I had trouble hearing. "Or would be when he grew up."

"Why . . . why would they think that?"

The young man's face was in the shadow cast by the peak above us, and I couldn't see his expression.

"It was like . . . sometimes he knew things."

"How do you mean? I don't understand."

"Knew things ahead of time. Before they happened."

I stood there trying to digest this information. Superstition? Grief hysteria? Now his words tumbled out.

"Once my uncle didn't come home during a storm, and it was too bad to go look for him. When it finally cleared, all the elders said to search the peaks, but Randy said no, to look in town. He said he could see him with a snow machine. Nobody listened. My uncle never had a snow machine. We looked for him for days, and he was finally found in a drift behind the school, frozen by some kids' old broken-down snow machine."

The boy turned and struck off along the side of the hill.

"Wait! Please wait! I . . ." I called, but he hurried on.

"You coming, Ms. Wright?" Randy's dad said from the trail below me. I looked around. I was now alone beside the path, struggling to understand what I had just heard.

Heaving a sigh, I went on down the hill.

I thought Ahtanguarak would lead me back to the city offices, but we walked right by them to an area of what looked like work sheds and storage buildings, zeroing in on a large structure that had windows on the upper floor only. He brought out a key, and we entered through a corner door and ascended a dark staircase. He flipped a light switch and moved aside for me to enter.

I stepped into Lower 48 suburbia, an affluent *tanik*'s playroom. A large-screen TV sat in front of a huge blue plush couch. To our right gleamed the Formica and chrome of a well-stocked wet bar plus microwave. Beyond lay a shadowland of pillows stacked atop a great waterbed.

Ahtanguarak laughed a laugh that was more like a giggle. "You see? Natives have more than dogsleds nowadays!" He threw off his jacket and went to the bar. "What would you like to drink?"

I stared at him in genuine astonishment. "Who does this place belong to?"

"Friends of mine at the borough," he said. "For the VIP traveler. Vodka? Rum? Whiskey?"

I didn't answer, continuing to look around. In one corner sat a stack of crates of whiskey. On the ottoman in front of the couch were several stray gloves and scarves.

"I thought Anaktuvuk was dry," I said.

"Oh . . . well," he said, taking two glasses out of a cupboard and opening a small refrigerator to extract ice. "It is. But just like in Utqiagvik, there are other . . . resources."

He mixed liquids into the glasses and brought them over to where I still stood, hesitating. I smelled a bubbly fragrance, guessed it might be vodka and 7UP, and wanted to pick it up and have a drink. Wanted it very much, actually, to sit and sip in this pleasant place, far away from the church. And the court. What would be the harm, really? Hadn't I earned a drink after a harrowing flight and even more harrowing funeral? Besides, over a drink, Ahtanguarak might relax enough to really share some information about Randy. And I could delay my return to the green mold, rancid lard, and cold bed awaiting me at my $180 quarters.

He placed the drinks on the ottoman, took up a remote, brought the TV to life, and clicked from channel to channel, settling on a scene of *tanik* teenagers walking down a New England road just as a red convertible filled with other teenagers overtook them. He ratcheted up the volume into a soundtrack of rock and roll, and I found myself reaching for the drink.

But in that instant my eye strayed toward the one window just above the waterbed. I saw the mountains looming dark against the starry sky above us and remembered I was in the "queen of the Brooks Range," as our pilot had put it. Alcohol was forbidden here, and we had just attended the solemn funeral of a young girl who need not have died. I had come here with my way paid by the State of Alaska to try to divert young Randy from following the same path she had taken.

I turned toward the door, glad I hadn't even taken off my coat. No sense trying to talk to this guy. Maybe Liz and I could come up with some other plan for Randy. Maybe Liz could explain to me what the pastor was talking about.

"Ms. Wright?"

"Uh, sorry—you know, I'm more tired than I realized. Very nice place here, but it's been a long day."

He didn't turn off the TV but put it on mute. "I thought we were going to talk."

"Was there something you wanted to tell me about Randy?"

"Well . . . it's not easy, you know. I thought we could just . . . visit a bit . . ."

Yeah, until you turned me in for drinking booze in a dry town, I thought. Maybe I wasn't quite as naive as Liz seemed to think.

"Good night," I said, shutting the door behind me. He was saying something, but I missed whatever it was.

Anaktuvuk looked more shadowy and felt colder than Utqiagvik as I crunched over the pale gravel, dreading a night beside a broken window and a morning of terror on the flight to Fairbanks. At least I had spent an entire day without obsessing over who had killed the Ipalook sisters, my client or someone else's. For a moment I wondered whether the evil of which Pastor Roghair spoke had claimed all three young women, and then tried not to follow that thought.

14

Even the strongest eagle cannot
soar higher than the stars.
ALASKA NATIVE PROVERB

I'M NOT ASHAMED TO SAY THAT AFTER I GOT OFF THE plane in Fairbanks, the first thing I did was walk into the landscaped island in front of the terminal and put my arms around the largest fir tree growing there, and then the birch next to it. Trees were the one thing I could never get used to being without in the Arctic. I longed to see them arched over residential streets, to hear the wind breathing among them, and to watch the magic lantern shows that sunlight stippling through their branches cast upon walls and floors. Movie theaters, malls, bars, lawns, and even gardens I could learn to do without, but not trees.

The prison was a low-lying blocky assemblage of blue paint and gray steel accented with abundant rows of accordion wire. Usually I was admitted right away, but this morning I inconveniently arrived during head count. I half wondered whether the delay was deliberate to discourage time-consuming public defender visitations, a tactic that would not be uncommon.

While I waited, the desk sergeant said I should look at the craft items inmates had made and put out for sale. I wandered through the glass cases in the waiting area, admiring the sleek ivory representations of the essences of seals, walruses, and whales, the Eskimo yo-yos made of crystalline polar bear fur, and a few elaborate skin dolls. I had seen most of the items before. In fact, I remembered wasting some time trying to persuade tourist tour bus representatives to have buses swing by the prison. The tourists could get some great buys of Native workmanship, and the inmates could make some much-needed money. But the big companies brought the tourists only to businesses with which they had lucrative contracts. Too bad, because ivory was less and less available. Killing walruses, the animals that produced ivory tusks, as well as polar bears and seals, was now illegal under the Marine Mammal Protection Act of 1972—except for Alaska Natives, whose history and culture of harvesting them sparingly stretched back into prehistory.

I came to two pieces I had not seen before, and my breath caught in my throat. One was a chalice of ivory on a plinth of baleen, and the other was a grail on a pedestal of bone. Both were wreathed with bas-reliefs of seals. In one, the seals chased each other, and in the other, in twining circles, they soared upward toward birds skimming the waves while polar bears peered down. One vessel had translucent sides so thin that the scarlet velvet fitted within glowed through. The other was fitted with a cover intricately rendered from fossilized ivory to resemble tiny pipe organs. They brought to mind the treasures of legend, the kind that were booty in ancient wars or stolen from great tombs at the risk of death.

"Oh, my Lord in heaven," I said.

The ID card read "Homage and Respect for the Spirit World of the Seals." It was signed by Bobby Nashookpuk.

The only art in my limited repertory that invited comparison was Ghiberti's friezes on the door of the Baptistery in Florence.

Nashookpuk's work showed sea creatures instead of saints, but on the larger grail there were also two human representations, a grotesque head exaggeratedly inhaling on one side and another blowing through pursed lips on the other—incubus and succubus, or the winds from Boreas and Zephyrus? Liz was so right to have sent me to see Nashookpuk. I should have known. Was the artist re-creating beautiful vessels to replace one he destroyed in his crime? Or that perhaps someone else had destroyed, for which he grieved? I would have to ask whether she knew the answer to this question, as well as to the riddle Pastor Roghair had raised.

"Ms. Wright, they're ready for you now."

I signed the log and submitted to a search of my purse, and then the guard conducted me down the hallway, through several buzz-lock doors.

"How's it going, Mr. Church?" I asked my escort.

"So-so, I guess. You must not be doing your job up there."

"How's that?"

"We're overloaded again."

"Sorry to hear that, but it's not me. Must be Anchorage."

"You coming to the next potlatch?"

"I hope so, but nobody's invited me yet."

Native potlatches at the prison were a genuine good time, and invitations were prized. Some years I got to go, some years not. Neither judges nor lawyers nor senators nor dignitaries attended unless they received a personal invitation from a Native inmate. The previous year I had been invited by one of my favorite check forgers. I got to sample a number of dishes including walrus meat, which was horrible and left a fishy aftertaste in my throat that lasted for days, and beaver, tough and oily. I skipped the moose, salmon, caribou, whitefish, and two kinds of muktuk (beluga and bowhead) but indulged in the three kinds of fry bread (plain, sugared, and with raisins), and berry pie. The event was held deep within the prison, beyond the usual visiting rooms, in a gymnasium that looked exactly like my high school gymnasium back in Kansas. After comments by respected Native elder visitors, the inmates graciously included everyone in the circle dance, an experience of community that generates a high of comradeship and belonging.

"You want to see your guys in any particular order?"

"Whatever's convenient. Thank you for your help."

He put me in the attorney interview room, with its carpeted walls, tiny table, and rickety chairs, and brought out, one by one, a teenage robber of pizza deliveries, a sad statutory rapist, a fellow who forged his grandmother's checks, two bootleggers, and Wiley Ungarook, who was in on a probation violation. I was disappointed to find that Wiley Ungarook's memory of the night Bernice and Wanda died had not yet improved.

It tired me to see several clients at once—to go over police reports with them, to ask about possible character witnesses, or, sometimes, potential treatment and rehab plans—but the necessity came with the territory. In the Lower 48, pretrial clients were held in local jails, not prisons, and public defenders could see two or three whenever time permitted. Utqiagvik's jail did not have room for them all, so the overflow was brought to the prison in Fairbanks to await trial. I had to schedule a whole day and night to fly to Fairbanks to see my clients.

Finally, Bobby Nashookpuk joined me, carrying a thick file. Nashookpuk looked like an illustration on a postcard of a classic Native Alaskan, with his regular features, closely cropped black hair, and neat goatee and mustache. There was nothing picture-postcard about his eyes, though. Those looked like illustrations from Dante of the suffering damned.

Usually for openers I made dumb small talk like "How have they been treating you?" or "How's the food?" But I couldn't bring myself to say anything so inane to this man from a remote Arctic village who was a world-class artist.

"Mr. Nashookpuk, I don't believe we've met before. My name is Rebecca Wright, from the Utqiagvik Public Defender."

We shook hands. I motioned to the chairs, but he did not sit.

"Liz Kanayurak tells me that you have called a lot. I am sorry I have not been to see you before. You've probably heard about the case of the Ipalook sisters. It's taking a lot of everybody's time."

He nodded gravely and cocked his head slightly to one side as if appraising me, whether for sincerity or legal ability or as a subject for a carving, I couldn't tell.

"Before we talk about your case, I want to tell you . . ."

What was it I wanted to tell him—that I was startled by the superb quality of his work? Or to congratulate him that he was able to work at all in this place? To offer to try to get him out at gunpoint if necessary? No matter his talent, I was a lawyer, not a groupie.

"I was looking at your chalices—your ivory and bone work—out front. The *Homage and Respect for the Spirit World of the Seals* is exquisite. Would you allow me to try to contact an agent to represent you? I truly believe your work deserves a much wider audience."

He turned his face away from me and flexed his shoulders slightly. Apparently, I had said a wrong thing, but I didn't understand quite how.

"If you like, we could ask Liz Kanayurak . . . or anyone you chose in Utqiagvik to do the contacting. You would probably make a lot of money."

This comment must have been even worse, for he now stepped toward the door. I was really screwing up this interview.

Mr. Church's head appeared in the narrow chicken-wired opening in the door.

"Everything okay, Bobby? You don't have to talk to anyone if you don't want to, you know."

Usually it was me they worried about, not the prisoners.

"I'm sorry. I'm here to talk with you about your case." I was groveling. I didn't want him to terminate the interview before we at least discussed his file. His was an old, post-conviction case that I likely couldn't even get reopened, but I wanted to do whatever I could for him.

Nashookpuk hesitated, then turned back toward me, and the guard's head disappeared from the window. He gave me some papers. He had made a timeline of the dates in his case, the dates of the incident, the charge, the conviction, and his unsuccessful appeal, plus notes about when his good time had been docked and he had been moved back and forth among institutions because of write-ups for failing urine drug tests. Cocaine. I had long ago ceased to be surprised at how much dope was available in prisons.

"Can I keep this outline, or is it your only copy?"

"You can keep it. I made it for you." The first words he had spoken to me.

"Thank you. I expect you are aware that once a person is convicted and the conviction is affirmed on appeal, it is very hard to get back in front of a judge. The court considers the case closed unless something unusual happens. New evidence. Or a change in the law that is so important it operates retroactively. I'm not sure I can do much for you, and I don't want to get your hopes up unrealistically."

The appraising gaze had returned.

"I know all that," he said. "The main reason I wanted to see you is about Amos Lane."

Warning bells now clanged in my head. Amos Lane was already my client. If a potential client began to tell me something about his own case that conflicted with Lane's, I should cut him off immediately or be prepared to withdraw from the one and not to undertake the other. You can't use one client's confidential communications against the best interests of another client. Experienced public defenders were supposed to see these entanglements coming and avoid them. Otherwise, the continual changes in representation would obstruct the court's ability to proceed with its caseload and bring the whole system to a halt.

On the other hand, if the time period of the other information was remote, if it didn't specifically involve negative or relevant data, sometimes there was turnaround room in the conflict rules. The Ipalook case was so murky that any new perspective might help. We had a duty to avoid developing conflicts, but we also had a duty to represent as many clients as possible.

"Amos was a neighbor when I was a teenager," he told me.

Okay. General info.

"We learned to hunt seals together."

All right.

"But then there came that bad year. And neither he nor I have ever recovered—but I'm the one in here, and he's still out there somewhere. Can't you—?"

I drew in a breath to ask him to stop, but hesitated. Perhaps he could tell me something from Amos's background that would help me understand my client better, or perhaps he had seen a violent side of Amos that developed young. Perhaps he even knew from friends or relatives some facts about the Ipalook case. I would have loved to have this information.

But not achieved through a violation of the canon of ethics. If I went that route, it would probably be found inadmissible as evidence and thrown out, anyway, along with me. I held up a hand, hating what I was about to say. One minute I was falling all over myself praising Nashookpuk's artistry, next I was listening avidly for gossipy details, and then I had to tell him to shut up. I wanted to yell, Tell me, tell me what happened—what do you know about Amos Lane? But I couldn't. I couldn't ask him that. His answer would lead directly into a conflict that would require me to exit both cases—and then to explain to Judge Jeffery the reason why. Then either Lane or Nashookpuk, or even the judge or my own agency, could file a complaint with the bar, which I would be hard pressed to defend.

"I'm sorry, I should have thought . . ." I began, staring at the much-folded piece of paper that he had painstakingly prepared for me. I had been so eager for information that I had thought maybe somewhere in the ethical rules there might be room for me to learn more about Lane's general background, and even a possible clue about the case, but I was as wrong as Public Safety had been in tape-recording our conversation.

I raised my eyes to the countenance of the finest artist I had ever met in person and managed to say, "Mr. Nashookpuk, I can't talk to you about any details about Amos Lane. I'm so sorry. You need to have your own separate attorney who has no ties at all to someone else's case."

Nashookpuk's eyes stared into mine as though searching whatever reality lay behind my *tanik* words. I wished I had never met Amos Lane and were free to represent Nashookpuk instead, to help him with his case, to find out whatever errors had been committed in it long before organized institutional public defense ever came to the North Slope.

"I promise you I will ask the Office of Public Advocacy to send one of their attorneys to see you."

Many clients would have attempted to change my mind or objected profanely to the waste of their own time in preparing paperwork and coming to the interview. Nashookpuk merely changed his expression from one of inquiry to mild contempt. "You need to know," he said. "Amos was never the same after that year." He knocked on the door for the guard.

There was nothing for me to say or do but to walk away.

On the way out, I spent all the Utqiagvik bucks I had on hand to buy both pieces of Nashookpuk's transcendent art from the display case in that grubby waiting room. I bought them because I wanted to have them around where I could see them every day, and as an investment in his future, and as an apology to him, as well as a salve to my own distress at not being able to represent him because of my other client, Amos Lane. Nashookpuk's words kept repeating in my head. "Amos was never the same after that year." How so? In what way? What had Amos become?

15

NOAA samples Arctic air, compares it with air sampled by NOAA's three other remote observatories [in Hawaii, Antarctica, and American Samoa], and then computes a baseline from which changes in time and space can be derived.

"BARROW, ALASKA, AS A WINDOW ON THE WORLD,"
NATIONAL OCEANIC AND ATMOSPHERIC ADMINISTRATION,
NOVEMBER 16, 2021

GOOD THING I TRAVELED WHEN I DID, BECAUSE AFTER I returned, Utqiagvik was hit with a cold so deep that even the planes quit flying. The place was always cold, of course. The constant cold kept the air so stable that if thunder ever occurred, that rare event made the Anchorage paper. Now Seismic Isaac announced on KBRW that the temperature had fallen to a hundred below. I doubt it actually got *that* cold, but I know it was colder than the usual thirty to fifty below because the planes had never quit flying before. I figured the hydraulic systems couldn't function. However, the trooper, who flew weekly escorting prisoners back and forth, said that a pilot had told him that in the extreme cold the directional equipment could no longer accurately track the horizon, so it wasn't safe to fly.

Standing at the kitchen window to mix my breakfast cereal, I noticed that the neighborhood looked strange. Smoke or steam or exhaust streams did not meander in their usual fashion but rose up straight as skewers. Curious, I stepped out the front door, and the air caught in my throat. Would this extreme chill freeze lung tissue? I didn't want to find out and came back in.

But cold never covered anybody's caseload.

When I first passed the Alaska bar and got a job in the Arctic, I knew I would need cold weather gear and drove up to the REI store in Seattle to browse their bargain basement. They had just received a shipment of factory-reject firefighter parkas. The labels claimed they were "designed for outdoor operations under Arctic conditions." Delighted to find such great parkas at a low price, even though they only came in standard emergency cobalt blue with reflective strips all over them, I put one on a credit card and proudly wore it to my first day at work. Liz laughed at me.

"Sorry, but you can't wear that. You'll freeze."

I tried to ignore her until October, when I began freezing.

Liz kindly gave me the name of a local skin sewer and told me to take her $1,000. The lady wrote down my measurements and fashioned for me a woman's calf-length parka covered in pale green velveteen, with a shearling lining, wolf trim, and a wolverine ruff, because wolverine, unlike other materials, does not collect hoarfrost. Next payday I bought Sorel boots and ragg mittens to go with it and was never again cold. I learned not to fear the cold.

Until today.

I brought out my personal emergency equipment: a huge, loosely woven blue-and-pink plaid mohair scarf that I had found at a yard sale. With it wound around my face, I could see through the open weave well enough to walk, and it usually tempered the worst of the cold before it reached my nose and mouth. The old scarf worked better than any of the several masks or balaclavas I had tried, which had caused sweating and itching.

Once I left the house, I could feel the icy air trying to enter my sleeves and burrow down into my boots. To see well enough to walk to the bus corner in the winter darkness, I had to push the scarf partly back from my face. Then the cold chilled my sinus cavities up to the plates in my skull.

When the bus appeared at the top of the slope and I sprinted the last few yards to meet it, my lungs recoiled and stiffened from the gasps of air that penetrated to them. The bus arrived in a cloud of ice fog, and the door wheezed open. I was relieved to climb on board because my fingers had become icicles sticking out of snowballs. If I had missed the bus, I would not have been able to work the key to get back into my house.

Only in this part of the world could you die from just standing too long at a bus stop.

On the second day of the extreme cold, the buses, like the planes, quit running. I rode into work with Tuttu Taxi, which never quit, and one of the bank tellers dropped me off that night at home, where I found Michael's pickup parked in its former place in front of my boardwalk.

A cautious hope stirred in my heart. He hadn't been over much since we drove out on Cakeeater Road. Perhaps he had come to be uncomfortable around me because I didn't get high like he did. Perhaps he preferred to be with people who did. But there was always a chance he would take a hard look at his addiction and decide he wanted to live differently.

We made scrambled eggs and toast for dinner, with the bacon I now kept stocked, and joked about when he showed up after hunting with the wounded hand. We watched a vintage movie, just like old times.

The next morning, Michael didn't get up to go to work. I thought perhaps the city had told employees to stay home because of the extreme weather. In order not to wake him, I tiptoed around while I took the dogs out and made breakfast. When I went to kiss him goodbye, I found him curled up in a fetal position.

"Michael? You okay?" I pulled on his shoulder.

He rose up, and before I could stop myself, I recoiled from him in shock. His eyes had the look of a dog who knew he was dying, and different colors of mucus ran from his nose.

"See you later," he mumbled, and returned to his curled-up position.

"Are you sick? You want to go to the clinic?"

He shrugged and turned his face away.

I sat back on my heels in concern. He looked sick, but I couldn't make him go to a doctor if he didn't want to go. Summoning an ambulance seemed a bit much. I would ask Liz what to do.

"Call me if you need me," I said.

With no buses available, the cabs all had wait lists, so I set out walking, swathed in my huge scarf over my parka. I remembered at the last minute to take a plastic sack of food for the dog.

When I rounded the corner, I couldn't see the dog. There was only a dimple in the fresh snow to mark the top of the stake to which she was tethered. No footprints led out to her.

I ran a few steps toward it but then slowed down because of the sharp air. I had to paddle and swim through the drifts with my mittened hands. Sinking down on my hands and knees, I flailed about in the whiteness to find her chain and follow it down hand over hand, remembering I had read somewhere that tethered dogs can go mad from the years of confinement and frustration and will disembowel or de-face anyone who comes within reach. But I had fed this dog. She knew me. Surely she wouldn't hurt me.

I broke through a crust frozen from her breathing and came face-to-face with the poor captive creature. Her eyes glittered yellow a few inches from mine. Reflexively I groped into her neck fur and unsnapped her chain. She shuddered all over as she realized what I had done. She bent her shaggy head and licked me once on my snowy exposed wrist, between the cuff of my parka and my mitten. Then she rocketed past me out of the snow.

By the time I scrambled free, she had reached the ocean, and I watched her running up the shore with the rippling gait of her wolf kin. She hadn't eaten the kibbles now scattered all over the snow. I stared after her until she was only a moving speck in the distance, heading toward the shooting stations out on Point Barrow.

I wondered whether locally it was considered a worse crime to free a dog than to bootleg vodka. I might soon find out.

LIZ WAS ALREADY at her desk that morning, though she didn't look very happy about being there.

"There's something the matter with Michael," I blurted out before even taking off my snowy gear, which was beginning to thaw and drip. "He looks terrible, and I—"

"There's something the matter with everybody in town today," she snapped back at me. "No planes, no deliveries. Everybody's strung out."

For the thousandth time in Utqiagvik, I felt like a fool. No planes meant no dope. Practically the whole town smoked either weed or something stronger, and whatever had been locally available was now long gone.

I unwound the damp scarf from my shoulders. "You don't have to be here, if you don't feel well," I said, in a low voice, so Carol wouldn't hear.

"Just as soon be here as anywhere," she said.

I was trying to bury myself in a file when Nelson Traverso, John Adams's attorney, walked in.

If I was nervous about the impending double murder trial, Traverso, wiry and energetic by nature, had gone into overdrive.

"I'm here to give you notice," he said dramatically, sitting down by my window box, which no longer held morning glories but some anemic impatiens. The morning glories had died in the absence of the midnight sun, and impatiens were the only flowers I could find that could survive a winter on fluorescent lights alone. "I'm going after your client."

"You're what?"

"I have no choice. Just giving you a heads-up. You'd do the same for me."

He had my attention. Amos had a great immunity agreement, but I didn't trust the State any more than he did. For Traverso to implicate my client in order to defend his was classic trial strategy, of course. If he had found explosive evidence against Amos, the case could still blow up in our faces, and the State would try to weasel out of the deal.

"Public Safety was right the first time when they tagged your guy," he said. "Ellingsworth made a big mistake when he switched to mine. I have no idea why Ed did it. Maybe John was easier to bully than your guy. I should have flown up here to talk to Adams when I first got appointed, but you know how it is."

I nodded. Yes, I knew how it was.

"Adams didn't understand he could ask for free counsel to be appointed. He didn't know he didn't have to talk to the detective at all. He's too damn polite for his own good. He just kept trying to answer the questions till he was saying whatever Ellingsworth wanted him to say. You've got to see the video—it's pitiful. Once I play it for the jury, they'll be ready to convict Ellingsworth, not John."

I tried to figure how much of this talk was Traverso whistling in the dark to keep up his own courage as he took a double homicide case to trial, and how much was clear legal logic. Traverso was smart and experienced. If he thought Ellingsworth had overstepped and that a jury might disregard Adams's confession—well, maybe they would.

Public advocates tend to follow one of two basic strategies. One type prefers to operate in trial mode. "Give us an early trial date," this counsel asks the court, invoking the speedy trial rule on each case and hoping that the overworked DA will make good settlement offers just to manage his calendar. This lawyer risks having five cases set for jury trial on the same day, with no way of knowing which will go first until the last minute.

The other mode is to avoid trial entirely by negotiating every case. This type of lawyer wants all the cases set as far down the road as possible, the more cases piling up, the better, with little regard for the clients who wait in jail. Trial witnesses lose their initial emotions and forget the details, and DAs get sick of lingering cases. The negotiator gets some great deals for his clients through sheer attrition but sometimes browbeats clients into admitting to things they didn't do because they've now been in jail long enough to be sentenced to "time served."

The better public advocates will choose the method that best fits the particular case. Traverso was a better public advocate. He had carefully researched the facts affecting both John and Amos and decided he had a good shot at prevailing at trial, and therefore he was not negotiating any plea offers. And he sought to try the case as soon as possible, before the State brought to bear any additional resources.

"So how are you going after Amos?"

"You got him immunity, and he has to testify."

"Right, but he's not going to admit to anything. Nobody knows for sure if he was even at the house that night."

"I can prove he was there."

"How can you prove it?"

"Doesn't matter. Once the jury gets a good look at your guy and hears there's no evidence against Adams—"

"There's evidence against Adams. He and Bernice had a fight, she threw her ring in his face . . ."

Traverso already knew all this, of course. He wasn't listening to me, anyway. He continued with his narration, or rehearsal, or whatever it was.

"We're going for broke," he said. "No lesser included instructions for manslaughter, no nothing. John goes up on the whole thing for fifty years, or he walks."

I tried to make an emphatic whistle, but it didn't come out quite right. One thing was clear. Traverso was no coward.

He said, "I don't think you quite get it."

"Get what?" I was willing to ask the dumb question. It's a sign of legal aptitude, you might say, because the dumb question is what others are embarrassed to ask and thus never learn the answers to.

"Amos Lane killed those poor girls. Everybody in town knows it."

"I don't know it."

"Yeah, well, you're the only one. He was drunk that night and prowling the streets. He flew into a rage at the baseball dugout. He was seen following the sisters up the street. Next thing anybody knows, they're dead."

"That's not proof. And you're skipping over several hours of alcoholic haze under the midnight sun during which drug dealers and other violent drunks were coming and going, including your client. We may never know what happened at that little house."

"The State has Amos's ripped shirt."

"Any of his clothing they have was seized illegally from a confidential treatment center, and I can get it thrown out."

"What about the appointment card? Going to get that thrown out?"

Here I felt a sense of slipping on ice under my feet. What appointment card? Had Joe not sent me everything? Of course, he no longer had a duty to send me anything at all, since Amos was never charged in the case. But I didn't want to let Traverso know he had worried me, at least not before he had tipped his whole hand.

"That all you got, Counselor? An appointment card?"

I hoped it wasn't one of those little cards that SATS gave patients to remind them of scheduled dates with therapists, especially if the patient named on the card was a certain client of mine.

He shut his mouth and abruptly stood up and moved to leave, as though he had already said more than he intended to.

"Hey," he said. "No offense. It's you and me against the State, right? As usual."

"I guess," I said, puzzled now by his change in demeanor. What *was* his whole hand? Maybe I should have just let him talk and never said anything at all.

"Wait. I have a question."

"What's that?" He halted, hand on the doorframe.

"The coroner said the bodies had been moved sometime after death. Who moved them? John or Amos—when they found the girls already dead after some drug dealer killed them?"

Now it was Traverso who was silent. Finally, he said: "Maybe you were right earlier. We never will know all the details. I'm due at the DA's. If I get anything over there that's of use to you, I'll pass it along, okay?"

"Yeah, thanks—we will, too."

He strode out the door, and Liz watched him go with curious eyes.

WEARY THAT NIGHT, I took a cab home. I recognized the driver from other trips, a slender Asian who was so quiet I hadn't gotten to know him as I had other drivers. Sitting in the musty back seat for the ten-minute drive, I felt a need to talk to some neutral human being who was not invested in any trial outcome.

"Where are you from, if you don't mind my asking?" I asked, in my most polite tone.

"Cambodia," he answered.

I didn't know much about that part of the world beyond images of sandaled men in orange robes carrying wooden bowls, Angkor Wat, and the genocide that occurred there in the past century.

"How did you happen to come so far to Utqiagvik?"

"War," he said.

"But why here?" I persisted.

"Well . . . settlement house in California, ad in paper for drive cab."

"Did you drive a cab in Cambodia?"

"No," he said. I could see in his partial profile that he was smiling now. "Monk."

"R-e-a-l-l-y," I said, impressed. "Buddhist?"

He nodded.

"How long? How many years?"

He hesitated, thinking. "Twenty-seven," he said.

Now I fell silent, out of respect for his history and sorrow at his fate. How could a person live that life there, and then this life here? I wished I had never bothered him with my questions; still, I was glad to hear of his service to his faith. We were nearing the turn at North Star Street, and I truly wanted to ask him one more question.

"Sir, do you mind if I ask you one more question?"

"Is all right."

"Uh . . . I believe one aspect of Buddhism is a focus on peace. Could you tell me . . . Would you mind . . . How does a person seek peace?"

It seemed like such a simplistic, dumb question, but I figured he knew more of an answer than anyone else I had met.

He was silent until we were stopped in front of my house. Then he said in a quiet voice, "Give up want."

I accepted this answer as I would an offering in a bowl, though I didn't understand it, and gave him all the money I had in my purse, which was about twice the fare.

Michael's truck was no longer parked in front of the house.

"Thank you for the ride. Good night. Thank you for the answer."

It was not until the dogs were fed and walked, and I'd eaten dinner and watched a program and was on my futon under the electric blanket, that I suddenly understood what the former monk had said. Give up want. Don't want a trial to go a certain way. Don't want Michael to do a certain thing.

Don't want outcomes. Don't want control. Perhaps peace is the only value one should want, but then one has to find the path to it.

I dozed off thinking that the cab driver had a twenty-seven-year head start on me.

16

Gifts make slaves like whips make dogs.
DANISH EXPLORER PETER FREUCHEN, QUOTING AN INUIT HUNTER WHO GAVE HIM NEEDED MEAT, SAYING HE DIDN'T WANT THANKS BECAUSE NEXT YEAR HE MIGHT BE THE HUNGRY ONE

I WAS TRIMMING MY FEEBLE, SCENTLESS PINK IMPATIENS and trying to give them enough water but not too much, when I heard Carol slam down her phone.

She stalked into my office. "I knew this was going to happen."

"What has happened?" The five local backup generators had failed, the ice was coming in, Alaska Airlines had canceled its Utqiagvik route—what?

"That was SATS. Liz is in detox."

I sat down heavily on my office chair. Carol came closer, enjoying her role as news oracle.

"Did she OD? Has she been arrested?"

"They said she wanted potato chips. She wants you to bring her some."

"This may be *good* news, that she's in detox."

"It's not exactly good news if now we don't have anybody to answer the phone or open the files. I've been trying to tell you we need a reliable person who can really help us."

I stood and took up my purse and my coat.

"You don't understand, Carol. Liz helps us more in an hour just by being here than some bureaucratic clerk could help us in a week. See you in a bit."

I left her standing there, knowing she would think my comment rude and that soon I would probably hear about it from Anchorage, but I was tired of waiting for Carol to catch on to what a law office was and how hard it was to run one in a remote area.

And Liz was my friend.

SATS was only a couple of blocks from the courthouse. I had never been farther inside the facility than the front desk and wasn't sure they would let me see Liz, since she was in the detox unit. Even if they didn't, she would get the message that I had come, and just that fact might help, too. I didn't think I could get away with claiming I represented her in order to be able to talk to her.

The cute receptionist explained that for permission to visit a client in detox, she would have to check with both the director, Pete Petersen, he of Amos Lane's arraignment testimony, and with Liz. I sat down among the plastic philodendrons and relentlessly pastel woodwork of the waiting room and tried not to be irritated by them. The cycle of addiction was such a heart- and family-rending process, and the addicts such damned souls, that I found lavender tweed wallpaper and matching molding so inappropriate, so disconnected, as to be annoying. No doubt the designer meant well, thinking to soothe raw feelings, needs, and desperation with nursery colors.

The receptionist returned with a smile. Both okays had been granted, and would I please follow her?

The detox was a couple of clinical bedrooms behind locked doors. It surprised and hurt me to see Liz's slender, restless form lying on a gurney, swathed in a much-washed hospital gown, her alert, almost feral face now still and paled to a sickly yellow. When she saw me, she sat up straight, and tears slid down her cheeks.

She put her hands to her face. Not the Liz I knew. I leaned in to hug her. When her sobs had subsided, we were both a little embarrassed, and I stepped away and pulled over a white plastic bucket chair to sit at her side.

"How're you doing, kiddo?"

She propped a pillow behind her back and took a minute to catch her breath. Then she said, "I'm lyin' here at death's door, and all I get is 'How're you doing, kiddo?'"

"What am I supposed to say? I don't know what to say. I never went through this with anybody before."

"You *taniks* are hopeless."

"I don't see any Eskimos here."

"'Cause I didn't call any. I could fill this whole building if I wanted to."

I didn't doubt her word. "So why didn't you call them?"

"I didn't want to worry anybody."

"Oh, I see. Me, it's okay if you worry."

"You worry all the time anyway. Speaking of worries, how's . . ."

"Liz, I left work and came over here because you're in goddamn detox, not to talk about my . . . So . . . what happened?"

She shrugged.

"I was afraid you OD'd or got arrested."

"There was this . . . party, see?"

"Yeah?"

"It didn't really start out as a party. Some people dropped by. Somebody brought something, and then somebody else brought something else, and it ended up being . . . a fairly big party. Know what I mean?"

"I guess," I said.

"The next morning, I woke up and looked around. Everybody was spread all over the furniture and the floor. And I had the craving already. I just wanted . . . one more. An upper, so I could get up. Or a downer, so I could go back to sleep."

I stared at my hands in my lap, listening.

"I started crawling around searching for anything that somebody had dropped. Checking people's hands, pockets, sleeves, cigarette packs, shoes for anything I could find. All of a sudden I thought, Fuck this! This is not the way I want to live my life, crawling around on the floor looking for leftover dope. I'm better than this. I've got kids. Someday I'll have grandkids."

I resisted an urge to holler, Hallelujah!

"Liz, I'll do anything in the world to help. I mean it."

"Except bring potato chips? Think of all the booze at your birthday party, and all I asked for was some lousy potato chips."

"Okay, okay. I just came straight here when I heard. Will they let you have potato chips? What's your pleasure, Ms. Kanayurak—salt and vinegar? Barbecue? I'll bring you six of each."

"What about your cases? What about the Ipalook trial?"

"Hell with 'em. You're getting well."

I kissed the top of her cigarette-smelling head and headed for Stuaqpak.

NELSON TRAVERSO COURTEOUSLY sent over John Adam's videotaped confession to the murders of his fiancée and her sister. Carol and I put the phones on hold to watch it. I dragged a folding chair into Carol's office, and we cranked up our video monitor, a hand-me-down from the DA's last inventory. The DAs had more money and better equipment than we public defenders did, and we were happy to get their hand-me-downs.

Ellingsworth began his questions with born-and-raised stuff, his voice heavy on the drawl. How long had Mr. Adams lived in Utqiagvik? All his life; he was born here. Where did he work? For six years he's worked at UIC. How long had he known Bernice and Wanda? All his life. They went to grade school together. How long had he and Bernice been together? They had been together a long time and gotten engaged only recently. They had a child, a beautiful daughter.

"Oh, you have a daughter, John? I have a daughter, too. What's her name?"

"Eqalin. Her name is Eqalin."

Here Adams began to cry.

Carol and I looked at each other in shared sympathy, for once agreeing with each other. Ellingsworth dropped the drawl and started in on Adams in earnest.

"You didn't mean for it to happen, did you, John?"

Adams shook his head, sobbing.

I made a note on my legal pad that his response could mean, I didn't mean to do it, or, I didn't mean for anyone to do it, or, I never wanted it to happen at all.

"You loved her, but you just lost your temper, right?"

Adams raised his tear-streaked face to Ellsworth in wonder at his meaning.

"I sympathize with you, man. Women can drive you crazy. We all know that."

Adams nodded dumbly and said, "But—"

"What did she do? Did she sleep with somebody else? That was it, wasn't it? We know Amos Lane was there sometime that night. He's kind of a big handsome guy, ain't he?"

I shuddered.

Carol and I both scribbled on our legal pads at that point. It was obvious that the detective had just lied to the suspect. No one knew for sure who had been at the Ipalook house that night, or when. The higher courts often upheld and approved this type of police misconduct, given the difficulties of the job. Basically, the case law said it was okay for police to lie, but to me it always seemed unfair and a violation of due process. I had often filed motions trying to get statements thrown out because the suspect had been tricked and lied to. I had never won one of these motions, but you have to keep trying. Sometimes a ripe case and a good motion can change the law.

"You were just so drunk you can't remember, right?"

Adams nodded.

"But you were the only one there when you were there."

"Uh-huh."

"You never meant for anybody to get hurt, did you?"

"I guess . . . I . . ."

I could see where this was going and wanted to yell at Ellingsworth, Leave the poor guy alone, you cop-in-a-nightmare! Cops like this detective were one reason I took special pride in serving as a public defender. Court was about the only place where the little guy got a chance to yap back at the authorities who had jerked him around.

I'd had enough of watching the anguish of a helpless man. Poor John Adams was not my client. Whatever he said or didn't say was not relevant to Amos's grant of immunity. Out of curiosity, Carol was making a rookie's mistake of spending time on what did not help cover her caseload, but she would learn.

She glanced up briefly when I went back to my office and watched the remaining three hours of the video by herself. At least for once we'd had the same reaction. We both felt sorry for the bullied defendant. Would the jurors as well?

THAT NIGHT, WATCHING an episode of *Poirot* on TV, in which a much more polished video confession appeared, I heard an odd banging sound. At first I thought it was the tundra wind rattling the kunnychuck, but when the noise separated into distinct knocks, I went to the door and found three of Michael's young cousins from the barbecue. They all wore solemn expressions, and one of them held a package. I couldn't remember names, but it was the girl who had gotten on my computer and two who had found leashes upstairs and walked the dogs.

"Hello, hello!" I said. "But Michael's not here right now."

"We know," the middle, older child said. "That's why we brought you this." And she held up a cigar box tied with a ribbon.

Mystified, I beckoned them inside, and we sat on the couch while I opened the box. Within I found three Tootsie Rolls; a multicolored woven yarn bracelet; a paperback youth edition of *Little Women*, somewhat worn; and a half-empty bottle of "Fresh" cologne. Love offerings, but why, and why now?

"Michael's gone and got arrested," the computer girl blurted out. "He took his paycheck to Fairbanks, and they picked him up at the bus station, is all we know."

"Auntie Mamie is so mad, but we don't want you to feel bad," the other two said at the same time.

The girls were too young to be telling me this news or for me to discuss it with them. Staring into their earnest faces, all I could think to say was "That's so sad. I hope he's okay. Anyway, I'm happy to see you. And these are lovely presents—I will keep them forever! Would you like some ice cream?"

"Yay!" They jumped up, glad their solemn mission was done.

We went into the kitchen to share out a quart of butter brickle. Then we watched two episodes of *Gilligan's Island*, during which, instead of Gilligan and Mary Ann, I saw a dark-haired stranger watching the dancers at Liz's party, cleaning a rifle at the kitchen table, driving me out on Cakeeater Road.

Then they said it was time for them to go babysit Angela. At the door, each hugged me hard.

"We were going to be in your wedding," one said.

"We liked you better than that other girlfriend he used to have."

"I was going to get a new dress!"

"Wait a minute," I asked them. In Utqiagvik, when someone gives you a gift, you're supposed to give something back.

I went upstairs to get my ivory rose earrings and wrapped them in a Kleenex.

"Please take these to Auntie Mamie," I said. "Give her my love and tell her she has beautiful granddaughters."

After waving goodbye and blowing kisses, I shut the door so

they wouldn't see me cry. I could almost have understood losing Michael to some girlish beauty. But to some damned substance? There would be no more barbecues, no dinners with a Cary Grant movie, and probably no electrician's license.

For every client whose life had been ruined, for the suffering of their families, and for my own sweet, precious, lost relationship, I hated addiction.

17

Every part of nature teaches that the passing of one life is the making of room for another.
HENRY DAVID THOREAU

THE IPALOOK TRIAL WAS A WEEK AWAY. IN THE MEANTIME, I had to focus on an unrelated misdemeanor jury trial. I was mulling over strategies for cross-examination while I locked my dead bolt and watched the bus stop on North Star Street, but I didn't see the bus. What I saw was a white bear coming out of the ditch on the other side of the road.

I stopped still, key in hand. All the warnings about polar bears flashed through my mind and, with them, the thought that I had never, ever expected to see one in person.

The bear ambled to the middle of the roadway and gazed about. I knew his beautiful, terrible self from photos, ivory carvings, and movies—the cute puppy ears, the sloping forehead, the long shank of his neck stretching out from narrow shoulders, the smooth haunches, the shaggy, boot-like ankles. Wind ruffled his thick yellowish fur, which turned crystalline and fleecy white on the tips. He glanced in my direction. He halted, still on all fours, and with his shiny black nostrils huffed the air. He stared at me almost cross-eyed, like I was an oddly behaving log or snowdrift. Then his eyes and ears snapped into radar lock, and he stood up to his full height.

He recognized prey.

For an instant, I registered the fact that, yes, he looked just like the bear in the glass case at the Fairbanks airport, all eight feet of him, and then came the awareness that we were not in an airport lobby and I was face-to-face with all the warnings I had not heeded. Terror seized me like I had never known before—not of death or of darkness but of being lifted into the air and hearing all my ribs snap, of claws raking through my eyes, of the bear breaking off pieces of me to eat while I still lived.

A gurgle came out of my throat. My right hand twitched as though to grasp some useless weapon I didn't have, and the key fell from my fingers. I wanted to retreat back into the doorless kunnychuck, but he would corner me there, and anyway, I couldn't move. I heard a strange loud scraping noise. Was there another bear I hadn't yet seen?

The bear dropped down to four feet and cautiously crossed the road toward me. He sniffed to the right and left and increased his pace. I could now have told him from other bears. He had a dirty patch on his right shoulder, and the opposite ear was ragged.

"Great God, let me die quick," I prayed.

I braced myself with one hand on the wall. I heard the humming of a mosquito near my ear and thought, I won't be bothered with mosquitoes much longer. Now the bear was so close I could have tossed him a biscuit. The sound at my ear turned into a buzz approaching from the left side, but I dared not look. If I took my eyes off the bear, he would be upon me. Maybe the droning sound was a plane. Maybe someone in the sky would watch me being eaten and I would not have to die alone.

"Hai! Hai!" a voice shouted.

A silver snow machine zoomed up behind the bear, its tracks screeching against the gravel of the road. The bear turned toward it and rose again to its full height. The metal beast charged between me and the bear. I jumped backward into the kunnychuck, and the bear retreated onto the road. The snow machine stopped, whined on the gravel, and ground its gears. I wondered why a snow machine was running when there was no snow. The bear stood still, watching the gasoline creature, and so did I. I saw two black-haired men astride the machine, and the one on the back held a long black gun. The machine leaped toward the bear, who batted at it with a great forepaw but missed.

"Hey! Hey, bear!"

They made another pass between the bear and me.

The men yelled at the bear as though he were a cow in a pasture. The snow machine bucked backward and then forward as they herded the white beast away from me, but it swerved back toward the house, reluctant to give up a catch to the machine. In all his life this polar bear had never known anything more fearsome than himself.

The rider on the back leveled the long black gun, and there came a deafening boom.

The snow machine paused.

The bear turned his muzzle skyward, as if testing a scent. Then he sat down hard on the road and looked around, puzzled. Another shot and the bear's chest heaved in response. The bear lay down on the gravel and sighed a long shuddering sigh.

The snow machine riders and I watched the bear die.

The driver climbed off the snow machine to check the bear, and the shooter walked over to me. It was Clair Okpeaha, my neighbor.

"Hello," he said, putting a hand on my shoulder and looking down into my face. "You okay? Some bears came into the landfill this morning. Don't you have a CB radio?"

I couldn't quite speak but managed to shake my head.

"Needs to be reported to Public Safety. Will you call it in?"

I bobbed my head up and down. Involuntarily, my eyes sank to the door key lying in the grit of the kunnychuck at my feet.

Okpeaha's gaze followed my glance. He picked up the key, unlocked the door, and handed my key to me. Amused, he went back to examine the bear. He and the driver felt its ribs and teeth and raised each foot to look at the claws.

Several people walked up from nowhere and gathered around the bear. I saw among them the elder Joshua Ahvakana.

"Nice job, Matu," he said to the driver. "Good shooting, Clair."

The driver raised a forefinger in acknowledgment. "I think I ruined my treads on the gravel," he said.

Behind me, inside the house, there was a ringing sound. It took me a while to realize that it was coming from my phone. I went to answer it, remembering that I had a trial set and that somehow I had to get to the courthouse, that prospective jurors would already be filing into the courtroom. I should probably call a cab instead of waiting for the bus. Maybe it was the court calling because I was late.

"Hello," a man's voice said. "I'm trying to reach Rebecca Wright."

"It's me. Uh, I mean, this is she," I said.

"Rebecca—hi! You're a hard person to find. What the heck are you doing in Utqiagvik, Alaska?"

"Huh?"

"I'm sorry—you don't have any idea who this is. Jim Stevens. From law school in Memphis. Remember?"

"Oh" was all I could manage.

"We were in Con Law together, and we used to have coffee sometimes, and there was that one day when you came in the lounge and said this dog had been hit and you needed somebody to take notes in class for you while you went to help it."

"Yes . . ."

"I heard you had been widowed. I'm sorry . . . the law school didn't have your forwarding address for a while, but then after that scholarship fund drive, they had your phone number."

"They did?"

"Listen, it sounds like I've called at a bad time. Let me give you my number, and if you feel like it, you can give me a call sometime."

I took out my little black book from the shoulder bag still slung around my neck. He recited his number and I wrote it down, tore off the slip of paper, and put it in my pocket.

"All right. Glad I reached you. You be careful up there."

I was silent.

"You're not going to call, are you?" he said.

"There was a bear, and I have a trial . . ."

"Oh. A trial. A bear? Okay, I get it. You're busy. I'm going to get off here. Good luck with your trial."

As soon as he hung up, I punched down the receiver hook and called Public Safety to come and look at the bear, and then I called Tuttu Taxi.

When I went back outside, Public Safety was already there, and an officer was prodding the bear and making notes. A couple of cars and more pedestrians had stopped to look, and now about twenty people were standing around the bear.

I walked over to Mr. Okpeaha and tried to shake his hand, but he was busy talking to the officer. I went to the driver of the snow machine and put out my hand and tried to say thanks, but he grabbed me first and hugged me and said he was glad I was okay.

I went to my neighbor again, remembering his ancestor who had run the thirteen miles from Walakpa Bay to tell the people of Utqiagvik that Will Rogers and Wiley Post had crashed and were dead. Clair had the matinee-idol handsomeness of Bobby Nashookpuk and had acquired a reputation for being an honorable and reliable neighbor. I thought he was the best neighbor I ever had.

"You were so f-f-fast," I stammered. "You were so brave. I was so scared. You were like cowboys—you drove the bear away. Thank you. Without you it would be me lying there in the road."

"Not much of you," he said, smiling. "I'm glad to get one. I got one year before last."

I looked again at the bear. Public Safety had stretched him out, and I could see the wound in his chest and the hole in his throat. The wind still ruffled the fur on his shoulders. The white bear was beautiful, but he was a killer. I was sorry he was dead but glad I hadn't died, especially that way.

A Public Safety officer came over to us. "Can I get everybody's names, please?" While he was jotting them down, he said, "This was a busy bear. A couple of hours ago he chased Mayor Ahmaogak up Momegana Street. The mayor had to dive into a dumpster to get away from him."

"That's why we were tracking him," Clair Okpeaha said. "Joshua followed him all morning."

"The bear was hungry," the snow machine driver added. "No meat on his ribs at all."

My knees trembled.

"Well, you can all read about it in the papers," the officer said. "This will make the Anchorage news."

The cab rolled up, and I got into it. When I reached the courthouse and went into the clerk's office to get a list of the venire, two clerks behind the counter stopped stamping and stapling papers to stare at me.

"Are you okay? You look like you saw a ghost," the magistrate's clerk said.

"There was a bear. A white bear came to my house. My neighbor Clair Okpeaha shot it. Am I late? Is the court waiting?"

BY THE TIME we finished selecting a jury, most of the jurors had heard about the bear on the tundra drums and probably felt sorry for me. After hearing from witnesses, they quickly acquitted my client.

I was putting on my parka to go catch the bus when I felt a scrap of paper in my pocket. It was a phone number. I remembered writing it down, and now I remembered who had called. Jim hadn't taken notes for me that day in law school. He came with me to try to help the dog, an old shepherd who died anyway, but at least didn't die alone. At the time, I was married and Jim was engaged to someone else. The paper seemed important, and I put it back in my pocket.

18

Time is an illusion.
ALBERT EINSTEIN

LIZ CALLED ME FROM DETOX AT TWO IN THE MORNING to say that Randy had not come home to his cousin's house. Randy's cousin couldn't go look for him because she was taking care of her niece's baby.

"Can you go look for him?" Liz asked.

I hesitated, remembering what a sleepless night would do to the next day's schedule. But how can you say no when your detoxing friend tells you that your suicidal teen client whose mom is dying is missing? I got up and called for a cab. I had no idea where to look for Randy, but I could ride around on Utqiagvik's thirteen miles of road to see whether I could spot him or find someone who might know his whereabouts. On impulse I took three of the half dozen twenties in my small cash reserve, just in case they were needed. Utqiagvik was the only place where I had ever kept cash at home. The Arctic cold seemed to operate as a burglar deterrent, and I had never worried about break-ins.

My driver was a lanky kid from Oregon. Cruising through

Browerville, he told me he worked three jobs—cab driver, janitor, and pizza delivery—and lived with his mom. So far he had saved $62,000.

"Sixty-two thousand dollars!" I said. "How old are you? If you don't mind my asking."

"Nineteen," he told me.

"What are you going to do with all that money? Go to school? Buy a sailboat? Start a business?"

"Right now, it's just fun to think about all of it in the bank with my name on it."

We were turning inland at the freshwater lagoon when I noticed a gathering of cars and four-wheelers beside a weathered box-like house. Several young people were going in the door. Could the kid in the middle be Randy? He looked the right size, with similar hair and his ever-present red satin basketball warm-up jacket, but the face was turned away, and I couldn't be sure.

"Stop!"

The driver stopped the cab so quickly I came close to bumping my nose on the back of the seat.

"I . . . uh . . . thought I might get out here and walk a bit."

The kid looked back at me, and then his glance slid to the house with all the vehicles beside it.

"You're not going in that place, are you?"

". . . No, of course not. How much do I owe you for the ride?"

"Well, let's see, so far it's . . . fifteen dollars."

No wonder he had $62,000 in the bank, I thought as I fished out one of my twenties. I got out, but he seemed reluctant to drive away.

"Watch out for polar bears on this side of town," he said.

It occurred to me I might know more about polar bears than he did. I said I would.

"And don't go in that house. It's a different kind of people."

Ruffled by his warning, I walked a few yards in the opposite direction from the house, in case he was watching in his rearview mirror. I could hear music that sounded like somebody's mixtape of favorite soft rock. I turned around and headed for the house.

At the door I paused to take stock. Perhaps, after all, I should pay better attention to what I was doing. Perhaps it would have been a good idea to put my remaining money in my sock, and at least make sure someone knew where I was.

"Sister Golden Hair" came on. I liked that song.

I stepped into the kunnychuck. The place was as dark as a cheap bar and smelled like one, that familiar amalgam of cigarette smoke, beer, a dirty floor, and urine. As I waited for my eyes to adjust, I also caught an outdoorsy scent from the damp fur jackets that hung on hooks on the wall.

There were several people gathered around a card table on the right and, to my left, a few couples dancing. I saw a doorway on the far wall, draped with a curtain. In the middle of the room, a mattress served as a sofa for several men deep in conversation. Beside them a large-screen television mutely played a Guns N' Roses video. With a start I noticed I was not the only *tanik* present. There was a second card table just past the mattress, and around it sat and stood the toughest, leanest, meanest-looking *taniks* I had seen since I handled a methamphetamine case in Harlan, Kentucky. The meth cases involved so many codefendants that conflicts of interest made representation difficult, and public defenders became road warriors as they tried to provide additional counsel to affected offices all over the state.

An image swam up in my mind of Officer Tidwell sitting beside my morning glories, telling me his theory of the Ipalook case. He said there had been a lot of dealers in town. Well, they were still here.

Good time to leave. I had tried. If Randy was here, I couldn't see him.

Someone jostled me from behind.

"Hi, honey, gotta bottle?" a male voice inquired.

He had been talking to the back of my parka, because when

he glimpsed my *tanik* face, he murmured, “Sorry.” He smelled of whiskey.

“Uh, no,” I said.

“S’okay,” he said. “I got one. You getsa next one, okay?”

“Uh, sure,” I said.

With an arm linked in mine, he propelled me into the smoky room. Several people turned to greet us, recognizing my companion.

“Is that your sweetie?” a voice called out to him. “You got a good one!”

The room broke out in laughter.

My new friend wore a man’s shorter parka, green with elaborate embroidery on the shoulders, and baggy white canvas pants. He led me to a table of poker players—fortunately, the nearer table, which was ringed with friendly Inupiat, not the second table full of scary *taniks*. Chairs were added for us, and the table became so crowded that we sat knee to knee and thigh to thigh. In an elaborate pantomime, with everyone at the table watching in silence, my escort threaded his right hand inside the left shoulder of his parka and withdrew from the sleeve an unopened plastic fifth of cheap vodka. One of the flat bottles, not the round ones.

The poker players cheered.

Maybe now would be a good time to leave, before drinks were served. I could just get up, smile at everyone, say I had to go pay the babysitter, and slip away. But that silhouette in the doorway had looked just like Randy. Liz’s mind would be eased, and mine, if I could find him. Here might be my only chance. If it wasn’t him, surely someone here would know Randy and his whereabouts. It wouldn’t hurt to stay a few minutes. I couldn’t afford to ride a cab all night.

My escort untwisted the top and tipped the bottle upside down. Nothing happened. The booze did not pour. I stared curiously at the bottle. A shaman’s trick?

“Frozen,” he said, amused at my amazement. “Buried in my cellar.”

I hadn't known vodka would freeze, but I guess if hydraulic fluid could freeze, so could vodka.

He had everyone's full attention, not just mine, as he withdrew a Zippo lighter from his parka pocket and began to warm the bottle, gently and carefully. He courteously handed it to me for a first sip. Not to be rude, I took a swig and passed it on. It tasted like rotten potatoes. Cheap booze is just as illegal as expensive, and if the bottle had not come in through the airport in legal fashion, I was now an accomplice to bootlegging.

Cheap booze also has the same effect as expensive stuff. After the bottle made more rounds and I had a couple more sips, just to be sociable, I found I worried less about any potential accomplice liability. I was there to look for Randy, after all. I could casually ask about him and might find out something useful. No doubt someone here was his aunt, uncle, or in-law, or past or present friend or auto shop customer. Randy himself might be in the back room with the curtained doorway.

Just as when I had played poker with Michael's mother, the deal rotated with each hand, and each new dealer called out a different style of poker as he shuffled. Creedence Clearwater replaced Axl Rose on the TV.

On my left, a diminutive fellow with a dark mustache asked my companion for his bottle. He passed it over, and it was returned to him empty of its last drop.

"Your turn now, huh?" my new friend said, nudging me in the midsection with an elbow.

"I guess so," I said, to be agreeable. "Yeah, maybe."

"Where you gonna get a bottle?" he persisted. "How big a bottle you gonna get?"

I realized he was not going to drop the issue.

I also realized I was ready for another drink myself. Watching them share the small, precious bottle had gone against my selfish *tanik* grain and made me thirstier. I had not grown up in a culture that valued and encouraged sharing, like the Inupiat's did, and was not good at it like they were. The problem was I didn't know how to get a bottle. The town was, after all, dry. Damp, rather. Same difference when you yourself were suddenly feeling dry and couldn't just go to a store and get what you wanted.

"You know where we can get a bottle?" I whispered to my friend.

"You got money?" he whispered back.

"Uh, sure," I said. But I had given one of my twenties to the cab driver and received in return only $5. Would $45 be enough to buy in Utqiagvik what in Fairbanks or Anchorage only cost $7.50? I had read in police reports that $50 was the going local rate. I didn't think the bootlegger would take a check.

My friend got up and crossed to a corner, where he burrowed under some jackets and found a telephone.

"Bubble-up?" he said into the mouthpiece. "I'm over at Porky's. You near?" He looked over at me, smiled a conspiratorial smile, and rubbed his fingertips together in the universal gesture for money.

"Cab outside," somebody called.

I followed him to the door and handed over my bills, thinking that bootleggers must circle-hover in cabs, like the Strategic Air Command antinuclear aircraft did at one time. He gave my money to a fair-haired girl-next-door-appearing young woman, who pulled a bottle from the shoulder of her apple-green baseball jacket.

"Fifty," the young woman said. "Who's she? This is only forty-five."

Mary-Jane-the-bootlegger scored over a 500 percent markup.

"Fifty a bottle, seventy-five if it's late or a holiday," my friend said to me.

"Is that the *tanik* price?"

"Always same price. Eskimo, *tanik*, same. Risky for her, you know." To the vendor he added, "It's okay. She's with me."

"If she doesn't want the bottle, I have other calls."

She took a step toward the opening of the kunnychuck. My escort took out a ten and handed it over.

She put the bottle into my hand and went out the door. It wasn't for me, I told myself. I would share it with my companion and the card players. Maybe they would share with me some information on Randy.

At that moment, a poker player turned off the TV and hollered, "Cops coming! Go home!"

Chairs skidded backward on the uneven linoleum. Shapes leaped up around me as it dawned on me what was happening and panic knotted my gut. Why was Public Safety coming? Was it for the bootlegger? And for me? Feet thudded past.

"Aiee-ee-eee! Aieee-eee!" someone keened.

The curtains on the back door parted and Randy came out, pulling down his sweatshirt over his jeans. A heart-wrenchingly beautiful girl followed him, petite and slender in her black parka and pants, her hair hanging heavy like a mantle of mink on one side of her delicate, startled face.

Randy spotted me and, with only the slightest double take, grabbed me by the wrist as he passed, his fingers gripping my flesh like steel pincers. I went along, reflexively tucking the precious bottle against my chest.

Outside, people hustled into cars or onto four-wheelers. Some strode up the road or out across the tundra. Motors roared into life, but I didn't hear any sirens.

Yet.

Randy waved at somebody. A dirty, cream-colored Datsun backed up beside us. Randy opened the door to its rear seat and shoved me so hard that I slid in headfirst on the upholstery. He hollered something in Inupiaq at the driver and shut the door against my feet, leaning on it until it latched. The car paused a moment with a shifting of the clutch, then leaped forward. I sat up. I could see vehicles and people dispersing in all directions, and now I heard the sirens.

A young kid with tinted glasses wearing a beaver-fur cap with earflaps was driving, hunched over the wheel. An old man with fluffy white hair sat in the middle, and a bundled-up woman leaned on the passenger door. They seemed to be arguing about which way to go. On impulse, I slid the flat bottle into the top of my sleeve, as I had seen others do.

We roared up one gravel road and down two more, passing from shacks and ranch ramblers to the center of Utqiagvik. Were they planning to hide in plain sight?

We stopped by a midnight-blue pickup with huge raised tires that was nosed up to the timber railing in front of Stuaqpak. Randy's beautiful young companion was perched on its hood, and Randy and a young man with a blond butch haircut and gunslinger eyes, in a leather jacket, stood before her. The three of them appeared to be arguing with each other.

"Why did Public Safety go out?" the white-haired man wanted to know when we piled out of the Datsun.

"Randy, Randy—are you okay?" I asked.

"What were you doing there?" Randy asked me.

"Who's that?" the young beauty asked him.

"I think they were just hoping to find somebody on probation who wasn't supposed to be drinking," my driver said. "Or maybe there was a warrant out for one of the dealers."

The elder gentleman patted my arm. "You all right?"

"Yes, I . . . uh, thank you," I said. "How about you?"

Randy asked my host-driver whether he could run me out to Browerville, but he shook his head.

"Would, but I can't—I gotta get home for the kids."

"Come on, we gotta go," the young beauty said to Randy, hopping down from the hood. "Cabs come here all the time," she said to me.

"I'm sorry to be trouble, but I . . ." I began, embarrassed and conscious once more of the sirens blaring in the distance. "I, uh, lent my money to a friend at the card game."

She glanced at the bulge in my sleeve. "You got a bottle, I bet," she said, and her eyes lit up with merriment at my expense.

"Chip in for cab money for my lawyer." Randy grabbed the driver's beaver hat and held it out first to the young gunslinger, who dug in his jeans and dropped in a ten while still glaring at Randy. Busted flat in downtown Utqiagvik, I was reduced to having my teenage client beg on my behalf.

"Oh, thank you, thank you," I babbled.

"In Utqiagvik everyone shares," the blue-eyed kid said. "Even with *taniks*."

The Datsun riders waved and drove off. The youthful goddess boarded the truck, and the boys leaped in after her. The truck backed up so quickly it seemed to be bucking and took off in the opposite direction from Browerville. Maybe they were going to Hollywood.

Downtown Utqiagvik, all block and a half of it, was perfectly safe at any hour, since there was essentially no street crime in town. I felt a bit lonely, though, suddenly on my own, but glad that tomorrow I could call Liz at the rehab and tell her Randy had a beautiful girlfriend, so maybe we could take him off suicide watch. Surely he would not want to harm himself when he had this relationship. Surely not.

A faded blue Public Safety Travelall lumbered toward me, siren no longer blaring. I wasn't worried about Public Safety anymore. I was just a private citizen standing on a public corner. I recognized the two officers from having worked with them on cases and gave them a polite wave. They looked at me curiously but did not stop. Since the jail was right across the street, they probably figured I had come into town to see some newly arrested client.

Then I remembered the bottle-bulge in my sleeve.

If necessary, I could argue that, for all they knew, I had purchased the vodka legally in Fairbanks and lost the receipt. This argument had never worked with a jury, but maybe the officers would give me a break.

I glanced at my watch and saw it was almost four. I went over to the timber railing in front of Stuaqpak and sat down. Time, the minutes and hours that had jerked forward so abruptly earlier in the evening, now stopped. Time in Utqiagvik did not proceed in orderly, measured steps as it did in other places, I had learned. Tonight I'd lost track of time—I had spent so much of it looking for Randy, and now I was wasting it.

Sleep deprived and slightly drunk, still sitting on the Stuaqpak railing, I pondered Arctic time. I remembered reading, on a pre-Michael Saturday night, a scholarly article by a fellow named Bluedorn at the University of Missouri who wrote that time was a "social construct" and there was no such thing as the "correct" universal time. For Arctic dwellers, "time" was more often defined by what others call seasons: time to clean out cellars in the spring, then to move to fish camp or go berry picking, then for fall whaling. When the first central schools were built in the 1950s, the Inupiat began to change their nomadic lifestyles so that their children could attend school. The end of the brief summer was no longer the time to get ready for whaling but to register children for classes.

Bluedorn argued that it was the use of machines—printing presses, huge looms requiring shifts of workers, and locomotives—that slotted Europeans into hours and minutes. At first, even trains were not "on time" because local times varied. The variations had not been a problem because no one got from place to place that fast. The growing networks of fast trains required fixed times to keep from running into each other. Time became standard, and the trains ran on schedules and timetables, and so did we.

Henry Ford made a watch that told two times at once, railroad time and local time.

Now time had become the pressure grid of deadlines and time clocks and schedules in which we all lived. "To everything there is a season, and a time for every purpose under heaven," King Solomon wrote 2,500 years ago, but time was different then.

As I waited for a cab to show up, I thought about the fact that we still had no timetable for the last night of Bernice and Wanda Ipalook's lives, no schedule showing what they had done that weekend, no outline that established what time each witness saw them. Because of the midnight sun, Saturday and Sunday had run into each other. We didn't know who their last visitor was. We might never know.

Could a jury figure out what happened to Bernice and Wanda? Jurors were collectively smart. I remembered hearing of a multiple axe murder that happened long before I came to Utqiagvik. The only suspect explained that his clothes were bloody because he tried to help the victims when he found them. No confession, no eyewitnesses, no fibers, and no fingerprints were presented at trial, but the jurors noticed something that had gone unseen by Public Safety, the DA, and the defense counsel. They observed drops of blood on the *back* of the suspect's parka. The jury decided the blood fell there when the defendant raised the axe over his head to strike again. They convicted him.

I looked at my watch once more—now 4:05—and then I took it off and shoved it into my pocket. Maybe I didn't need to know the time of day anymore.

The sound of a motor approached, and a Tuttu Taxi appeared from behind the church.

"Where you want to go?" the driver asked in an accent I didn't recognize. The escape adrenaline had not subsided, and I didn't feel tired enough to go home and sleep.

"Uh, take me to the edge of town," I said.

"Which edge?"

"The prettiest," I said.

"I take you to my favorite."

Unlike most cab drivers, who wore jeans, this one had on nice slacks and a harmonizing jacket. I couldn't see much of his face, but he might have been Asian. The large cell phone on a battery pack at his side chimed, and he took it up.

"No, no, I say to stack second shipment and send first back. They will have to—I don't care. Yes, all the way to Anchorage. Right size here by Tuesday or lose sale. Yes, yes. That right."

He hung up and waved his hand toward a café we were passing, where a few lights burned.

"New people, always everything they all screw up," he said.

"Oh, you work there too?" I asked, used to the Utqiagvik custom of multiple jobs.

"Is my place. I own," he said.

I studied the back of his head and saw the nape had many gray hairs. His piece of Utqiagvik real estate with a going business on it would be worth . . . My eyes were registering dollar signs when he pointed to a snapshot rubber-banded to his windshield visor.

"Bride arrive soon. Money enough now."

"How nice. Where is your bride?"

"Korea, of course. Parents arrange. You surprised? Work better, parents arrange. Parents know better, you know?"

I didn't feel I had an opinion worth giving on the subject. "Congratulations to you both. Many happy years," I said.

He nodded and murmured something, and we set off through the early morning fog. Tethered dogs appeared and disappeared beside us like in a shaman's dream. Once we reached the tundra, the mist closed down around us so completely that the road disappeared, and the driver paused the car. I lowered my window and wisps of cloud came inside, smelling like dew. Forms took shape in the haze, silent silhouettes with oddly burdened heads and a plodding gait. Caribou, or their ghosts, one after the other, antlered or smooth, great and small. I lost track of how long we watched them. We seemed to have entered a different kind of time.

An opening appeared in the vapor, and I saw an expanse of white plain. We drove among the caribou and toward the plain for perhaps one minute or one mile—now time was distance—until a lake came into view. The driver stopped, and I got out and walked to the edge of the water.

It occurred to me that I was now less of a *tanik* than I had been this time yesterday, or when I had first driven out to this place, what seemed a long time ago, with Michael, in the white limo. All this time I was learning how much I did not know. Some say this realization is the beginning of wisdom, when you cease to believe that you or your culture have all the answers.

I got back in the car and asked the driver to take me home. I still had time for a little nap before work. Maybe this time tomorrow, Liz would still be sober, Randy would still be alive, and we would begin to have some answers in the Ipalook murders.

19

The shaman is the figure at the beginning of history that unites the doctor, the scientist and the artist into a single notion of care-giving and creativity.
TERENCE McKENNA

THE IPALOOK TRIAL LOOMED ON THE HORIZON LIKE an avalanche. The State planned to prove that John Adams murdered his fiancé, Bernice Ipalook, in a fit of jealousy because she had been with Amos Lane, then had killed the only eyewitness, her sister, Wanda. Nelson Traverso, counsel for Adams, would show the jury that it was my client, Amos Charles Lane, who had strangled the sisters while in a drunken rage.

Jury selection was scheduled to begin midweek; opening statements, probably the following Monday.

Meanwhile, I still had to keep up with my other cases as best I could and, in Liz's absence, the ringing phone. For a break one morning, I grabbed the mail pouch and trudged the two blocks to the modest clapboard structure that served as our federal building.

The lobby was gritty underfoot, and a dormitory smell arose from the old men in fur jackets who sat along the window ledges. I joined the line at the counter, eavesdropping on the chatter.

"Manu, when you back from Anaktuvuk?"

"Lend me some of your bingo money, man."

"Perry, you got fat. Too many Eskimo donuts."

"Not fat. Muscle. Alma work him out every night."

"And sometimes at lunchtime."

When the lady ahead of me finally finished visiting with the postal clerk in what I recognized from court as Tagalog, it was my turn.

"Hello, lawyer lady," the bright-eyed Filipina clerk said.

"Hello, Miss Pretty. Do you have any mail for the public defender?"

She brought out a packet of mass mail items and added a four-inch stack that was already bundled for us. I took the load and was smiling my thanks when a bony hand grabbed my wrist. Startled, I looked around to see who it was but saw only cream-colored wall. I was staring over the head of a tiny woman with a wizened face like the dolls that craftspeople make out of dried apples. She wore a green babushka and was muttering something to herself.

"Yes, ma'am?" I said, trying to be as polite as a *tanik* could possibly be, since she was an elder.

"More death coming," she said, now plucking at my parka sleeve with a crooked forefinger.

Not sure whether I had understood her correctly, nor whether she herself understood what she was saying, I said again, "Yes, ma'am."

"I saw him. He follow them up the road."

I stared into her glistening eyes. We mirrored and magnified each other's alarm.

"Laughing—they were laughing. He give Bernice a ride."

"He did?" I said, mesmerized.

"Three deaths. Three sisters. Now more death come."

I shook my head to break her gaze. No, there would not be more death. Amos Lane was under lock and key at SATS. John Adams was at FCC until the trial started. Randy Ahtanguarak had a beautiful girlfriend to live for. The old lady was wrong. And what three sisters? I knew of only Bernice and Wanda.

"Public Safety never ask me," she said. "They never ask about that old death. About Harriet."

"Oh? What about Harriet?" I was suddenly alert.

"Hate. You hate?" she said.

"Hate who?" Did she mean the follower of the girls, or rapists and murderers, or death itself?

"Public Safety," she said, and turned away and walked out the door.

I stood a moment looking after her, teetering on a discarded catalog underneath my feet. Then the fur-clad lady in line behind me began to push forward, and I followed the elder lady out of the building, but when I got to the street, she was nowhere in sight.

Trudging back to the office, I could not help wondering whether I had just heard a prophecy. I knew some Natives said that shamans could predict the future. This lady did not look like the artists' renderings of shamans on the postcards at the airport, but who were they to know what a shaman looked like? I had learned by now that many *tanik* expectations had no basis in reality. Whoever or whatever she was, surely her prediction was wrong. It had to be wrong. I hoped it was wrong.

AFTER I MADE a last-minute scan of witness statements, another effort to clarify the elusive timetable of events on the weekend the Ipalook sisters died, it was almost seven by the time I left for the Browerville bus.

Now there was no pickup truck in front of my house, but there was a dark shape on the boardwalk. The dog I had liberated from the snow waited in front of my door, standing and gravely wagging her tail as I approached. I reached down and gave her apple-domed head a pat of welcome.

"How did you find me, ice dog?" I said. "I could use some extra company."

I looked up and down the street before opening the door for her. Public defenders were not supposed to appropriate local people's dogs, even abandoned ones, but I didn't want to see her chained again. The ice dog walked inside as calmly as though she had been raised in hotel lobbies rather than on the tundra. My lab and terrier got to their feet when they saw and scented her—and the cats had already disappeared—but neither rushed forward nor barked. The newcomer paced through the living room and kitchen and went up to the sleeping loft and back down while I watched, hanging up my parka and gear.

She settled herself on the braided rug in front of the natural gas heater. My dogs approached her in turn. She allowed them to sniff her muzzle and waved her tail briefly to acknowledge the presence of each. Then she closed her eyes for a nap.

I realized that for the first time, I was in the presence of an alpha female. While I walked the other dogs and fixed myself some dinner, she did not disturb herself to pay us any attention, and only occasionally opened an eye to observe me if I spoke to her.

"Ice dog, I don't want to call you ice dog anymore. I'm trying to remember the words in Inupiaq. *Siku* is 'ice,' right? 'Dog' is *qimmiq*? How about Siku? Will you answer to Siku?"

I had a feeling that she wasn't going to answer to much of anything.

In the middle of dinner and the TV news there was a knock at the door, and she got to her feet. The other dogs barked. I went to the door, expecting Michael, but opened it to find an entire Native family—mother, father, and three children, the middle child six inches shorter than the tallest and six inches taller than the littlest—standing on my planking.

"You have our dog," the lady said.

"What dog?" I stalled.

"Our sled dog that you took."

"I didn't take her, she came here."

"How'd she get loose? You let her loose, didn't you?"

"You weren't feeding her."

"She's still our dog."

With that response we had reached an impasse. I reflected for a moment on how the newspaper headline would read: "Public Defender Steals Native Kids' Dog." Then I thought of Siku, as I wanted to call her, dragged back out to the inevitable chain on the ice.

"Would you like to sell her?" I heard myself ask.

The mother and father conferred.

"How much?" the mother asked.

I wasn't in a mood to quibble. "Two hundred and fifty dollars," I astonished myself by offering.

Another conference.

"Deal," the lady said.

I invited them in, but they chose to stay on the ramp while I made out a check.

"She wasn't really our dog," the woman explained when I handed her the little slip of paper that ransomed Siku's freedom. "We were just keeping her for some friends who had to go to Anchorage for medical. Sometimes we forgot to feed her."

I nodded as though this explanation made everything fine and shook hands with each parent. They left happy.

"You are the most expensive sled dog ever to come out of this town," I said to Siku when she had settled again in her premier spot in front of the heater. She gave me a couple of thumps of pelt-heavy tail. I noticed she had made no effort to greet the family who had come to see about her, and that her golden eyes had narrowed to slits until the door was shut behind them.

I wasn't interested in TV anymore. As on several pre-Michael nights in Utqiagvik, I found myself standing at the kitchen window, looking out over the patchy grass toward neighboring houses, staring up the empty street, wishing some store, some lounge, some café were open so I could drop by for a few minutes to be around other people without having to represent them or be responsible for their fates.

A dog tethered nearby howled. The howl was answered from far out on the tundra, first from beyond the Naval Arctic Research Laboratory, then from the other side of the airport. Several howlers joined in a chorus, their wails rising and falling, ceasing and beginning again. I knew the voices from the tundra were not dogs. The singing of wolves was higher pitched and ululating.

Shivering slightly, I tried to think of someone to call who might be willing to talk for a while without recognizing the ring for the distress signal it was. Ruefully, I remembered Della, who had brought me the shell for Randy's mom. Tonight she might say she was too busy to talk, as I had once been too busy for lunch with her. I couldn't call Liz at detox. She was supposed to be concentrating on recovery.

I remembered the phone call on the day the bear came to the door and wondered whether the little scrap of paper was still wadded up in my parka pocket.

Utqiagvik was four hours behind his time zone. It wouldn't be so terribly late in Tennessee.

My fingers found the wad of paper in the velveteen lining.

"When the night has been too lonely, and the road has been too long," I hummed to myself as I dialed the number. The phone rang many times. I had almost replaced the receiver when a sleepy voice answered.

"Oh, dear. I woke you up. I'm so sorry . . . I, uh . . . Time is so different up here. I'll call another time—"

"Alaska! Wait—it's Rebecca, isn't it? I'm glad you called. I'd about given you up. I, uh, wanted to see how you were doing, and to catch up . . ."

I sat down on the stairsteps and told him about the heavy caseload and the stress and the big salaries and the beauty of the caribou in the fog and the lousewort on the frozen gravel and watching the dawn at different hours of the day. He understood about the caseload. He was opening his own practice and working extra hours to get it started. He understood about the stress. He and his wife were divorcing, he had moved into an apartment, and his teenage children did not visit very often.

By the time I got to bed, I was so tired that I fell into a stonelike sleep until Siku came up and butted her head against my knee. I told her to go away. She persisted. I decided it might save time to go ahead and find out what she wanted. Then I could go back to sleep.

I stepped into my suede clogs and my fleecy robe and followed her downstairs. She trotted to the front door expectantly.

"Housebroken already?" I hoped so.

We went out into the predawn ether, that time of Arctic night (or day) when it is so cold and so still that the air seems incapable of sustaining life. Odd that the aurora was out in the summer. Waves of green light rolled above us like the surfing combers at Mākaha. This was not the tame rainbow of light that is printed on travel posters to lure the Japanese to expensive Fairbanks hotels in hopes of favorable conception under the northern lights. This aurora was the kind that is so potent Natives say you can hear it.

I hoped against hope Siku would jump off the boardwalk and squat right away so I could get back onto my cozy futon mattress before I was totally, irrevocably stark-staring awake. Maybe she just wanted me to see the nice aurora, and then we could both go back to bed.

But she trotted over the boardwalk to the road and stood there, waiting for me to catch up with her. Wondering what her needs were, hoping it wouldn't take long to meet them, I followed, feeling buyer's remorse over my purchase of her. I suppose it should have been an option to just leave her out on the tundra with the aurora—God knew she was used to the tundra—and go back to bed, but she seemed to have a purpose, and I wanted to know what it was.

She was trotting toward the ocean now, toward the place where I had first seen her tethered. Some kind of roots ritual? I had about had enough cold air, and my feet were chilling quickly. I was deciding to make myself turn back, with or without Siku, when I noticed some forms out on the tundra between the road and the ocean, shapes that hadn't been there before. A circle of dark shadows, arranged like the spokes of a wheel, with a snowy circle in the center. At first the silhouettes were still, then they began to move. They were dogs. They were sled dogs, each looking very much like the dog I was with.

Who had put in a new dog yard? And so quickly? I was glad to see it. Perhaps now there would be more dogsledding. I liked to see the sleds glide by, and to ride when I could. Quiet but swift. No wonder my new dog wanted to come out to greet the new neighbors. They might all be her cousins. No doubt she had even more cousins than Michael. But now she was sitting down in the middle of the road, watching very intently and not moving closer to the circle.

Then I saw that there was a man standing within the circle. He stood in the hub of one of those dog-tethering arrangements designed for quick release in areas that flood. Each chain has a loop at the end, and all the loops are staked to the earth with a single great pin that goes down through the middle of all the loops in the center of the wheel.

I tried to see in the darkness who the man was but couldn't make out his face. It was a Native man with long black hair. It didn't look like Michael. Was it Amos? He was sliding the stake out from the loops of all the chains. Surely it wasn't Amos. Amos was supposed to be in the treatment facility. He couldn't be out here at night. Could he? The dogs sprang to their feet just as Siku had done when I set her free, shaking, sniffing, testing whether they really could move or not. One raised a muzzle and yapped out a quick bark; another leaped in the air. At once all the dogs charged the center of the circle, snarling and howling, growling and roaring. I stepped back and raised a forearm to my face in defense. The man went down, screaming, in the rattle of chains and the snapping of jaws. His shrieks and the baying of the dogs rose around Siku and me, unbearably loud, becoming a great crescendo of sound that ascended into the aurora above.

I shook my head and tried to focus my eyes but could no longer see well what was happening. The noise subsided into whimpers, and the aurora faded, reverberating faintly, while I stood there, mute and frozen.

Now there came a new and different noise. It was so different from the dog noise that I had trouble recognizing it, though it resembled the aurora in the way it rose and fell. The noise went on and on until I fully opened my eyes into the darkness of my loft and realized that the phone was ringing downstairs. Groggy, I crept down to it using both hands on the railing.

Siku slept peacefully in front of the guttering stove, with the other dogs arrayed on the floor around her.

"Hello."

"Rebecca, I wouldn't wake you, but I wanted you to hear it from me," Liz said.

"What is it?"

I huddled on the bottom stair around the phone, my feet burning with cold and my shoulders shaking with dread at what she might say. She didn't speak again right away.

"It's Randy, isn't it," I finally said.

There came an odd, muffled sound from her end of the line. I waited wearily for her to tell me that Randy had gotten hurt—that he had been snowmobiling and crashed, or had OD'd and been resuscitated, or possibly that he had a gunshot wound in the arm or leg, inflicted on him or by him—and that he was now at the hospital with his mom.

Liz began sobbing into the phone. I waited, wrapping my arms around myself.

"His mom died," Liz said. "Last night around eight."

"Oh," I said.

"Randy and his girlfriend—"

"Oh, God, no . . ." Suddenly I knew what she was going to say.

I didn't think I could bear this news any more than Liz could bear to tell me. I saw again the curtained doorway and Randy emerging with his young love from their dark sanctuary, remembered the suffering in Randy's eyes while he sat in my office chair, recalled the picture of him in a basketball uniform on his father's desk in Anaktuvuk.

"They went out on the ice and . . ." She took a deep breath. "He shot her, and then he shot himself."

I rocked back and forth. "Sweet Jesus, dear Lord, help us . . ."

"She's not dead. That kid with the blue truck, he found them. Randy was already cold. She was all bloody but not dead."

I stared blurrily around my little kitchen. The refrigerator still whirred. The blue plastic jug of distilled water sat half full on the counter. The grayish window curtains hung at the dim window. Stupidly, I wished Randy had lived until the Adams trial was over. Maybe things would have been different then. I could hear, through the phone wire, Liz's low, keening moans.

"Liz, tell them to give you something so you can sleep for a while."

"What are you going to do?"

"I don't know. I may get up and go to work."

"That's what you always do."

"I'll come and see you over the weekend."

Numb, I hung up. I wanted to scream—I wanted to howl like the dogs and wolves. I wanted to lock myself in some library and read every book until I found one with answers.

Instead, I put on my parka and stepped into my boots and went outside with the three dogs. The midnight sun shone down upon us like it had the night the Ipalook sisters died, almost exactly one year earlier. The snowy owls were out, soaring and circling as they searched the tundra for mice and lemmings. Tonight the magnificence of these airborne icons seemed muted. They were neither comfort nor company.

Why, Randy?

I found myself thinking of the hunting lodge at Mayerling where the heir to the Austro-Hungarian Empire killed his beautiful young lover and himself in 1889. Like Randy, Rudolf had everything to live for—more than everything. Also like Randy, he was unable to find a future for himself. Randy couldn't see beyond his mother's tragic death, his father's indifference, and the confusion of the two cultures clashing around him. The prince lost hope in his own youthfully liberal ideas in the face of the emperor's militant conservatism, his father's refusal to listen to him, and the conflicting nationalisms that raged around them both, which eventually sparked the First World War.

No future, no hope.

Yes, I might as well go to the office. It was useless to try to sleep. The cases had to be done. There were always more cases. Someday I might be able to face the fact that Liz and I should have been able to save him, but I couldn't bear to now.

20

The crow wish'd every thing was black, the owl,
that every thing was white.
WILLIAM BLAKE

The trial of State of Alaska v. John Adams
Utqiagvik, August 1, 1994

THE COURT BUILDING WAS RINGED WITH CABS, CROWDS surged through the normally quiet hallways, and the bailiff had to shut the doors to the courtroom for fear of fire-code violations. Those who could not get into the courtroom stood or sat on the mezzanine and waited for an opening. The mounting tension affected everyone in the courthouse. Normally courteous clerks snapped at one another, and ordinarily patient cops jostled people into line.

I asked Liz to go to the courtroom and update me as each witness was called so we could anticipate when Amos would be brought over from SATS. I was relieved to have Liz back. She had gained a little weight and looked good.

"Hey, listen," she said. "I lent Amos one of Jeff's shirts to wear. If they let him out tonight, will you make sure I get it back before somebody shoots him?"

"Thanks for doing that for him."

Liz shrugged and headed for the courtroom.

Carol was working on her misdemeanor docket and I was sweating over an outline of the events of last July 31 for the last time when the DA's secretary, Carolyn, poked her curly gray head in the door and said, "We need a favor."

"What's that?" I called back, not really knowing how the public defender could help the DA in the middle of a trial, especially one in which we had a vested interest in the star witness, even though we did not represent the actual defendant.

"Joe and Pat are in court all day. I have to go to the hospital to get some medical records. Dr. Sanderson is due in at eleven."

"Dr. Sanderson?"

"Defense is calling Dr. Ofshe, the false-confession guy, so we got our own expert. I have to lock up my office while I'm gone. Can you let Sanderson come over here? Get him some coffee, show him where the men's room is . . . until I get back?"

"Yeah, sure," I said, glad to do her a favor, since she had done so many for us, like copying a whole set of the Ipalook witness statements.

Unfortunately, I remembered only later that I had a Children's Services hearing at eleven.

"Carol, you don't mind babysitting their witness, do you?" I hollered in her general direction. "I forgot I have this hearing to do."

Carol came to my door and mumbled something and went back into her office. I didn't quite catch her answer and assumed she would help out. It was little enough to ask. Expert witnesses were usually interesting to talk to.

But when I returned from my hearing, I found the door wide open with neither Carol nor Liz present. A bespectacled and bewildered gentleman sat stiffly in the chair beside Liz's empty desk.

I was pissed.

Abandoning our office, with its equipment and confidential files—especially on a hectic day like this one, with the courthouse filled with strangers, without so much as a "be right back" note on a locked door—was inexcusable. I was tired of picking up the slack for both Liz and Carol. This breach was too much.

But it wasn't this poor gentleman's fault.

"You must be Dr. Sanderson. Welcome to Utqiagvik. Is your testimony scheduled soon?"

He stood and we shook hands. "They told me to come here . . ."

"Yes, of course! Sorry, we're a bit disorganized today—we don't usually have this big an event taking place."

I probably would have invited him to lunch, or at least steered him toward Pepe's North of the Border, but at that moment Carolyn emerged from the elevator and she, with many thanks, took Dr. Sanderson off my hands.

If I had been granted a moment to sit among my new crop of morning glories to catch my breath, the rest of the day might have gone differently, but right then Carol popped out of the stairwell. One look at my face must have told her that this time she had gone too far. She hurried into her own office. I followed her.

"Carol, we need to talk."

"About what? I just got back from the jail, and I have to do some phone calls." She tossed her lank hair and lifted her chin.

"Now."

"Just this one call—"

"Right now."

She sat down at her desk, dropped her purse and files, and swiveled to face me.

I remained standing. "I asked you to see about an expert witness this morning."

"That was the DA's witness, not ours."

"Lord knows they've done enough favors for us."

"I don't see why I should have to take care of somebody else's witness. The DA has more people than we do."

"It's called working in a law office and being part of a legal community. And because I asked you to. And because anybody would know better than to go off and leave the office open. Can't I count on you?"

She sat there jiggling her knee like a teenager.

"Liz should take care of it. That's her job, not mine. I could cover the trial. It's not my fault she's a druggie."

"Sometimes she's more help to this office than you are."

"Yeah, and how much help are you running around with your local cokehead boyfriend? People ask me . . . Honestly, it's embarrassing. I haven't told Anchorage yet, but I will. It makes us look bad."

I heard steps behind me. I hoped it wasn't the DA's secretary asking for another favor. Or an auditor from Anchorage. I turned. It was Liz. She was looking at Carol with a peculiar expression on her face. I wondered how much she had heard. Liz had such an aura of personal toughness that if I had been Carol, I would have shut my mouth when she came in the door with that light in her eyes, but Carol nattered on.

"You might as well hear this, too, Liz. Anchorage already knows that you don't show up half the time. Honestly, you people just don't have any conception of the nine-to-five."

Liz was half smiling now, but the smile didn't reach her eyes.

"Yeah, you're right—we don't much care about your *tanik* nine-to-five. *Us people* took about thirty seconds when the bear came to Rebecca's door."

I opened my mouth to agree, but Carol put her foot in it first. "You should never have let her get involved with that Michael, Liz—he's a coke freak. She probably has the stuff in her house."

Liz took a step toward her.

"You stupid *tanik* bitch," she said in a voice so low I had to strain to hear. "You ever bad-mouth her—or him—again, you're going to wake up somewhere regretting it, and that's a promise. You come up here for your Utqiagvik bucks, or because no other office will take you—you think you know law, and you don't know shit—you hear me? When all *you people* finally go back home and blow yourselves up, we'll still be here, like always."

"Liz, I . . ." I began.

"You better get down there," Liz said to me. "They're taking Dr. Ofshe out of order, since he has a plane to catch. Here. I got you a transcript of Ofshe's deposition. The State is playing the Adams confession tape now, and then they're going to call Amos Lane."

She shoved a sheaf of papers at me. "I wouldn't have your job for nothing," she said.

Carol stared at Liz like she had never seen her before.

In silence, I gathered up my file and headed for the courtroom. Clattering down the utility stairs in my court heels, I reflected that the tensions of the past year had grown so great I no longer cared about the trial outcome, just that the case should be over. I couldn't go on worrying about what Amos had done, or not done, while I tried to support Liz and run an office, and grieved for Randy, and missed Michael. Today, if Lane and Adams duked it out in full view of the jury, if a family member had a heart attack and during the distraction Lane and Adams both ran out onto the tundra, it was all okay with me, so long as the ordeal was finished.

At the courtroom door, a calm descended upon me.

"The horse is made ready for battle," I remembered, "but victory rests with the Lord."

To the best of my ability, I had spent much of a year readying this horse, right or wrong, and it was all I could do. If Ellingsworth had overplayed the odds, if Traverso had gambled on the wrong pony . . . I had done what I could for my own client, and stayed in my lane. The system didn't work if you tried to run anybody else's race but your own.

I pulled on the curved wooden handle and went inside.

The courtroom was even more crowded than when I had attended Amos Lane's arraignment dragging my suitcase. Inside, the already-breathed air was hot and oppressive. I stood by the door for a few moments to get my bearings. Since Amos was a witness, not a defendant, no seating provision had been made for us, but Judge Jeffery would want him in place when his time came. It was up to me to make arrangements.

The lights were dimmed, and the jury was watching Ellingsworth's video of Adams's so-called confession. I studied the jurors for their reactions. Many were slumped in their chairs with heads averted or had arms crossed over their chests. I knew enough about juror body language to recognize that they didn't like what they were seeing and were resisting its impact.

In the video, Adams looked exhausted, grief-stricken, and confused. The off-camera voice of Ed Ellingsworth kept prodding him.

"You didn't mean to do it, did you, man?"

Mutters and mumbles from Adams and a shake of the head.

"Women are just so infuriating sometimes. We understand—I've been through that, too, man. Sometime I'll tell you. Just man to man. But right now, if you can talk about it, we can get you some help, and you will feel so much better, and then you can sleep. Don't you want some help?"

John raised his tear-streaked face toward Ed, and in his eyes I saw a soul suffering from sorrow and trauma in abundance, but guilt? I hadn't seen guilt in his face before, and I didn't see it now.

Some of the jurors appeared angry. Were they angry at Adams for murdering the sisters? Or at the detective for the way he was badgering a bereaved man? The two women nearest the prosecution table glared at Ellingsworth where he sat with his henchmen, the Fairbanks and Utqiagvik DAs and Officer Marten.

"She threw the ring at you, didn't she, and you lost your temper, like anybody would have done," the off-camera voice persisted. Adams squirmed in his chair. Three jurors in the back row squirmed in theirs.

The trooper, sitting on his stool in the well of the court, beckoned to me.

I went up the aisle as unobtrusively as possible and bent my head down to his shoulder. He smelled of bitter sweat. This trial had made even the imperturbable trooper worry.

"I'm going to go get Lane soon," he whispered.

"Any way we can get a table and a couple of chairs?" I murmured.

"I'll find something," he said.

I nodded without speaking and took his seat when he got up and left. Now I was only about three feet from the screen. From that close angle, I found it increasingly unbearable to watch the inquisition of Adams. I remembered the deposition transcript Liz had put in my hand and bent my head to read it in the glare from the video.

"Dr. Richard Ofshe. State v. Adams, 4BA-S93-734-Cr." was the label. I paged through the part about his educational background and professional experience and stopped at the first question directed to him about types of false confessions.

> When it comes to the study of false confessions, there are generally recognized to be three kinds of false confession. The first kind is what's called a "voluntary false confession." A voluntary false confession is usually the sort of thing that happens when a crime has been committed that gets a lot of attention and someone who is often mentally ill wants attention and will call the police or show up at the police station and will simply walk in and without the police doing anything say "I committed the crime." But it's false.
>
> The next kind is called a "coerced compliant false confession," and what this refers to is the fact that sometimes in response to police interrogation, which can be and often is a very distressing situation, an individual who in fact is innocent and knows that he or she is innocent, will sometimes just give up and

> knowingly give a false confession because they can no longer stand the strain of the interrogation. It just gets to them to the point where they no longer care, and to end the interrogation they will simply give a false confession.
>
> In order for that to occur the interrogation must get intense and usually will occur when the interrogators have overstepped and done things that they shouldn't do. But the key thing is that the person knows that they're giving a false confession at the time they do it.
>
> The last kind of confession is the most complicated. It's called a "coerced internalized false confession." And what that means is that an individual is persuaded by the tactics that the interrogators use and actually believes, that it is more certain than not, that they probably committed the crime they're being accused of even though they have no memory of having done it.

Holy crap, I thought to myself, this stuff is dynamite. It was going to blow Adams's so-called confession right out of the water. The jury would see that the words coming out of his mouth were Ellingsworth's, not his. The jury had just watched the video of Adams being bullied, and now they would hear from a qualified expert in whose opinion Adams's confession was false. I was grateful to Liz for getting me a copy of the deposition. I tried to read as much as I could before the trooper returned with Amos.

> The interrogations of August 19, 31, September 2 and September 3 are examples of improperly applied accusatory interrogations. Now, the term "accusatory interrogation" has a particular meaning. Police

> officers are advised in the training manuals that train interrogators that an accusatory interrogation is when you get in somebody's face so to speak, when you say, "you did it, I know you did it," and the officer goes in with the intention of getting the person to confess. That kind of interrogation officers are advised to only do when there is strong evidence showing that this person committed the crime. Part of the reason for that is that once an accusatory interrogation begins, certain tactics are used in interrogation and those tactics can be very dangerous.

Ofshe had earlier supplied a definition of a false confession obtained by coercive interrogation. Now he applied that definition to the present case.

> The interrogations starting on July 19th were all accusatory interrogations. These interrogations were, in my opinion, poorly done. They caused Mr. Adams to become confused and to distrust his own memory of what happened over that weekend. Mr. Adams was pressured to agree to a story of the crime that was actually made up by Investigator Ellingsworth. Mr. Adams was pressured to make guesses about how the crime happened and, in my analysis it becomes clear that where those guesses can be evaluated, they're wrong.
>
> Many people think that the most important part of an interrogation is when the person says, "I did it." But that's not the important moment. What's important is getting from the suspect the story of the crime in the suspect's words and getting the suspect to contribute details about the crime that only the guilty party could know.

When the trooper tapped my shoulder, I startle-jumped six inches.

He had brought two folding chairs. I glanced up at Judge Jeffery, who frowned down at us for making a commotion while court was in session.

The Fairbanks DA was motioning for the video to be cut off and was getting to his feet.

"Anyone want a stretch break?" Judge Jeffery asked the jurors.

Hands shot up. Judge Jeffery adjourned us for half an hour, and the whole courtroom went into motion.

Good. We would have a moment to get organized.

"Thanks so much, Pete. Any chance of one of those small tables?"

I thanked the trooper, and when the crowd had cleared, he brought in a table.

Amos's face was blank. He wore chains on his ankles, waist, and wrists, and black sweatpants and jail scuffs. The borrowed Western-style shirt, in a Stuart green, red, and yellow plaid, was stretched taut over his massive shoulders. Even if it wasn't a very good fit, Amos was lucky the judge had allowed him to wear it. I debated whether to ask for the chains to be removed and decided to do so as a matter of basic dignity. I noticed Amos appeared to have freshly washed his hair and was wearing it loose about his shoulders instead of tied back.

His time had come. I didn't know which way to hope anymore: that Amos would honor his immunity agreement and testify clearly and well so he could be released today, or that poor, suffering John Adams would be exonerated and get to go home. Were those results mutually exclusive? After all these months of work, I still didn't have the answer to that question. Who left the Ipalook girls last, an angry boyfriend or a drunken stranger? Perhaps I was in some sort of denial, refusing to objectively face that I might have obtained immunity for a double murderer, but it still seemed to me that Amos might, indeed, have gone home with the sisters, spent some time with them, and left them alive and well.

Amos and I installed ourselves at our table and chairs, and the trooper returned to his stool near the clerk's enclosure.

"How're you doing?" I asked Amos.

A shrug of lips and shoulders. "I don't feel like talking to no damn jury."

I was trying to master my own nervous apprehension. "Amos, you have no idea how lucky you are to get immunity in a double homicide. Immunity is what everybody at FCC wishes they had. All you have to do today is testify truthfully, and you get out of jail tonight."

"They want me to say I was with those girls."

"Well, weren't you?" It occurred to me I had never directly asked him that question before. The question was not, Did you hurt them? The question was, Did you go there—watch TV, drink beer, play cards, whatever—and make John Adams jealous?

He didn't respond.

"Amos, I thought we went over all this before. The State needs you for their case. If you can tell the jury you went to see the Ipalook sisters Saturday night, it will help them argue that John Adams went over there Sunday morning."

"But what if I was never there?"

"Amos, I can't tell you what to say. Nobody can. But the State is expecting you to say you were there. Traverso, Adams's attorney, is going to ask you if you were there. You can't take the Fifth and refuse to answer anymore because you took the immunity deal. You have to answer their questions, all their questions. Just remember you can't be prosecuted."

"You got any paper?" he asked.

"What?"

"I need some paper."

I picked up the nearest legal pad from the defense table and tore off a couple of blank pages from the middle of it. I also appropriated a ballpoint pen from the several scattered over the State's tabletop.

"Here."

He arranged his long legs under our small table and began to doodle another firebird like the one he had drawn at his arraignment. The handcuffs on his wrists did not seem to impede his sketching. I supposed he was used to them.

Adams returned to his place. He and Lane exchanged measuring glances. Judge Jeffery swept into the courtroom, and we reconvened.

The judge asked for preliminary matters, and I stood to request that my client's shackles be removed. The judge looked inquiringly at Assistant District Attorney Pat Doogan, the veteran attorney with the military haircut to whom Fairbanks had entrusted this high-profile prosecution. Doogan always looked to me like either a sun-beaten yachtsman or a British field officer. He, too, rose to his feet.

"Your Honor, under the unusual circumstances of this case, and since Mr. Lane is not a defendant here with a defendant's rights in the presence of a jury, we ask that the shackles remain."

Ordinarily Judge Jeffery allowed all reasonable requests to afford dignity to everyone, but apparently even he had concerns about these particular circumstances.

"Since Mr. Lane is only in court to give his testimony, we will grant the State's request."

"Sorry," I whispered to Amos.

He shrugged.

Doogan and I sat down.

Judge Jeffery addressed the courtroom. "We are back on the record in the case of *State of Alaska versus John Adams*, 4BA-S93-734. We are ready to hear the testimony of Amos Lane. Ladies and gentlemen of the jury, Mr. Lane has been granted immunity from prosecution in exchange for his testimony today. You should evaluate his testimony like that of any other witness. You can believe all of his testimony, part of it, or none of it."

Some jurors regarded Judge Jeffery attentively, some of them stared at Amos, and others gazed wearily at the tops of their knees.

"Your Honor, the State calls Amos Lane to the stand," Doogan said.

For a moment, Amos looked into my eyes. I tried to meet his gaze squarely, to read whatever lay within, and could not. In utter silence except for the jangling of his chains, limping slightly on his maimed feet and shackled ankles, he made his way to the witness chair, the trooper hovering nearby.

Unlike most judicial officers, Judge Jeffery did not ask witnesses to swear, only to affirm, and he did not require the use of a Bible.

"Do you affirm that you will tell the truth, only the truth, and the whole truth?" the clerk asked.

Amos answered yes and settled into the hot seat.

Doogan took him through questions of where he was born and raised and asked about his previous rape conviction, so it would have less impact when Traverso inevitably brought it up. Amos answered everything directly and clearly, and I began to relax a little. So far, so good. He was coming across as dignified and truthful. Most of the jurors gazed at him with what seemed to be impartial interest. Adams stared stonily at the witness.

"Now, Mr. Lane, I need you to focus on the weekend of July 31 and August 1, last summer."

"Yes, sir."

"That particular weekend you were participating in alcohol treatment at SATS, isn't that correct?"

"Yes, sir. I'm an alcoholic. I'm in treatment for it."

"How long have you been in treatment now?"

"Almost a year, man. Takes a while."

"And last August you had a weekend pass to be out of the building?"

"Yes, they told me I had been doing good in my program, and so I got to visit my relatives that weekend."

"The whole weekend or just Saturday night?"

"Just Saturday night."

"And did you visit your relatives?"

"Yes, I did."

"And what did you do there?"

This was new territory to me. Amos had never trusted me enough to give me any info about his whereabouts or activities that evening. Along with everybody else in the courtroom, I hung on his every word.

"We played cards."

"You played cards. And did you have anything to drink?"

"Yes, I did drink. I wasn't supposed to, but I did. It was Saturday night, and they had lots of booze on hand. I . . . uh, I had a relapse."

"You had a relapse."

"Yes, relapse is part of recovery. My counselor said so."

"How much did you drink?"

"It's hard to say. Maybe a bottle. Maybe a bottle and a half."

"Maybe a bottle and a half. Of what?"

"Um, vodka. Like I say, they had lots on hand."

"How long did you stay at your relatives'?"

"Oh, it was . . . until eleven or so."

"Then what did you do?"

"Went to the Saturday night sober dance at the community center."

"So you got there a little after eleven?"

"Yes. Something like that."

"Were you on foot?"

"No. My uncle, he lent me his three-wheeler. I was riding his three-wheeler."

"Okay, so you'd been drinking, you were driving your uncle's three-wheeler, and you went to the dance at the community center. How long did you stay there?"

"Couple hours."

"Then what did you do?"

At this point, Amos began to seem less comfortable in his chair. He shifted in the seat and squared his great shoulders as though Jeff's shirt was binding him. I looked again at the jury. He had their full attention. Heaven only knew what they had already heard about Amos Lane, before or during the trial.

"Oh, I was just out cruising. Sun was shining. It was nice to be out."

"You were out cruising. Where?"

"Oh, around town."

"Did you see anybody you know?"

Amos considered a minute. "Yeah, I saw my cousin."

"Who's your cousin?"

"Nate Olemaun."

"You saw your cousin Nate Olemaun. Where was he?"

"He was at the ball field with a bunch of people."

"Okay, and then what did you do?"

"I, uh . . . cruised around some more."

Amos was fidgeting now. Doogan plodded on in workmanlike fashion.

"You cruised around some more. And at some point that evening did you see Bernice and Wanda Ipalook?"

"Yeah, I saw 'em."

"You saw Bernice and Wanda Ipalook that night. And where were they?"

"They were . . . they were walking along the road."

"What road?"

"Road between Stuaqpak and their house."

"Saturday night, July 31, last year, you saw Bernice and Wanda Ipalook walking along the road between Stuaqpak and their house. About what time was that?"

Amos now appeared irritated. He flexed his wrists against the cuffs and pulled at the chains attaching them to his steel waistband. Two jurors flinched. Reflexes of fear or pangs of pity? Maybe the damn things were hurting him.

"I don't know, man, what time it was. Midnight sun, Saturday night, you know—I had a few drinks, what the hell."

"And so you followed Bernice and Wanda to their house?"

Nelson Traverso was on his feet. "Objection. Leading."

I didn't understand why Traverso was objecting now. Doogan had asked plenty of leading questions before this one. Traverso had no reason to protect this witness. On the contrary, he wanted him to spill his guts. Perhaps just to give emphasis to this important part of his testimony?

"Sustained."

"Very well, Your Honor. I'll rephrase. Where did the sisters go? Where did you follow them?"

Amos took more time to respond to these questions than he had to any of the others, as though the DA were coming closer to an area marked in red letters "DON'T GO THERE."

"I followed them partways."

"What do you mean you followed them partways?"

"I followed them along the road a little ways."

Now it was the DA who hesitated. He seemed uncertain how to prod Amos, who was supposed to be the State's own sweetheart witness, into providing the needed information. Could it be that he should have asked me to go over Lane's testimony with him ahead of time? It was always so hard to cover every single thing needed to get ready for a trial, even a major trial. The DAs had many resources at their disposal, but sometimes even they cut corners or overlooked important points.

"How . . . how were the Ipalook sisters then? How were they behaving?"

"They was drunk, man—they was stumbling all over the road."

There was a disturbance behind us, among the spectators. Judge Jeffery looked up sharply from his perpetual notetaking. The bailiff glided past me through the pony gate into the pews where an older woman, probably a member of the Ipalook family, had burst into tears. She got up to leave, and a neighbor helped her out. The bailiff supervised their exit while the entire courtroom waited, and then returned to his post. I noticed then that there were two additional deputies standing in the back of the courtroom.

"I know this testimony is difficult for many to hear," Judge Jeffery said, "but I have to advise everyone that we will have order here. Anyone who cannot maintain order will be escorted from the courtroom."

I glanced at John Adams and was startled by what I saw. The man who was so meek and weary and broken in the video now sat bolt upright like a warrior at attention and stared fixedly at Lane, only a few feet away from him on the stand. Adams was not shackled, and his fingers flexed in and out of fists.

"They was drunk and yelling and hollering," Lane went on, more rapidly now. "They came up to me and they grabbed on to me and they kept saying, 'Come on over and visit, we got a bottle. Come on over, sweetie, and play with us.'"

"And so you went over, right?"

"No, no, man—I never went in there."

"You never went in there?"

"No, I never did."

"You never went in the house with Bernice and Wanda Ipalook."

"No, sir. Never."

Doogan now addressed the court. "Your Honor, I ask permission to show Mr. Lane two items that have been marked as State's exhibits—I believe it's numbers 24 and 35." He consulted a chart on his table.

"You may hand them to the bailiff."

Ellingsworth selected two objects in plastic evidence bags from the table in front of the judge's bench and held them up for the bailiff, who came for them and handed one to Amos in the witness chair.

"Will you please tell the jury what this is, Mr. Lane?"

Amos stared at the bag and turned it over a couple of times. "Don't know what it is," he mumbled.

Here the clerk raised a hand and said something directly to the judge.

"Mr. Lane, I am directing you to speak clearly so the tape recorder can record your testimony."

"I don't know what it is," Amos repeated, a little louder.

"Mr. Lane, would it help your memory if I advised you that the evidence tag on this object says it is a rubber grommet—the little rubber cover that goes on the end of the key. That it came from what has been identified for the jury as the key to your uncle's three-wheeler, and that it was found in the living room of Bernice and Wanda Ipalook's house, found tangled in some blankets there?"

There was more rustling behind me. John Adams started out of his chair, and Traverso put a hand on his shoulder and pushed him back down. Amos said nothing in response to the DA's question. Doogan pressed on.

"Mr. Bailiff, please retrieve item 24 and hand item 35 to the witness."

The bailiff complied.

"Mr. Lane, I don't believe you will have any difficulty identifying this object. Please tell the jury what it is."

Amos stared at the item in his hand, and his face seemed to tighten up until it looked like one of the wooden masks depicting howling spirits worn in clan dances. My heart slid into my throat. I should have asked Traverso for the complete, final list of evidentiary items. I should have gone over them one by one with my client. But, like Doogan, I had anticipated straightforward testimony from this man. I had worked hard on establishing a timetable of witnesses when I should have focused on the physical evidence. Something unexpected always happens in trials. That's why they're scary. That's why they're called trials.

What was this item? I had the skidding-on-ice, impending-car-wreck feeling I hate to have during a trial.

Amos tilted his head down toward his lap so that no one could see his expression. We waited on him.

"Mr. Lane, please identify the object."

Utter silence in the courtroom.

"Your Honor?" Doogan said.

"The witness is directed to answer the question," Judge Jeffery said.

Amos did not respond.

"Very well," Doogan said. "Your Honor, we ask that the projector screen be lowered."

If Doogan had neglected to rehearse some points, he had obviously prepared for this particular moment and choreographed it carefully. Slusser and Ellingsworth jumped up in unison to activate the projector and lower the lights just as the screen came down. A minute of fiddling with the projector and then the screen came into bright focus. We saw on it a SATS appointment card for Monday, August 2, at 10:00 a.m.

The name of the person who had the appointment was Amos Lane.

"Your Honor, we ask that the record reflect that Exhibit 35 is an appointment card for the Substance Abuse Treatment Services for Amos Lane for Monday, August 2, of last year, the Monday following the weekend during which Bernice and Wanda Ipalook died. Now, Mr. Bailiff, please read for us from the evidence tag the place where this item was found."

The screen retreated, and the lights came back on. The bailiff went forward and retrieved the plastic bag containing the card from Amos and then paused, hesitant, in the middle of the courtroom. I didn't recall a similar request ever having been made of a bailiff, and apparently the bailiff did not either. The bailiff looked to the judge for direction. For a moment everyone in the courtroom remained as still as though we were under a spell in a fairy tale.

"Bailiff, hand it to me. I will read the exhibit tag," Judge Jeffery said.

The bailiff handed up the bag to the bench. Judge Jeffery studied it a moment and then read, slowly and clearly, "State's Exhibit 35. SATS appointment card. Found under the body of Bernice Ipalook."

We had all been staring at Amos and overlooking John Adams. Adams made it over his table and through the well of the court with his hands stretched toward Amos's neck before the trooper tackled him on the steps to the witness box and bowled him sideways out of the way. Amos had stood to meet him with a headbutt before the bailiff realized what was going on. The bailiff managed to push Amos, who had no leverage on his shackled and maimed feet, back in his chair. Someone screamed. I scrambled out of the way, between the side of the jury box and the judge's bench. Judge Jeffery banged his gavel, and I saw his other hand hover near the alarm button under the bench.

The two deputies ran forward from the rear of the courtroom to assist the trooper and the bailiff. The DAs sat transfixed at their table. Some spectators surged forward to get into the melee, and some tried to leave the courtroom. A few jurors half rose, but most cowered back in their seats.

"Clear the courtroom!" Judge Jeffery ordered in a louder than usual but otherwise calm voice.

The trooper and a deputy dragged Amos toward the holding room door. The bailiff and a deputy took Adams by each arm and pulled him toward the judge's chambers. The jurors looked back and forth between the two men, stunned in place.

"Clear the courtroom!" the judge repeated.

The outer door opened, and the courtroom suddenly seemed cooler. I hovered at the back of the crowded aisle until I could slip out the side door downstairs to my usual retreat, the back door exit of the courthouse. I had to get some air.

And to figure out what had just happened. The appointment card had set Adams off. Had he gone for Lane out of jealousy? Had we just glimpsed the jealous rage in which he had killed the sisters? The appointment card seemed to show how physically close Amos had been to Bernice at some point. How else could it have been found beneath her body? Or did Adams jump to the conclusion that the presence of the card proved Lane had killed the sisters, and he lunged forward seeking revenge? Jealousy or revenge: which was it?

The trial was supposed to reveal the truth. Maybe the jurors could see it. I couldn't.

JUDGE JEFFERY RECONVENED the trial later that day, but the DA did not recall Amos Lane, and I did not return to the courtroom. Neither side asked for a mistrial, which either could have probably obtained. Neither side wanted to have to redo jury selection and testimony. Both sides wanted this jury to end the waiting and resolve the case.

The clerk kindly called our office to let me know that the jury had retired to deliberate around six. I wanted to stay at work until they came back with a verdict, but at seven thirty I gave up and went home. They might deliberate all night.

From home, I called the jail at half-hour intervals. The guards who housed John Adams would know his fate as quickly as anyone else I could reach by phone. Sergeant Rosas was on duty, and he teased me about my curiosity.

"Who are you hoping gets fried, Mrs. Rebecca?"

"Not funny, Sergeant Rosas. You know Alaska doesn't have the death penalty."

"Too bad."

At nine fifteen, he had the news I was waiting for.

"Has the jury come back?"

"Yes. It's over."

"Do you still have John Adams, or has he been transported to FCC?"

"He gone."

"Gone where?"

"He gone home. Or to some party. The jury say not guilty."

"Not guilty. Wow!"

"Your star client, he back."

"Back. Back where?"

"Amos Lane back in jail now."

"He can't be in jail. He got immunity."

"What's immunity?"

"He can't be charged with the Ipalook murders. He got a deal for his testimony. Look in your file. I made sure there was a copy of that order in the jail file."

"We have new paper now. Not charged with murder. Charged with perjury."

"Perjury." John Adams's jury did not believe he had confessed. They believed that the physical evidence, the key grommet and the appointment card, showed beyond reasonable doubt that Amos Lane had been with the Ipalook sisters the night they died. It was obvious to the jury, and to the State, that Amos had lied when he testified that he had not been there. He was under oath when he lied, the definition of perjury.

I sat down on the bottom stair by the phone, digesting this news.

"Yeah. I have cousin on jury. They no like video. They say can't tell what happened."

I was still thinking.

"Lane want you come see him."

"Thank you for the information, Sergeant Rosas."

"Yes, you welcome, you bet. You get some sleep, Mrs. Rebecca."

"You too. Bye."

I dropped the phone on the floor, picked it up, hung up the receiver, and went into the kitchen, where I burrowed into the back of the cupboard for the bottle of vodka I had been hoarding ever since I bought it from the bootlegger. I poured myself a half water glass, thinking the vodka would help me sleep, but I was wrong. The futon seemed too thin and the covers too light. When I turned on the electric blanket, I was more comfortable, but then thoughts began zooming around in my head, returning over and over to one issue. One, that from the outset the midnight sun had skewed the case. The sun dazzle blurred the time sequence of events that weekend. Friday ran into Saturday and Sunday, and witnesses couldn't remember exactly when they saw the sisters. Was it after John Adams had gone home on the last bus of the day? Only the timing of the bus schedule was certain that day. Did anyone see them alive after Amos had returned to SATS? No one could be sure.

The coroner testified that the bodies had been moved after death. Why, and by whom? Neither the State nor the defense had answered these questions or even attempted to address them.

In the darkness of my second-floor cavern, weary but sleepless, I considered one possible explanation. Maybe Amos, hungover after the night of the midnight sun, had noticed his appointment card was missing and had gone back to the Ipalook sisters' house to look for it. Perhaps it was he who had moved the bodies, searching for the incriminating card, though he never found it in the tangle of blankets and clothes. But the State had found it, and now the jury had seen it and had freed John Adams.

The jury had spoken, but the Ipalook murder case had not been solved.

21

In God's wildness lies the hope of the world—the great fresh unblighted unredeemed wilderness.
JOHN MUIR

THE TRIAL WAS DONE, BUT LEGAL SPARRING WENT ON in Amos's new case. There was DNA evidence that appeared to confirm Amos had been with the sisters that night, but I managed to get it suppressed because the statistical sampling of "Eskimo DNA" was insufficient for comparison purposes. Also, Judge Jeffery agreed with us that Amos's shirt with the missing button had been illegally seized from SATS and prohibited its use as evidence.

The State intended to try Amos for perjury based on the appointment card and the key grommet. Then I filed a motion for change of venue. Judge Jeffery again agreed with defense, although reluctantly. He wrote:

> The Court finds the present case highly unique . . . Because of the nature and dynamics of rumor in a small town, it is impossible to determine through voir dire what actually has been overheard, and how it may have affected the attitudes, conscious

> or unconscious, of potential jurors . . . The cost and logistical problems of moving the case to Fairbanks pale in comparison with the problems of re-trying the case [if it was overturned on appeal].

Once the venue was changed, I expected that the DA would make us a reasonable settlement offer. DAs do not like to travel to unfamiliar jurisdictions where they may not possess as much clout with court staff and local police, and where they may have to work harder. Truth be told, by then they were tired of the case, and they came up with an offer that Lane accepted.

Amos pled no contest to one count of perjury. He acknowledged that the State had compelling evidence he had been at house 1541, but he never admitted that he was there, much less that he had hurt anyone. True to form, he never admitted anything at all during the entire duration of both cases, the double homicide and the perjury charge. He was released for time served.

Ellingsworth, whose decision it had been to focus on Adams rather than Lane as the perpetrator, adopted a lower profile within the Department of Public Safety after this case. As far as I knew, he wasn't demoted or reassigned, but he no longer served as lead investigator. I would have liked to debrief the Ipalook murders with him and to find out whether he had plans to indict anyone else for the crimes, but I never had the opportunity. He seemed to avoid me.

John Adams, cleared of all charges, returned to raising Eqalin, with the help of the entire Ipalook family, and was warmly welcomed back to work at Ukpeagvik Inupiat Corporation on the weatherization project.

"YOU'RE NOT COMING back to Utqiagvik, are you," Liz said. It was not a question.

"Of course I'm coming back. It's just a long weekend. Jim was going to be in Seattle for a meeting and he invited me for a visit, is all. I'm going to finish that part of my vacation that got interrupted last year when the Ipalooks were murdered."

"Sure. You haven't seen him in ten years, and he just happens to be coming all the way to Seattle from Tennessee. Sooner or later, you're going to marry him and move down there, and then they'll send up some asshole who doesn't even try to get to know anybody here like you have."

"Maybe I tried to get to know some people too well."

She shrugged.

"I'm not going anywhere if I can't find somebody to dog-sit."

Liz looked at me with her stubborn you're-a-dumb-*tanik* expression. I didn't know what to say. If she didn't want to help with something, she wouldn't, and wouldn't even try to find someone who would.

"I can dog-sit for you," Carol said.

We both turned and looked at her.

"Hey, I like dogs, too, you know," she said, with a sheepish smile.

Perhaps she did like dogs. It was also true that she had only a cubbyhole apartment, and at my place she would have a whole house, such as it was. Or maybe it now occurred to her that if my permanent departure was imminent, she might like Utqiagvik better when she became directing attorney of its public defender's office, for lack of anyone else willing to come up to the Slope.

Or perhaps she simply wanted to help. For once.

"Much appreciated," I said, in all sincerity. It occurred to me that her role in the office had not been an easy one. She had suffered newbie jitters when she first came up to the Slope. Utqiagvik seemed strange to her, and Liz and I were already tight. She'd had to learn not only to manage a whole caseload on her first legal job but how to navigate the Arctic as well. No wonder she had seemed mulish at times.

Liz found me a flight for the following Friday. The Tuttu Taxi that picked me up for it was prompt, but the driver was unfamiliar.

"Where are you from?" I asked, the usual question from one *tanik* to another, as we cruised up North Star Street toward the airport. I was enjoying the sun dazzle for once, since I would soon fly past it into evening darkness.

"Macedonia," he said. "Like Alexander."

"No kidding. I don't think I've ever met anyone from Macedonia before. You've traveled even farther than Alexander. Do you go home to visit?"

"Can't. They kicked me out."

"Who kicked you out?"

"My country. I don't have a country anymore."

I decided not to inquire how he ended up in Utqiagvik. I had met others here who were stateless, or who were escaping a relationship or the law. It was better not to ask for details.

"That must be hard," I said, "not to go home."

He shook his head under his porkpie hat. "Alexander was buried in strange lands, too."

I was going to say that no one knew where Alexander was buried, but ahead of us some moving figures caught my eye.

"What's going on there?" I said.

"Oh. That's the grave of Randy," he told me. "Randy Aht . . . Ahtang . . . He was . . . some kind of basketball hero. Now the kids come here with candles."

"Stop. Please stop a minute."

"I thought you had to catch a plane."

"I'll just be a moment."

He pulled over, and I climbed out into the chilly dust of the roadside. We were at the small graveyard between Browerville and Utqiagvik, near the saltwater lagoon. Snow fences leaned crazily among the tundra hummocks, and a few crooked crosses stood in puddles. A teenager sat on a tarp at one of the graves, and near him several candles in votive holders flickered feebly . Two more young people who looked vaguely familiar, probably from bus rides, made their way toward the site, carrying more candles. The kids wore candy-apple-red satin athletic jackets like Randy had worn, the fabric too thin to keep them warm.

I bowed my head and prayed that Randy might have peace, and his friends, some hope.

Something in the sight of the young people's pilgrimage to Randy's grave troubled me, beyond the ongoing grief. Did his spirit remain with us? Was that why they came? What kind of spirit was his? I tried to remember Pastor Roghair's counsel about the shamans and apply it, but once again I was out of time. There was never enough time. There hadn't been enough time since I came to Utqiagvik. The cases went on, the cases had to be heard within constitutional limits, and there were always more cases. I had buried the shock of his suicide, of his suicide pact with his beautiful young lover, inside me, like the winter snow buried everything each year. Perhaps some other day, some other year, there would be time to try to understand.

I got back in the cab.

"Did you know that boy?" the driver asked me. "They say he killed himself."

"Yes, I knew him. Randy Ahtanguarak. Yes, he did."

"That's sad," he said. "I'm sorry."

"Thank you."

"There's a lot they don't know about Alexander's death . . ." he began to tell me, and I would have liked to hear, but we reached the terminal.

The man from Macedonia carried my suitcase all the way inside and refused a tip but accepted a hug. I checked in at the small counter and found a place to sit among the travelers, leaning my head against the wall and watching the now-familiar scene. Babies bundled in parkas, chubby kids racing each other back and forth, and over all of it, I caught the familiar scent of seal oil.

The face of an old man standing near the door reminded me of the masks sold to tourists—a disk of stiff caribou hide with seal-fur ruffs for eyebrows and mustache and goatee, a scrap of silky fox pelt on top for hair. But it was a real face, not a mask, strong and gaunt, as though the man had survived hunger in the January cold.

The elder walked stiffly toward me and bent and looked into my face.

"How are you?" he asked. "You look better than when I last see you."

I stood up and extended my hand. "I'm fine, Mr. Ahvakana, thanks to you. If it hadn't been for you and my neighbor, I would be lying out on the road somewhere."

"Only a little of you," he said, his eyes crinkling up. "Are you going out to shop?"

"No, sir, just a visit."

"And are you coming back to Utqiagvik?" he asked, taking my hand in both of his.

It seemed an odd question, but perhaps he thought most *taniks* left sooner or later. Sure, I would be back next week, but I didn't know for how long. I had begun to wonder whether it was time to move on, time to leave before I burned out, time to go before I started making too many mistakes. With such a huge caseload, mistakes in strategy, in priorities, or simple oversights were inevitable. So far, by stretching every effort and all my energy to their limits, I had avoided making major mistakes. I couldn't work at maximum speed forever. Perhaps if things had been different with Michael, or if I could have planted a tree or two . . .

Ahvakana was apparently used to my not being a very good communicator. He released my hand and patted my shoulder.

"A safe trip," he said. "Return before the new snow." He went back to his place by the door.

I boarded the flight and settled into my seat, staring out the window at the clouds to gauge the weather for the trip. They were clumpy. The air would not be smooth. I had lived in a Native community for nine years; perhaps now I was no longer entirely a *tanik*. I had at least picked up a few Native habits, such as being sensitive to weather.

Just as we ascended, I saw a familiar battered pickup roll into the parking area. Michael got out, curled his fingers into the chain link, and stared upward at the plane.

Had Liz told him I was leaving and that he should come to say goodbye—or to ask me not to go? I hadn't even known he was back in town. For a moment I wondered what I would have said to him had he arrived in time. I used to be so glad to see his truck parked by my boardwalk because it meant a good evening ahead. He would have started dinner or already walked the dogs. One of his sisters or small nieces or nephews, also spotting the truck, might drop by. If something went wrong with the water faucet or the TV, he would fix it. The truck meant warmth and belonging and safety.

I remembered riding out with him in Debra's shining limo, but then the trip in his truck on Cakeeater Road.

I mashed my cheek against the cold aircraft window for a last look as I was carried upward. Perhaps it wasn't really him. Perhaps it was an illusion born of longing and hope and sun dazzle. As I well knew, the endless sun played tricks with your senses, and I couldn't be sure. In Utqiagvik I had learned that there were a great many things about which I couldn't be sure, like time, and even justice.

We flew into the sun, and his image faded.

22

The wolf and the shaman are of one nest.
ALASKA NATIVE PROVERB

LIZ CORRECTLY PREDICTED THAT JIM STEVENS AND I would grow a relationship, though it took a year of startlingly long-distance phone bills, with only one more visit. Then Jim left his native Tennessee, where he had been a prosecutor, and I left Alaska, and we boarded all our mutual dogs and cats and eloped to New Orleans. I had two hours to shop for a wedding outfit and found a beautiful white suit with faux fur cuffs, on sale, that was only one size too big. Jim wore a tweed suit and a bright tie his daughter had given him. I thought he looked quite distinguished, with his straight mustache and close-cropped hair. We stayed in the Quarter at a former Creole townhouse, where a juvenile court judge met us in the courtyard for the ceremony. A girl can't get married without flowers, so I borrowed a white orchid in a basket from a doorway, and then put it right back.

The following week, Jim and I reported to our new jobs with the Kentucky Department of Public Advocacy. Since we had each practiced law for over five years, we were not required to take the

Kentucky bar exam, only to submit to vetting: fingerprints, criminal and traffic records, documents of any personal litigation, all previous addresses, contact information for every previous employer, and school transcripts, plus a hefty fee. Jim worked in Paducah, I supervised a small office in Madisonville, and we lived halfway between, in the woodsy community of Kuttawa. The caseloads were heavy and the commutes were long, but the home was happy.

Every day was a tree reunion for me. After all those years without them, once again I could watch the magic lantern show of their leaf shadows on the wall, walk in the tealike fragrance of the forest, and run my fingers over the shaggy bark of the hickory and smooth beeches.

Madisonville is in the coalfields, 3,300 miles away from Utqiagvik, and was founded in 1807, almost a hundred years before the first Anglo, Charles Brower, settled on the Arctic coast. I couldn't stop comparing the two places. In Kentucky, the judge left the windows of his chambers open to catch the breezes off the shade trees in court square. In Utkeagvik, you could not open any windows in the airlocked courthouse. When there was time in the morning, the Kentucky judge welcomed local attorneys in chambers for coffee. In Alaska, the ban on ex parte communication, which forbids counsel who represent parties with pending cases to speak separately with the judge hearing their cases, was so strict that attorneys entered chambers only during trials, with a clerk present.

The public defender's office was tucked into a strip mall and had plenty of parking, a good thing because now, for the first time in nine years, I had a car. My four-year-old, low-slung black Mitsubishi Galant drove so easily that it went faster than I realized or intended. I got two speeding tickets and had to attend traffic information school.

An hour's commute, when you drive carefully, gives you lots of time to think, sometimes about matters you might earlier have buried in in busyness. I thought about Randy's suicide. I was constantly reminded of him, anyway, since Kentucky is a basketball state. Seeing the kids walking downtown in bright basketball jackets always brought him to mind. I went over what Liz and I had tried to do for him and questioned what other remedies we might have attempted or solutions offered. Liz had found him housing, but he rarely stayed there and preferred to couch surf with friends. I tried to be available when he wanted to talk but was often in court when he dropped by. Yes, I gave him the chambered nautilus for his mother and flew to Anaktuvuk to talk to his father and went looking for him the night no one knew where he was, but nothing had helped.

I wondered what he and his beautiful young lover had said to each other when they lay down on the ice to die, and if they pursued some goal in the afterlife. Can there be a valid consent to a pact for suicide, or is the first death always murder, in anyone's culture? She had survived, thanks only to the kid with the gunslinger eyes and the blue truck, and I prayed that the rest of her life would be easier.

I pieced together events and references I had not thought connected before, like the prophecy of the elder lady at the post office, and Randy's Anaktuvuk friend telling me that Randy knew things before they happened, and the unnerving sight of young people in basketball jackets bearing candles to his grave. When I had half-jokingly suggested to Della that I didn't want a postcard from Palau, I wanted a seashell—she had showed up when it was needed with one of the most beautiful shells in the world for Randy's mom. Pastor Willa told me people had advised her to work with shamans when she first came to Utqiagvik, and she responded that she couldn't know when they sought good or evil. The elders advised the archaeologists not to interfere with a shaman's grave, and when they persisted, a storm reburied the site. Perhaps forces far more powerful than Liz or me wanted a different destiny for Randy.

Then my outsider's mind drew back from contemplating mysteries it could never understand. Accepting his loss, I gave some money in Randy's name to the Madisonville high school basketball team, a donation that will recur annually, to help with their travel to events. Randy was probably their first Inupiaq supporter, a small memorial in honor of his talents, his suffering heart, and what he might have been, in either culture.

STARTING NEW IN a different office provides an anti-burnout break, of sorts, but the pace soon picked up in Madisonville. My first trial involved a young soldier who had recently broken up with his girlfriend, an exotic dancer. Her small son suddenly accused him of abuse. I think the prosecutor had doubts about his own case, because he offered my client a sweetheart deal if he would make an admission. The young man said, "I'm not admitting anything. I didn't do it." We went to trial, risking the serious mandatory penalty, on the theory that the mom had "implanted" the memory in her child. In closing, I told the jury how I grew up remembering my grandfather's funeral and the sweet smell of the flowers as I peered over the edge of the casket, where he lay so still and wouldn't answer me. I found out later my mother thought I was too young to attend and left me with neighbors. I had only heard about the casket and the flowers from relatives. The jury listened, and acquitted.

Another case, a juvenile matter, did not go so well. My teenage client, who was Black, and a bunch of other kids had gathered after school at their hangout in a cemetery, where two classmates had vowed to fight. Everyone wanted to see the action, and there was plenty. Kids took sides, and a melee ensued. One young person did not go home that night. On the basis of no evidence at all, my client was singled out as a suspect. I met with him and three dozen family members and friends and neighbors to encourage—actually, to implore—him to take the case to trial. I knew, of course, that, unlike in Utqiagvik, Anglos were the majority in Madisonville, and that in the past jury selection had been skewed against seating Black jurors. But times were changing, and a recent Supreme Court case had leveled the playing field for jury selection. To my disappointment, the family feared the risk, and the consequences even of an acquittal, and the young man took the plea deal offered: manslaughter, six months to serve, and probation until he turned eighteen. I told Liz about this case, which was, in a way, similar to her own.

AT FIRST, LIZ and I stayed in touch by phone. These were the years when the internet exploded, and soon we were friends on Facebook. I got to see pictures of her children as they grew up, and then her elfin granddaughter, Aaryana. But I worried about the family. In photos, both Liz and Jeff seemed to age quickly. Late in 1999 came the hard news that Jeff had lost his struggle with cancer. Liz left Utqiagvik. She went to work for one of the oil companies in Prudhoe Bay, then moved to Anchorage to be close to her sister, Deva. Sadly, she began to suffer from chronic obstructive pulmonary disease.

On August 2, 2020, Deva messaged me that I should call her. She told me Liz was gone. We cried together over the phone, 2,800 miles apart. I had continued to hope that Liz one day might come down to the Lower 48 on a holiday, or I might have reason to visit the Slope, and we would see each other again.

Deva created an unforgettable service for Liz in Anchorage. I sent a bouquet of lilies and attended via live stream. Native ladies had cooked all day for a potluck at Deva's house, which Liz would have loved. She would have been proud of her daughter, Jaeleen, slender, like her mother, and elegant in a chic black dress, and of the way her son, Orin, tried to support and take care of his sister.

I wished I could hear her call me a hopeless *tanik* just one more time. I'd always thought that someday I could persuade her to become a professional paralegal, and that she, in turn, would teach me how to truly share, but we ran out of time.

ONE WINDY, GOLDEN September afternoon, a package with a Fairbanks postmark arrived for me at the front desk of the Madisonville public defender. It was carefully wrapped in layers of brown paper and tied with stiff twine, but bore no return address or name.

"Your old friends sent you some whale blubber, I bet," Angie, our secretary, said. She liked to tease me about my former job being in a place so far away and frozen and strange. Angie was a coal miner's daughter, as she often proudly said. I did not mention to her that Kentucky customs sometimes seemed as inscrutable to me as those in Utqiagvik, as did the accent.

Fortunately, Angie was a dog lover, too, and didn't object when I brought my ice dog to the office. Siku was very attached to me and didn't like to be left behind in the fenced yard, especially if it was hot. She loved the Kentucky woods and creeks, though, and the backwoods dogs also recognized her alpha-ness and deferred to her and paid her court.

I carried the package into my office. Outside the window, maples and ginkgoes in glowing fall regalia bordered the neat lawns and gingerbreaded houses of Main Street, but there was no ocean where you could glimpse gray whales scratching their bellies on the gravel, and there were no snowy owls soaring overhead like curious angels. In Utqiagvik it would be time for fall whaling.

I cut the twine, peeled back the paper, and found inside a miniature basket sled made of bent and dried willow strips, fine and patient Native craftmanship, if not the spectacular skill of Bobby Nashookpuk. Bobby's work had now found a wider audience and was featured in online galleries at hefty prices.

I knew in my heart that Amos Lane had sent the sled. Michael was not a craftsperson, and in any case, there was now a permanent line between him and me. Anyone else would have left a return address. I turned the piece over and over in my hands, stroking the small ribs and runners, smoothing the miniature doeskin travel bag. It gave off a fragrance of shellac and oil.

Perhaps Amos sent it as a thank-you for my hard work on his case. He had been well represented. The immunity deal itself was not the result of great legal effort—it arose from Ellingsworth's error in prosecuting John Adams—but the motions in the perjury case were skilled attorney footwork, if I do say so myself. So why did the gift feel to me like a payoff?

My internal jury was still out about Amos, and he remained as vivid in my memory as Liz or Randy or the elder Joshua Ahvakana. I remembered Amos's dignity in the face of condemnation and his hopes of returning to his art of ivory carving. I prayed for him that the artistry had triumphed over whatever other nature lay within.

I didn't put the sled in a drawer or on a shelf. I put it front and center on my desk, where it would always remind me of the North Slope, and of learning there how very much I do not know.

THE SLED REMINDED me to check on Amos from time to time. Eventually he became a presence on YouTube, first in a podcast, *Coffee & Quaq*. He and his sister Eunice also appeared in the Affinityfilms series *Save Our Sisters Alaska,* which documents the missing and murdered Indigenous women who were overlooked by authorities.

In spite of the odds again him, Amos succeeded in doing what he told me in the Utqiagvik jail he dreamed of doing: He took up professional ivory carving and opened a shop in Anchorage. YouTube videos by Frozen North Media showcase his work under the titles "Amos Lane Inupiaq Artist" and "Amos Lane Creations."

But Amos continued to drink, as I heard from Liz's family, and he also did drugs, lots of drugs. Sometimes when he was high or drunk, the old rage erupted. On April 11, 2016, KTVA News in

Anchorage reported one such incident. The headline read, "Man Who Broke Officer's Face During Arrest Pleads Guilty to Felony Assault."

I read the article and looked at the video. Anchorage police officer Ian Fletcher had attempted to arrest Amos for violating his conditions of release in an earlier case, but Amos punched him in the face and ran. It took several officers to catch him, even with his maimed feet, and to subdue him, even after he had been tased twice. The unfortunate Officer Fletcher had to be hospitalized for surgery for a "blowout orbital fracture."

I remembered Nate Olemaun telling me when I interviewed him about the Ipalook case, "That guy's as strong as four bears."

I found online a video of the sentencing hearing and heard Amos's familiar voice tell the court, "My apologies to Mr. Fletcher and family, community. I'm thankful nobody got hurt any more than what's been said. I will take this, and we'll go on with our lives." He sounded truly remorseful and utterly sincere.

The miniature sled accompanied me when I moved on to other public defender's offices, including the post-conviction specialists in Eddyville and a larger office in Clarksville, Tennessee. I took particular pride in serving in the Tennessee office because we had our own investigator, so we could rely less on the State's version of facts, and our own social worker, to develop rehab programs for clients who needed them. We had a heavy caseload, but among all the new charges and crowded dockets, I never forgot Amos Lane, even after I retired from the full-time practice of law.

I TRIED TO think of Amos's file as closed, as one of the hundreds I had completed and put away in boxes, but some cases take on an afterlife of their own—and some are interconnected in ways that defy human understanding. Years later, there came a revelation that shocked me, and I am a career public defender who thought I had lost the capacity to be shocked.

Perhaps I should have seen it coming and should have tried earlier to answer the nagging question in my head. In 1994, Liz said Bobby Nashookpuk was scheduled for release from prison in 2060, and I wondered what he could have done to merit such a harsh sentence.

I tried looking him up but got no further than the Department of Corrections online page showing his institutional number and location. I turned to a commercial search service, one of the reputable ones that had previously given me good information on other clients. They responded that the history for Bobby Nashookpuk was "not available" and refunded my money. Huh? I had never received that result before.

I quit searching. He was not a client. His history was none of my business.

But every time I looked at *Homage and Respect for the Spirit World of the Seals*, for which I had bought the lockable glass case now installed in a corner of my living room, I wondered again: Why was this fine artist serving so much time?

Finally I burrowed through several pages of the Alaska Court System online search instructions, submitted a formal request to the Records Division for whatever information could be found on the history of Bobby Nashookpuk, and began a correspondence with the court bureaucracy. I learned that Alaska criminal court records dated before 1990 are not available online. I asked how one could search for them and found that one has to contact the trial court where they were handled. So where would the records for Point Hope be? Point Hope cases went to the Kotzebue court, in the Northwest Arctic Borough, instead of to Utqiagvik, in the North Slope Borough, because Kotzebue was geographically closer. I was discouraged with the process and ready to give up the effort, but a kind and conscientious deputy supervisor in the Anchorage Records Division, Kevin Kackman, joined the search. He found that the old Nashookpuk records had been inadvertently tagged with an identifying number that was incorrect by one digit, and had therefore been "unavailable." Kackman sent me the records.

I wish he hadn't.

The criminal complaint I received stated that in Point Hope in 1985, Harriet Lane, Amos's mother, was the victim of a rape so brutal that she died the following morning of injuries sustained during it. The alleged perpetrator was Bobby G. Nashookpuk.

Other documents showed that he pled no contest to second-degree murder and was sentenced to twenty-five years. He got out in 2002, spent ten good years in Fairbanks, then committed two more serious sexual assaults, for which he is now incarcerated with a release date of 2060.

I saw the suffering in Nashookpuk's eyes when I met with him at Fairbanks Correctional in 1994, while he was serving his first sentence, which I did not know at the time had anything to do with the Lane family. Perhaps in some way, in his ivory *Homage and Respect* chalices, he had, indeed, sought to re-create the beautiful vessel he had destroyed. He tried to talk to me about Amos Lane then, but I cut him off because Amos was already my client. Perhaps I should have disregarded the conflict of interest rules and asked him what happened years earlier in Point Hope and why he was serving so much time. Pete Petersen at arraignment, and Nate Olemaun in his living room, had told me about Harriet's terrible death, but Nate had said that her murder was never prosecuted, that only one man of three had been charged, and only with rape and not homicide, so I had missed the link for all those years.

AMOS LANE'S LAST CASE

June 20, 2022, Fairbanks, Alaska

WHEN I CHECKED ON AMOS LANE WITH MY NEW LAPtop in our small upstairs home office, with its slanting ceilings and one window looking into maple treetops, his name came up in several articles in the Anchorage and Seattle papers. A reckless driving incident had escalated into a police chase. According to KTVF in Fairbanks:

> An officer-involved shooting took place early Monday morning in Fairbanks, fatally injuring one man and sending two to the hospital.
>
> According to a dispatch report issued by the Alaska State Troopers (AST), at 2:55 a.m., AST entered a chase with a 2011 Ford sedan near the Mitchell Expressway and Airport Road, ending the chase when conditions became unsafe.
>
> Six hours later, AST located the same sedan driven by an adult male. Once again, the driver failed

> to pull over for troopers near Peger Road and Phillips Field Road.
>
> AST and Fairbanks Police Department (FPD) pursued the sedan to 23rd Avenue and Cushman Street, forcing the vehicle to stop at around 9:15 a.m.
>
> The driver then produced a handgun, pointing it at a female passenger, who was the only other occupant in the vehicle.
>
> AST and FPD fired their duty weapons at the driver when he failed to follow commands, fatally wounding him.
>
> The female passenger was also injured by gunfire and is being treated at an area hospital for non-life-threatening injuries.
>
> During the incident, a trooper was also struck by a bullet and has been treated and released from an area hospital.
>
> Police opened the area back to the public around 12:30 p.m.

An update added, "The driver has been identified as 57-year-old Amos Lane of Anchorage."

Stunned, I read and reread the reactions that Fairbanks residents posted about this news. Here, almost thirty years after the deaths of Bernice and Wanda Ipalook and the acquittal of John Adams at trial, Amos Lane's online jury had convened. In an inversion of time that Einstein would have understood, the sentence had already been passed and executed.

> "So officers failed to de-escalate a potential hostage situation, and now a man is dead, the passenger and an officer is injured when no one could've been hurt. Yeah, great job . . ."

"Good job officers. It's hard to stop crazy."

"Squarebanks is getting unsquared. What's in the air, water? It'll soon be SCAREBANKS."

"You are all forgetting this was someone's son, brother, or Dad have some respect of people involved."

"I'm sorry to the officers involved who now have to live with this for the rest of their lives, just because they were doing their job to protect our community."

"Sad. It sounds like the police sure shot him a lot."

"The only one who shot anyone that day were the officers. They shot the police officer, they shot the woman, and they shot Lane. I personally know Amos Lane and he was an amazing man. He didn't deserve to die."

"I love how if the police hadn't done anything, y'all would be mad."

"So sad dude. I'm glad she's ok tho!! He probably would have killed her."

The article included a picture of the crime scene. My former client, Amos Charles Lane, the tundra hunter from Point Hope, the carver of walrus ivory, died on the pavement in front of a Subway sandwich shop, a laundromat, and a tanning salon.

I searched online for other information about Amos's last years, sitting so long at my desk that sunlight began to fade from the maple leaves outside. For the first time, I listened to the *Coffee & Quaq* podcast that was part of the *Save Our Sisters Alaska* campaign. I heard again a voice that remained familiar from so many court hearings, jail interviews, and telephone conversations. He told the interviewer how his mother's death in 1985 had set him on a path of rage and self-destruction that he still struggled to escape, though he had then been clean and sober for six years. I knew from other cases how the trauma of violence can trigger cycles that repeat within families and generations, but I had not known all its impact on Amos's family. Three years after Harriet died, Amos's father, Lennie Lane, blaming himself for Harriet's death, took his own life.

At the end of the podcast, the interviewer asked Amos what he wanted now, and what might give him closure and some peace.

"My parents got buried in different places," he said. "I want to bring my dad's body back to bury next to my mom's."

I once read, in school so many years ago, that in the whole history of human communication, there are only three basic stories to be told about human lives. The first is about undertaking the heroic task, to slay evil or to rescue good. The second story centers on a great quest for God or knowledge or art. The third tells of the simple desire for love and family. In his last years, what Amos wanted was to put back together the family he lost at fourteen. I cried for him.

THE FACTS OF Amos Lane's death were as ambiguous as those of the murder of the Ipalook sisters. The superficial interpretation is that the shoot-out with police demonstrated his violent nature and confirmed that he was responsible for that double homicide almost thirty years earlier. Public Safety made a serious mistake in charging Adams instead of Lane, who should have been taken off the streets decades ago.

But there is also a different version. Amos's family and friends set up a Facebook page called "Justice for Amos Lane 'Kupuyu.'" They say he was the victim of a brutal overreaction by racist cops to what started out as a traffic stop. Amos was shot seven times, and his passenger was hit once, as was another officer. Some believe that police were hounding Amos in retaliation for the 2015 incident when Amos "broke an officer's face." Many say Amos's death was unnecessary and a tragic loss for his beloved sisters and daughter, as well as for the ivory-carving community in Anchorage.

Additional facts supporting this version may arise from the lawsuit filed by former officer Alex Valdez on June 19, 2024, against the City of Fairbanks and the Fairbanks Police Department. A stray bullet struck him during the 2022 shoot-out. Valdez claims that his ability to make a living was impaired by this injury, which resulted from the reckless and excessive use of force by the officers.

There's a third possible explanation of Amos's end, as plausible as the others. Perhaps it was a suicide by cop. Amos was fifty-seven. His most recent photos show his hair had grayed and his posture was skewed, perhaps because of his maimed feet, and he appeared to be missing teeth. And addiction always takes a toll on both body and spirit.

Amos was street smart. He would have known that if he pulled a gun, the officers would open fire—he raised, though did not shoot, his weapon. Liz's family told me the woman in the car with him, Eunice Toorak, was the mother of his child, not some random kidnap victim. Amos may have feared going back to jail and grown weary of being haunted by the terrible death of his mother, his own wrongdoings, and the tyranny of addiction. Death by firing squad is quick.

THE TINY, WIZENED elder lady told me at the Utqiagvik post office, shortly before John Adams was brought to trial for the deaths of Bernice and Wanda Ipalook, that there were three victims, not just two. The Ipalook sisters died in Utqiagvik on August 3, 1993, during that weekend of dazzling, blinding midnight sun, when the Native community believed that Amos Lane had killed them. Later I found that Amos Lane's mother, Harriet Lane, was murdered in Point Hope on July 9, 1985, also in the days of endless light. There were, indeed, three victims, sisters, in death, of the midnight sun.

I HAD READ everything I could find. I switched off the laptop and took up Amos's miniature sled, brushing off the dust that had settled on it. I wished for some wise person to talk with, someone who knew Amos, someone who knew Randy, but Liz was gone, and I couldn't talk to Michael. I thought of the trusted elder Joshua Ahvakana. I remembered how he had walked out on Cake-eater Road to study the tundra weather, how he and other elders patrolled the community when the white bear came in—their vigilance had saved my life—and how he had blessed me when I was waiting at the air shack to fly out of Utqiagvik. I wanted to see his kind eyes and to feel his hand on my shoulder. Perhaps he could explain to me how one death leads to others. Perhaps he would tell me, We know the wolf and the shaman are of one nest, but we don't always know who around us is creator, or destroyer, or both. Let us no longer seek Anglo justice or Native justice. Let us seek peace. Soon the snow will come and cover us all.

A door slammed below.

"Rebecca?"

"Coming."

I put the sled back in its place on my desk and went downstairs. There was still time to walk in the woods before nightfall.

ACKNOWLEDGMENTS

If it takes a village to raise a child, to produce a book it takes an online community of remarkably skilled and persevering specialists, such as Elizabeth Kracht of Kimberley Cameron & Associates and Kate Hirons Editorial Services. Thank you.

© Greg Sand

REBECCA WRIGHT STEVENS is a retired public defender with a double major in English and Spanish from the University of Kansas in Lawrence and a juris doctor degree from the University of Memphis. She lives with her husband on top of a mountain in East Tennessee. Find out more at rebeccawrightstevens.com.